Globe Law and Business

Online Dispute Resolution

Law's Future in the Digital Age

Max Barrett

Author
Max Barrett

Managing director
Sian O'Neill

Online Dispute Resolution: Law's Future in the Digital Age
is published by

Globe Law and Business Ltd
3 Mylor Close
Horsell
Woking
Surrey GU21 4DD
United Kingdom
Tel: +44 20 3745 4770
www.globelawandbusiness.com

Online Dispute Resolution: Law's Future in the Digital Age

ISBN 9781837230587
EPUB ISBN 9781837230594
Adobe PDF ISBN 9781837230600

For Athena

Table of contents

[Some] disputes are not suitable for decision by the courts. Some ... are so numerous that the courts would not have sufficient judges to cope with the amount of work involved ... And, more often than not, expedition and economy are essential factors which, it is thought, the courts do not provide.

Denning[1]

[C]ases where the controversy turns not upon the rule of law, but upon its application to the facts ... make up the bulk of the business of the courts. They are important for the litigants concerned in them ... But they leave jurisprudence where it stood before. As applied to such cases, the judicial process ... is a process of search and comparison, and little else.

Cardozo[2]

By the turn of the [twenty-first] century, the paper world familiar to lawyers for centuries had largely given way to today's electronic regime ... New technology also entered law offices and courtrooms ... The COVID-19 pandemic ushered in yet another wave of rapid technological innovation ... [N]ow we face the latest technological frontier: artificial intelligence ... AI obviously has great potential to dramatically increase access to key information for lawyers and non-lawyers ... But ... [m]achines cannot fully replace key actors in court.

US Chief Justice John Roberts (2023)[3]

Acknowledgements

I am grateful to all at Globe Law and Business for seeing this book through to publication. At home, Agapi has, as ever, been a rock of support throughout the writing and publishing process – thank you, Agapi. My three children – Athena (to whom this book is dedicated), Petros and Mikhalis – were all hugely supportive and patient as I spent hours reading and writing. My mother and brothers have, as always, been thoroughly encouraging. My late father, I know, would also have been encouraging had he been here – though insisting, no doubt, that I continue to do some physical exercise every day to keep ill health at bay. Finally, I am grateful to my former judicial assistant, Ms Hodel Herlihy, for doing a proofread of a late draft of this book.

This book is written in my personal capacity and not in my capacity as a judge. It is not intended as legal advice and should not be relied upon as such. I hope that readers will find it an enjoyable and informative read.

All author royalties earned on sales of this book will be donated to the Red Cross's Ukraine Appeal.

Honourable Mr Justice Max Barrett
High Court of Ireland
August 2025

Preface

ODR is not science fiction.
Susskind Report[4]

A defining feature of traditional courthouses is their architectural design. Towering columns, imposing façades and grand entrances have long conveyed law's majesty. Traditional courtroom interiors have been arranged to reflect a strict hierarchy: judges elevated above all others, court officials beneath them, then the lawyers and disputants, with any spectators relegated to the beyond. The influence of ecclesiastical architecture on judicial buildings – particularly in Britain and its former colonies – underscored an almost religious reverence for legal institutions. Yet even before the COVID-19 pandemic, the traditional courtroom was beginning to decline in significance. In the United States, it has been estimated that over 90% of civil cases are presently resolved without trial, largely due to the rise of alternative dispute resolution (ADR) methods such as arbitration and mediation.[5] The pandemic accelerated this trend, forcing trials online and fundamentally altering the once-universal perception of physical courtrooms as the place where justice fell necessarily to be discharged. The pandemic-driven shift to virtual trials challenged long-held assumptions about courtroom trials as the gold standard for due process. It invited a reimagination of the judicial space and the role of courts and courtrooms. Following the pandemic, courts and court services faced a critical crossroads: should they return entirely to physical proceedings, or should they embrace a new, digital model of proceeding?

One concern about online proceedings is the potential erosion of gravitas. Physical courthouses typically accentuate the solemnity of legal proceedings. Some fear that moving trials online may strip the court process of this majesty. Such concerns echo debates from an earlier era regarding the intrusion of television cameras into courtrooms. A landmark case in this regard was *Estes v Texas* (1965).[6] There, the US Supreme Court ruled that televising a criminal trial violated a defendant's right to due process. The court was concerned that television broadcasting of proceedings could distort proceedings, affect jurors and even lead to pressuring of witnesses. Justice Harlan's concurring opinion in the case outlined concerns that remain relevant to online trials today: the potential for spectacle over substance and the risk that judges or jurors might render decisions swayed by public perception rather than legal principle. Of course (at least in the United States), legal attitudes towards televised trials soon evolved. By 1981, the Supreme Court had completely reversed course, holding in *Chandler v Florida*[7] that courtroom broadcasts were not inherently unconstitutional. Over time, American courts established guidelines for televised trials, balancing transparency with fairness. Today, televised trials are routine throughout the United States.

The transition to online trials appears to be following a similar trajectory. While the COVID-19 pandemic forced courts to embrace remote hearings out of necessity, the experience also demonstrated that virtual proceedings are not only possible but sometimes preferable. While courts may have returned in large part to in-person hearings, few (if any) jurisdictions have completely abandoned the online elements of their processes. Even so, it would be a fool who denied that what might be styled as a shift to digital presents challenges. Virtual trials can alter courtroom dynamics, affecting the spatial semiotics and interpersonal interactions that shape advocacy and testimony. Lawyers worry that remote hearings make it harder to assess witness credibility, maintain jury engagement and foster collegiality among legal professionals.* There is also the question of how legal education should adapt, with existing and future lawyers already needing to be trained in both online advocacy and traditional courtroom skills.

Ultimately, the justice system must balance tradition with innovation. The grandeur of courthouses once served as a powerful reminder of the law's authority, but in more egalitarian times, justice must also be accessible and adaptable. The challenge ahead is not architectural; it is conceptual. If the physical courtroom is no longer the sole forum for justice, how should one define the judicial process in the digital age? Full square and centre in the process of redefining the judicial process (and the doing of justice) in the 21st century and beyond is the concept of online dispute resolution (ODR). ODR – in particular, court and court-connected ODR – is the particular subject of this book. It comprises the following chapters:

1. **"ODR in brief"**: This chapter considers how ODR uses artificial intelligence (AI), automation and technology generally to resolve disputes more efficiently.

---

* The Chief Justice of the United States, John Roberts, in his end-of-year report to the federal judiciary in 2023, touched on how physicality matters, for example, at criminal sentencing hearings, observing (at 6) that for sentencing judges, "Much can turn on a shaking hand, a quivering voice, a change of inflection, a bead of sweat, a moment's hesitation, a fleeting break in eye contact". But as a justification for in-person hearings, this line of reasoning seems rather to wilt in the rise of holography (telepresence) as a science. As one learned commentator has observed, holography means that jurors and others can clearly see the behaviour of all involved in litigation, facilitating them deter dining credibility. (See Exon (1), 18–19.)

2. **"The courtroom redefined":** This chapter considers how the COVID-19 driven shift to digital courtrooms has demonstrated that ODR can be accessible and efficient.
3. **"The Susskind and Briggs Reports":** This chapter considers the Susskind Report and the two Briggs Reports – three eminent publications that address the rollout of ODR in the United Kingdom.
4. **"Two UK examples of ODR in action":** This chapter considers the operation of the UK Traffic Penalty Tribunal (TPT) and Money Claim Online (MCOL) process.
5. **"ODR in the United States":** This chapter considers how ODR in the United States has demonstrated its effectiveness in dealing with high-volume, low-complexity cases, although challenges still remain.
6. **"The US National Center for Technology and Dispute Resolution":** This chapter considers some codes on ODR drafted by this eminent American thinktank.
7. **"The California Access to Justice Commission and the future of legal technology":** This chapter considers some reports of the California Access to Justice Commission which highlight the potential of ODR to remediate gaps in the existing offline justice system.
8. **"Two US examples of ODR in action":** This chapter considers the ODR models of Michigan and Utah, both of which (in their own ways) showcase the best of ODR.
9. **"Three Canadian examples of ODR in action":** This chapter considers three Canadian ODR platforms that likewise showcase the best of ODR.
10. **"ODR and the European Union":** This chapter considers the approach of the European Union to ODR.
11. **"ODR and China":** This chapter considers how China's centralised ODR has become something of a world leader in the field.
12. **"ODR and artificial intelligence":** This chapter considers how AI improves ODR efficiency, while raising concerns – for example, as to bias, ethics and fairness.
13. **"Blockchain":** This chapter considers the efficiencies and deficiencies of crowdsourced, blockchain-based ODR.
14. **"Cybersecurity and chatbots":** This chapter considers how cybersecurity is critical to ODR's legitimacy and the role and weaknesses of chatbots.
15. **"Guidelines on ODR mechanisms":** This chapter considers how and why ODR must align with human rights principles.
16. **"Two European charters":** This chapter considers how the European Ethical Charter and the Framework Charter on AI may better ensure accountability and fairness when it comes to AI-informed ODR.
17. **"ODR and people in need":** This chapter considers how ODR must be

designed to empower, not exclude, those already affected by access to justice issues.

18. **"Domain name dispute resolution":** This chapter considers the successful domain name dispute resolution process operated by the Internet Corporation for Assigned Names and Numbers (ICANN).
19. **"ODR and specific sectors":** This chapter considers aspects of ODR in the context of asylum/immigration, consumer, criminal and family law cases.
20 **"Conclusion":** This chapter brings together some key points from the preceding chapters.

Appendix: ODR and international bodies. This appendix considers how global and regional bodies such as the Asia-Pacific Economic Cooperation (APEC), the Association of Southeast Asian Nations (ASEAN), the Organisation for Economic Co-operation and Development (OECD) and the United Nations Commission on International Trade Law (UNCITRAL) have addressed ODR to date.

Each chapter is succeeded by 10 key learnings (often accompanied by counter-observations) and preceded by 10 brief takeaways that a person tasked with constructing an ODR platform might glean from the chapter in question.

Save where unavoidable – such as where a piece of quoted text uses gendered language – I have sought in this book to use gender-inclusive language.

An earlier draft of this text contained a multitude of footnotes, usually referencing a source text and page number. In a bid to make the book more user-friendly, where a footnote usefully adds something to the main text, an asterisked footnote has been included at the bottom of the relevant page. Otherwise, all footnotes have been converted to numbered endnotes that appear towards the end of the book. The result is a text that is easier on the eye and a more engaging read.

1. ODR in brief

ODR … encompasses a broad array of technologies used to resolve a growing variety of business and consumer disputes … Courts have implemented ODR for low-dollar personal injury claims, landlord-tenant, small claims, and minor traffic and code enforcement violations. ODR presents opportunities for courts to expand services while simultaneously reducing costs and improving customer experience and satisfaction.

Joint Technology Committee[8]

Traditionally, dispute resolution has always been associated with a place, ie, courts … Owing to the circumstances induced by the COVID-19 pandemic … traditional notions of dispute resolution have come to be challenged. In these trying times, technology has emerged as a harbinger of change and neutralizer of circumstances. At the helm of this technology revolution, is Online Dispute Resolution – ODR.

NITI Aayog[9]

Improving ODR: 10 key lessons

- Define the purpose of ODR.
- Start with high-volume, low-complexity cases.
- Prioritise user accessibility.
- Integrate customisation and AI capabilities.
- Emphasise procedural justice.
- Address the digital divide.
- Learn from existing platforms.
- Balance automation with human oversight.
- Evaluate performance with rigorous metrics.
- Use ODR to complement, not replace, traditional courts.

The term 'online dispute resolution' emerged in the 1990s and has since evolved considerably.[10] In particular, digital consumer transactions have surged and a need for an effective means of resolving the multitude of related disputes arising has presented. Today, ODR represents a dynamic and transformative approach to resolving disputes through the use of technology. The primary focus of this book is the use of ODR to support or replace court adjudication – what is sometimes referred to as 'court and court-connected ODR'. The particular challenge presenting for court systems is that if they do not move with the times, they may find themselves increasingly supplanted by an ODR system for which there is a clear global demand.*

As to what constitutes ODR, as the OECD has recently observed, there is no universally accepted definition of the concept.[11] The OECD suggests, by way of shorthand definition, that the term refers to "the use of digital technologies and data to support dispute settlement within and beyond the court".[12] It also notes that the two common and essential elements of every definition of ODR are the types of dispute resolution processes covered and how digital technologies and data are applied.[13] Separately, the European Bank for Reconstruction and Development (EBRD) has defined 'ODR' as the processing of certain cases entirely online from the point of filing the claim to the point of pronouncing judgment, reaching a settlement or terminating a case in any formal manner.[14] Whether a dispute resolution process needs to be conducted entirely online for it to constitute ODR is a moot but ultimately semantic point. Information and communications technology (ICT) has been incorporated into numerous dispute resolution systems in a manner that complements or supplements processes which include online and offline work.[15]

From the outset, it is vital to clarify a distinction that forms a foundation of this book: the difference between ODR and ADR. Traditionally, 'ADR' has referred to flexible methods for resolving disputes alongside or completely outside the public court system. It encompasses approaches such as arbitration and mediation which offer parties a way to settle their differences without involving the formality, length and expense of litigation.

One common misconception is that ODR is merely ADR adapted to the digital age – that is, ADR conducted with the help of technology. This viewpoint fundamentally underestimates the transformative potential of ODR. ODR is not simply 'e-ADR' or a digital replica of traditional methods. Instead, it represents a paradigm shift in how disputes are managed and resolved. ODR integrates cutting-edge technologies – including AI and machine learning (ML) – to automate processes, provide tailored solutions and create curated platforms that serve as tools of justice.**

---

* A survey published by the World Intellectual Property Organization (WIPO) in 2021, analysing trends in the use of ADR in intellectual property (copyright and content) disputes in 129 countries across all regions, describes ODR platforms as having enjoyed a "renaissance" in recent years, operating in parallel and in conjunction with 'traditional' court systems (WIPO (1), 52).

Figure 1: Some principal forms of ODR

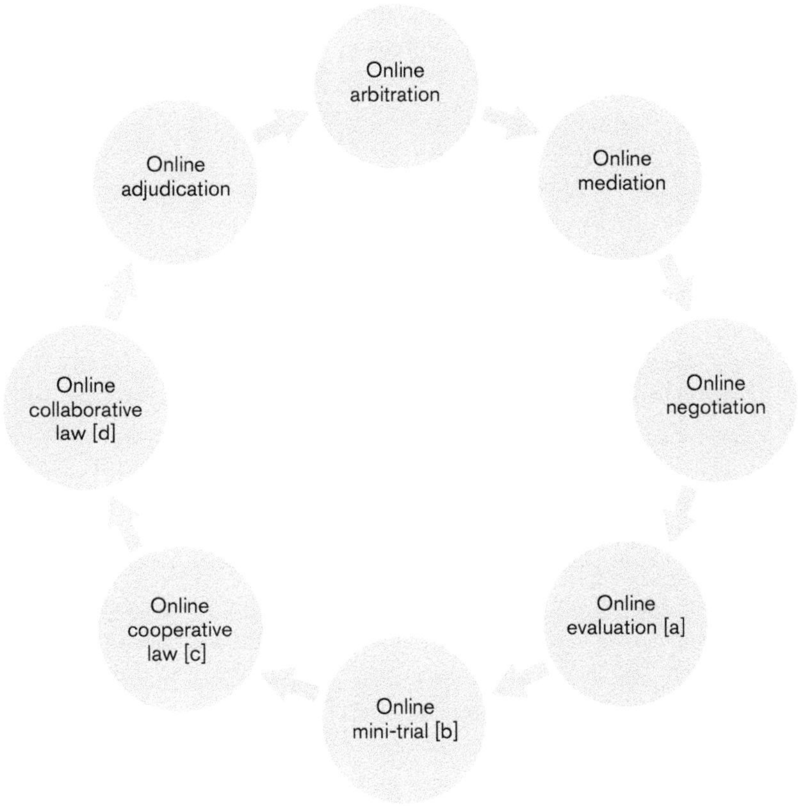

[a] Evaluation: Expert makes non-binding recommendation.
[b] Mini-trial: Jury of peers gives non-binding determination.
[c] Cooperative law: Lawyers and other professionals seek to help clients through to resolution.
[d] Collaborative law: Cooperative law and disqualification agreement which provides that if either party elects to sue, the existing lawyers are disqualified from acting.

** The European Ethical Charter on the Use of Artificial Intelligence in Judicial Systems and Their Environment (2018), which is considered at some length in Chapter 16, contains a glossary which defines 'AI' as comprising "techniques whose aim is to reproduce, by a machine, the cognitive abilities of human beings". Current developments seek to have machines perform complex tasks previously carried out by humans. However, the term 'artificial intelligence' is criticised by experts who distinguish between 'strong' AIs (able to contextualise specialised and varied problems in a completely autonomous manner) and 'weak' or 'moderate' AIs (high performance in their field of training). Some experts argue that 'strong' AIs would require significant advances in basic research, and not just simple improvements in the performance of existing systems, to be able to model the world as a whole. The AI-informed tools discussed in this book are developed using ML methods – that is, 'weak' AIs. As for ML, this – per the glossary to the charter – "makes it possible to construct a mathematical model from data, incorporating a large number of variables that are not known in advance. The parameters are configured gradually during the learning phase, which uses training data sets to find and classify links. The different methods of machine learning are chosen by the designers depending on the nature of the tasks to be completed (grouping). These methods are usually classified into three categories: (human) supervised learning, unsupervised learning and reinforcement learning".

ODR is inescapable: as one learned commentator has observed, even "dispute resolution services that do not necessarily see themselves as 'on-line' will continually need to adapt to take account of the increasing availability and quality of new forms of communication".[16] This suggests that the best definition of ODR may well be the more expansive one of not merely the automated online resolution of disputes, but the more general application of technology to the peaceful resolution of conflicts.[17]

Unlike ADR, which typically relies on human intervention, ODR actively employs technology as a core component of dispute resolution. Its scope extends far beyond livestreaming court proceedings or facilitating virtual mediation sessions. So, for example, ODR may rely upon automated dispute resolution (ie, systems capable of resolving disputes without human involvement, often using algorithms to generate outcomes based on predefined criteria), script-based solutions (ie, tools that guide users through structured processes, enabling swift and effective resolutions) and curated platforms (ie, dedicated online spaces designed to support dispute management, offering resources tailored to specific dispute types).

ODR involves a fundamental reimagining of justice in the digital age. Unlike ADR, which is primarily reactive, ODR has the potential to be proactive, helping parties to avoid disputes altogether or helping to contain disputes before they escalate. This shift is not merely about efficiency or cost (though it can assist with both); it redefines the very nature of access to justice. The OECD has recently remarked of the concept of access to justice and the beneficial role of ODR in this regard that:

- *Access to justice for all is a fundamental underpinning of democracy and the bedrock of a strong social contract ...*
- *Access to justice refers to the ability of people, businesses and communities to prevent conflicts and obtain effective, fair, equitable and timely resolution of their legal and justice-related needs ...*
- *ODR holds significant potential to enhance access to justice ... by making dispute resolution more affordable and accessible ... by providing timely access to information ... [and] by expanding the options available for individuals and businesses to resolve disputes.*[18]

ODR provides global reach (resolving disputes across borders with ease, making justice accessible to individuals and businesses worldwide), inclusivity (bridging gaps for those unable to access traditional systems due to financial, geographical or physical barriers), and transparency and accountability, using data and AI so as better to ensure consistent, fair and impartial outcomes at the end of dispute resolution processes.

The development of ODR can be traced back to the rise of online transactions in the early 1990s. Small-scale disputes, often involving modest amounts and geographically distant parties, created the need for efficient resolution mechanisms. Over time, ODR evolved through three transformative stages:

- *Stage 1 – eBay leads the way:* In 1999, eBay introduced an online mediation platform for disputes between buyers and sellers. From resolving 200 cases in its first two weeks, the system grew to handle over 60 million disputes annually by 2010. This pioneering effort showcased the potential of ODR to manage high volumes of cases effectively.
- *Stage 2 – The ODR platform boom:* Inspired by eBay's success, numerous ODR platforms emerged, such as Cybersettle, the Mediation Room and Smartsettle. These platforms demonstrated that diversity in approach is an asset. Each succeeded by offering innovative dispute resolution mechanisms.
- *Stage 3 – Governments join the movement:* Governments soon recognised ODR's potential. In 2004, New York City introduced an ODR system with Cybersettle to expedite personal injury claims. Similar initiatives followed worldwide, such as the Civil Resolution Tribunal in British Columbia, the Online Dispute Resolution Centre in New Mexico and MCOL in the United Kingdom. This global rollout of ODR schemes has led to a diverse array of platforms, including private platforms, court-connected systems and government-operated solutions.

ODR addresses many of the shortcomings of traditional court systems, offering significant advantages over these systems. These include the following.

First, *cost-effectiveness*. Litigation can be prohibitively expensive, discouraging individuals and businesses from seeking justice. ODR reduces costs by reducing or eliminating travel costs, expediting resolution and (often) minimising the need for extensive legal representation. Indirect costs, such as lost productivity and investor confidence, are also mitigated. That said, a careful cost-benefit analysis falls to be undertaken when deciding whether to establish an ODR platform. This is because while ODR eliminates many traditional costs, it also introduces new ones, such as platform fees and cybersecurity and other IT-related expenses. Additionally, those unfamiliar with the online world require extra assistance (the provision of which is a further cost of ODR rollout).

Second, *convenience*. ODR simplifies dispute resolution. With asynchronous communication and online processes, parties avoid travel and can resolve disputes at their convenience. That said, while such flexibility is valuable, some complex disputes may require real-time, offline engagement.

Third, *customisability*. The integration of AI with ODR enables tailored dispute resolution processes, enhancing efficiency and user satisfaction. That said, excessive tailoring may run the risk of inconsistent outcomes in fact-similar disputes. Moreover, undue reliance on AI mechanisms may reduce transparency if the decision-making process is not clearly explained or understood.

Fourth, *accessibility.** By reducing procedural complexity and allowing disputes to be resolved from home, ODR is more inclusive. Its less adversarial nature should encourage participation, especially among those who may feel intimidated by traditional litigation processes. That said, it does require a level of technological competence and internet access that not all users possess.

Fifth, *bias mitigation.* Where visual contact is unnecessary, ODR should minimise unconscious bias – a form of bias that occurs when one employs behavioural, verbal and visual prompts to make quick assessments of people.[19]

In a text-based dispute, personal characteristics such as ethnicity, gender, sex and status are harder to know and hence are less likely to play a part in the outcome. As one learned commentator has observed, the anonymisation presenting in text-based dispute resolution reduces the prospect of bias arising from how something is said[20] (ODR schemes can, of course, include a visual element if that is considered necessary – though once it includes a visual dimension, the potential for unconscious bias arises again.)

ODR, it has been suggested, goes beyond the technological enhancement of court-connected ADR and entails a transformative change in how conflict is resolved by the courts, with the full potential of this changed process as yet unrealised.[21] In short, ODR is not just a tool. By leveraging technology, it democratises access to justice, reduces the burden on courts and provides a more user-centric approach to resolving disputes. As this book shows, ODR has already transformed the legal landscape, and its journey has barely begun.

In 2019, various American judicial officers and court administrators, all of whom had been tasked with establishing ODR systems, published a helpful article in which they identified various questions that court administrators similarly placed could usefully consider.[22] A similar exercise, with answers provided by reference to the contents of this book, is undertaken below.

Q: *What key issue are you trying to resolve?*
A: Inefficiency in traditional offline dispute resolution.

Q: *What key difficulties present as regards the current approach to dispute resolution?*
A: Complexity, cost and judicial involvement in routine disputes.

---

* Digital accessibility is often conceived in terms of universal usability, "enabling diverse populations to successfully and independently use the web for meaningful goals" (Sela (2), 141). In its work on ODR, the Hague Institute for Innovation of Law has offered an eight-point plan as to how complete accessibility can be attained in practice: "1. Goal 100% access to justice for family justice, then employment ... etc ... 2. Ministry of justice and parliament set concrete goals and terms of reference. 3. Courts obtain freedom ... [re] procedures; and to set and use court fees ... 4. Suppliers of innovative ... [ODR] procedures can ... get access to market ... 5. Complainants get fairness ... justice ... [and] lower costs ... 6. Defendants do not need to fear procedure ... [and] pay fair share ... 7. Lawyers litigate less, serve more clients ... [and generally benefit] ... 8. State monitors, pays less in subsidies, [gets] more satisfied citizens ..."

Q: *Why do you think ODR might usefully be relied upon?*

A: ODR offers an online solution to the issues identified in the previous answer and offers greater accessibility to existing court systems.

Q: *How will you know when the key issues presenting are resolved?*

A: By applying metrics such as 'reduction in case times' and 'improvements in user satisfaction'.

Q: *Who needs to be involved in the redesign process?*

A: Ideally, all relevant stakeholders.

Q: *What does the present offline system currently involve (step by step)?*

A: Typically, case initiation, document submission, preliminary hearing, evidence exchange, substantive hearing and judgment.

Q: *Where and how would ODR fit in the redesigned system?*

A: By serving as a crutch to offline proceedings or offering a novel online alternative for various dispute forms.

Q: *What additional ethical, procedural or system rules might an ODR system require?*

A: Online evidential, procedural and privacy rules seem most likely to be required. Provision will also be needed as regards human oversight, language assistance, legal compliance and secure communication.

Q: *Who can best meet your specifications?*

A: Most likely to be of assistance are qualified market vendors with necessary expertise and some experience of creating ODR platforms. Existing in-house IT teams, though they will obviously play an important role, seem unlikely to possess the specialised experience of qualified market vendors.

Q: *Is there enough value to move forward with an ODR solution?*

A: This will depend on the relevant cost-benefit analysis. As a rule of thumb, if ODR improves on the existing process without any procedural or ethical concerns, it may be worth proceeding with.

Q: *How will people engage with the system?*

A: Typically, via a secure, user-friendly interface that allows diverse users to access the platform, submit documents and communicate securely.

Q: *How will you obtain feedback on, and continuously improve, the system?*

A: Typically, this is done by way of performance assessments, system audits and user surveys.

Figure 2: Greacen's 18 steps

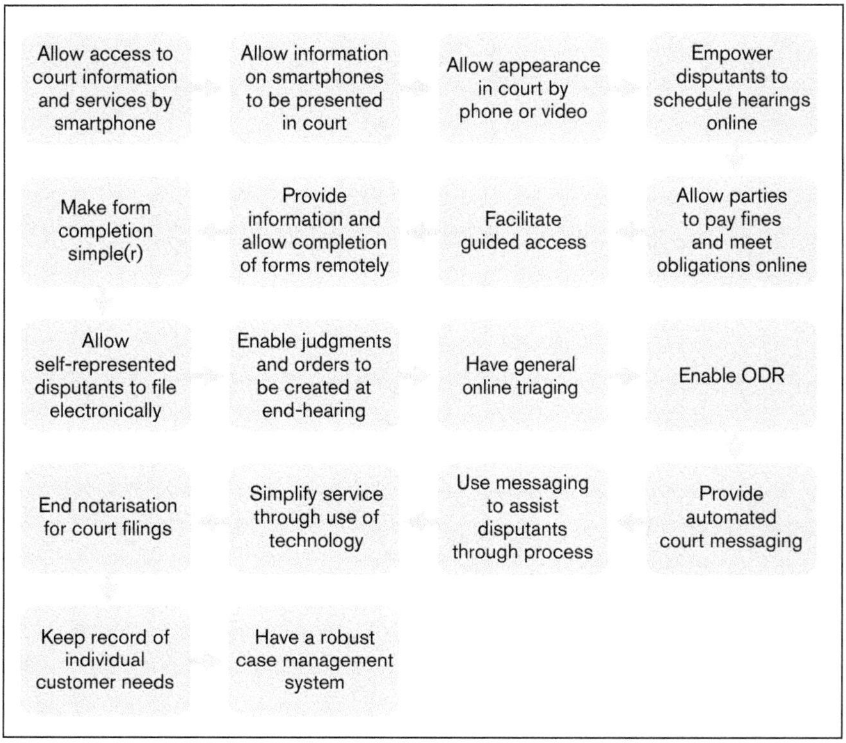

Writing in 2018, Greacen (in a report done under the auspices of the Institute for the Advancement of the American Legal System)* identified 18 ways in which American courts should use technology so as to serve their customers better.[23] The suggestions are summarised in Figure 2. Among the benefits which Greacen attributes to greater use of technology are the following.[24] Pleadings should be more complete and more readable. Court hearings should be less time-consuming. Swifter despatch of simpler cases should give judges more time to decide more complex cases. Courts should be enabled to produce written judgments and orders at the end of hearings. Parties should better understand court processes and orders. Proceedings should become less confrontational and conflict driven. And public perception and the standing of courts should improve. Although Greacen's publication was written in the American context, there is no reason to believe that its analysis, observations and conclusions do not have wider resonance. The fact that the study is now almost a decade old

* Operating from the University of Denver, the Institute for the Advancement of the American Legal System is a national, independent research organisation that proposes solutions aimed at making the civil justice system of the United States more just.

shows just how far the United States and its legal academics and professionals have already journeyed, when compared with many other jurisdictions, in terms of academic consideration and the practical implementation of ODR.

Key learnings

- *Define the purpose of ODR.* ODR should not be confused with ADR that is conducted online. It is a distinct system that uses technology to create entirely new pathways for dispute resolution. That said, while ODR can introduce novel dispute resolution pathways, it still operates within the broader spectrum of existing resolution methods.
- *Start with high-volume, low-complexity cases.* The success of ODR initiatives in jurisdictions such as the United States demonstrates that platforms work best when they first target disputes with high case volumes and low complexity. However, this approach may unduly slow the fullest rollout of ODR.
- *Prioritise user accessibility.* A cornerstone of successful ODR systems is accessibility. Even so, accessibility efforts must be balanced against security and procedural safeguards if an ODR system is to earn public trust.
- *Integrate customisation and AI capabilities.* AI and other advanced technologies allow ODR platforms to offer tailored dispute resolution processes, including automated decision making and guided, script-based solutions. The practical challenge lies in ensuring that these technologies enhance rather than replace human judgment in complex disputes.
- *Emphasise procedural justice.* Beyond cost savings and efficiency, ODR systems must ensure that users feel the process is fair and transparent. However, while ensuring transparency is undoubtedly important, excessive emphasis on the procedural may unduly slow innovation.
- *Address the digital divide.* An ODR platform cannot succeed if it excludes users due to a lack of technological literacy, access to reliable internet or hardware limitations. Again, a careful balance likely falls to be applied by policymakers if all efficiency gains are not to be lost.
- *Learn from existing platforms.* The evolution of ODR, from eBay's pioneering system to government-operated platforms such as MCOL, offers valuable lessons for the would-be ODR platform provider. However, too rigidly following past models may stifle innovation.
- *Balance automation with human oversight.* While automation can streamline processes and reduce costs, human involvement remains necessary in certain areas, such as complex disputes or cases requiring mediation. That said, excessive human oversight in an ODR system could negate the efficiencies that automation seeks to achieve.

- *Evaluate performance with rigorous metrics.* A robust ODR platform requires regular assessment across multiple dimensions, such as user satisfaction, case resolution times and cost efficiency. Again, caution is required: quantitative assessments alone may fail to capture the rich detail of user experience.
- *Use ODR to complement traditional courts.* ODR is viewed by some as a tool to enhance the justice system, not as a wholesale replacement for in-person proceedings. To be guarded against is an overly cautious approach that prevents the fullest rollout of ODR.

2. The courtroom redefined

Going to court can be nearly impossible for individuals who live at a significant distance from the jurisdiction of the dispute, making it almost impossible to enforce the terms of a divorce decree, resolve a traffic citation received while traveling through an area, or address the issue of a non-paying tenant. ODR allows parties in different locations or jurisdictions to resolve disputes without the cost and complexity of trying to meet at the same time in the same place.
Joint Technology Committee[25]

The future of justice should be conceptualized beyond the confines of brick and mortar. As has been said, courts should be a service not a place. It can be a service that is accessible, formidable, intelligible, pervasive, robust and designed with an outcome-oriented framework … Today, the next generation's revolution of the dispute resolution ecosystem, world over, comes through the vehicle of technology.
NITI Aayog[26]

Improving ODR: 10 key lessons

- A physical courtroom is no longer invariably essential.
- Technology has a long track record in aiding legal reform.
- Digital courtrooms improve access to justice.
- Efficiency and cost savings are core benefits of ODR.
- Technology enhances transparency and accountability.
- Resistance to change must be addressed with evidence.
- Procedural safeguards are critical.
- Systems must be carefully designed to avoid bias.
- Hybrid models may be the best solution.
- Imagination is key to transforming justice.

The physical courtroom, steeped in tradition, is facing an uncertain future. The COVID-19 pandemic highlighted what had been quietly unfolding for decades: the evolution of courtroom practices through technology. By the early 21st century, innovations such as e-filing of documents, electronic court records, video conferencing and assistive technologies for people with disabilities were already reshaping court systems. The pandemic accelerated this transformation dramatically, pushing courts worldwide into adopting remote hearings as an emergency response to unprecedented challenges.

The sudden shift was remarkable. Judges, lawyers and disputants turned to platforms such as Microsoft Teams and Zoom, with documents being shared through Google Docs and email being used for service and notice. What began as a temporary measure soon became the new normal. Some began to question whether in-person hearings were still necessary, labelling them unaffordable and even unnecessarily quaint.

While the pandemic served as a catalyst, the roots of digital courtrooms run far deeper. As long ago as 1931, *The Times* reported on an innovative approach in Manchester, England, where microphones and recording equipment were installed to create a permanent record of proceedings.[27] By the 1970s, videotaped evidence had made its debut in cases such as *McCall v Clemens*[28] in the United States. Although these innovations initially failed to gain widespread adoption, they set the stage for a gradual transformation of the traditional courtroom experience. US District Judge Carl Rubin's high-tech courtroom (back in 1991) is a landmark example. Handling a securities fraud case involving over 1 million documents, he arranged for the digitised on-screen display of exhibits and depositions for jurors. While some criticised the approach, arguing that it detracted from the focus on witness testimony, Rubin's efforts foreshadowed the digital integration that is now reshaping courtrooms worldwide.

As mentioned, the COVID-19 pandemic exposed the potential of online courtrooms to operate efficiently in a digital environment. Courts adapted quickly, embracing technologies that allowed for remote hearings and asynchronous communication (whereby parties could upload documents to a platform at their convenience, while opposing parties accessed them and responded later). These processes offered significant advantages:

- *Efficiency and speed:* Online systems streamline routine cases, freeing judges and lawyers to focus on complex matters requiring human insight. That said, they may also lead to inefficiencies, such as IT failures, connectivity issues and delays caused by the unfamiliarity of some with digital platforms.
- *Increased accessibility:* Remote hearings can help to eliminate barriers such as geography and cost, making justice more inclusive. Care, however, is required as they can also create new barriers for those who do not have reliable internet access or lack digital literacy.

Figure 3: Some e-court initiatives in common law jurisdictions

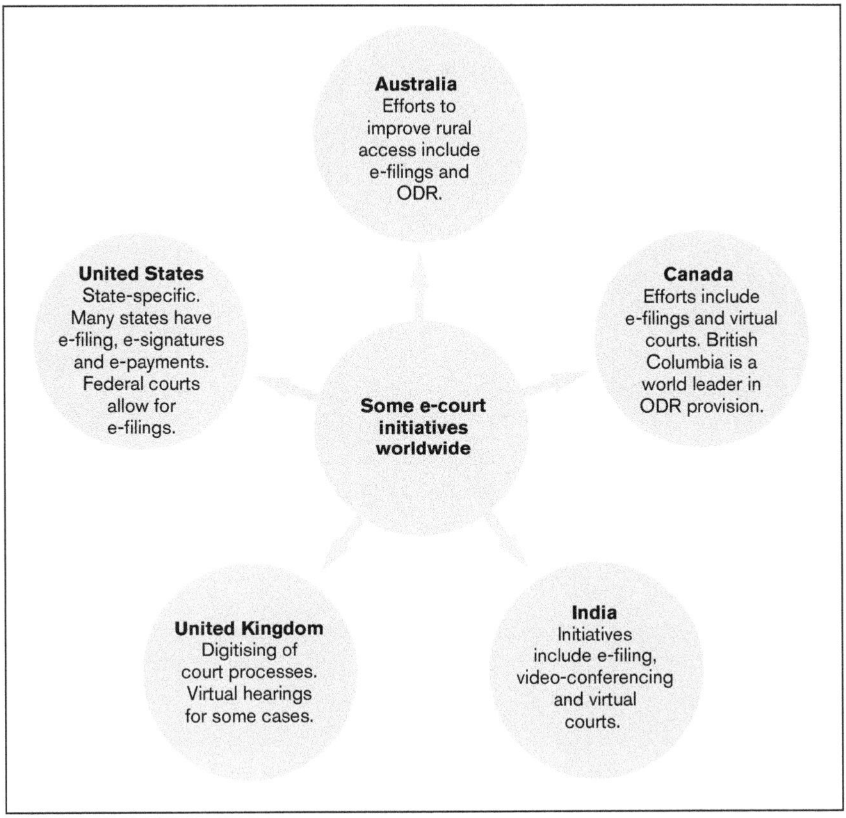

- *Transparency and accuracy:* Digital records provide a detailed, permanent archive of proceedings, potentially reducing errors and increasing accountability – though they inevitably raise concern about cybersecurity and data breaches.
- *Bias elimination:* By removing face-to-face interactions, online systems can help to eliminate biases related to race, gender and appearance. That said, they can introduce new ones. For example, if judges rely more on written submissions, this may disadvantage the less literate.

Resistance to change has often slowed technological adoption in the legal field. Judge McCrystal, reflecting on his videotaped trials in the 1970s, was harshly critical of the legal profession's lack of imagination, observing:[29]

> *November 18, 1971, the date of the first reported jury trial in which all testimony was pre-recorded on videotape, is now a part of American judicial history ... As with most innovations in the law, comments from the legal community ranged*

from "It's a gimmick," to "Wait and see," to "It's an idea whose time has arrived." The preponderance of the comments were predictably of the "wait and see" school. This school has long been noted for its lack of imagination, but, unfortunately or not, it represents the professional consensus among lawyers and judges.

The advantage that proponents of ODR currently have in their favour is that, thanks to the COVID-19 pandemic, a great many people have actual experience of the successful rollout and operation of online technology, whether in the legal context, the work environment or otherwise. The pandemic demonstrated that much of what certain courts handle – traffic violations, minor infractions and administrative tasks – is well suited to online resolution. By embracing ODR platforms, courts can recreate themselves as more accessible, efficient and user-focused institutions.

Former Chief Justice McCormack of Michigan has observed that the COVID-19 pandemic was not a disruption that anyone wanted, but it may have been the disruption needed to transform the judiciary into a more accessible, transparent, efficient and customer-friendly branch of government.[30] In the aftermath of the pandemic, hybrid and even online hearings have become more common in many jurisdictions, marking one of the most profound shifts in courtroom practice in centuries. Technology-enabled courtrooms now offer undeniable advantages – reduced costs, enhanced accessibility and improved evidence presentation – all pointing towards a future where traditional courtrooms, long romanticised by Hollywood, are no longer the default forum for dispute resolution. This integration of technology into courts has yielded perhaps five key advantages that are repeatedly highlighted throughout this book.

First, *greater accessibility*. Technology facilitates access to a broader range of legal services – for example, enabling people in rural areas to connect with lawyers and participate in proceedings without travelling. This improved accessibility has even been touted as the greatest virtue of ODR, enabling (as it does) the traditional geographical and infrastructural constraints of offline dispute resolution processes to be avoided.[31]

Second, *streamlined processes*. Automation reduces bureaucracy, expediting tasks such as document filing and evidence submission. That may be one of its attractions to policymakers. Remarking on the increased digitisation of family court systems worldwide, one learned commentator has noted the appeal of automation in an age of public austerity cuts.[32]

Third, *enhanced accuracy*. Access by the judiciary to better data practices and tools entails a number of potential advantages, such as better marshalling of information, access to more pertinent information and even access to prediction-oriented methodologies. This contrasts favourably to the position that continues to present for many courts whereby their use of raw, potentially useful information can be somewhat inefficient; without improved data practices and tools, data may be plentiful but essentially indigestible."[33]

Fourth, *cost reduction*. Remote participation allows foreign witnesses to testify without the expense of travel and other logistical costs. This is particularly attractive when it comes to low-cost e-disputes with a cross-border dimension. Without the benefit of ODR, such disputes might otherwise go unlitigated. As one learned commentator has observed, the traditional processes of ADR and litigation involve significant fees and travel costs, which may be so great as to render the arbitration or litigation excessively expensive; by contrast, ODR provides a route to justice that entails non-prohibitive costs.[34] That said, as mentioned previously, there are some extra costs occasioned by ODR, such as platform fees, cybersecurity and other IT-related costs, and assisting those who find themselves on the wrong side of the digital divide.

Fifth, *improved transparency*. Digital platforms can enable wider real-time public and press access to hearings, enhancing accountability and openness. Even so, this is perhaps the greatest weakness of ODR systems to date – especially when it comes to public access – as although media access can readily be accommodated in online processes, a fully satisfactory means of ensuring access for the general public has thus far tended to elude ODR system designers.[35]

The advancements touched upon above (greater accessibility, streamlined processes, enhanced accuracy, reduced costs and improved transparency) all point to the growing attractions of an inevitably more online future for court systems worldwide. However, ODR technology, while promising, is not without its challenges. So, for example, in the United States, the Brennan Center for Justice (an independent thinktank closely associated with New York University School of Law) has given a somewhat tepid response to increased use of remote video technology in court, opining that "Judges should adopt the technology with caution".[36] Thus, it has pointed, among other matters, to studies of videoconferencing in courts which suggest that bail is set at a higher amount when set remotely; immigrants tend to be less believed and more often deported when their hearings are conducted remotely; children, when viewed remotely, tend to be viewed as less accurate, believable, confident and consistent; video conferencing can make attorney-client communications more difficult; and it can be harder for self-represented disputants to obtain representation and other support by keeping them away from a physical courthouse.[37]

All that said, the Brennan Center acknowledges the potential of virtual proceedings to enhance access to justice through reduction of costs and an increase in accessibility.[38] And in any event, while the issues identified are undoubtedly concerning, they are not insurmountable. To begin with, videoconferencing as a technology seems likely to be replaced by holography – that is, the use of light transmission to broadcast a three-dimensional image of a person into a place where they are not physically present.[39] This will have the result that one can have an almost traditional, in-person, face-to-face form of communication with a person who is in a remote venue. In the meantime, there are practical steps that can be taken that should allay the types of concern identified by the Brennan Center, such as the following:

- *Bail being set at a higher amount:* Possible solutions to this deficiency include judicial training and guidelines on potential bias introduced by videoconferencing; formal comparative analyses being undertaken of online/offline bail amounts and corrective steps taken if and as appropriate; and the introduction of better audio and video to make the process more akin to real life and less susceptible to the types of bias identified by the Brennan Center.
- *Treating with immigrants:* Possible solutions to this aspect of matters include judicial training and guidelines on the potential bias introduced by videoconferencing; and ensuring that immigrants have access to good-quality interpretation and are provided with adequate legal support and, in high-stakes cases (eg, asylum claims), the option of an in-person hearing.
- *The poor view taken of children's evidence:* Possible solutions to this deficiency include judicial training and guidelines on potential bias introduced by videoconferencing; more child-friendly virtual court settings; and the engagement of suitably qualified personnel to assist a child who is giving testimony.
- *Lawyer-client communications:* Possible solutions include providing lawyers with private virtual meeting rooms to meet with their clients; and providing asynchronous communication channels (eg, secure text) in circumstances where, for whatever reason, real-time communication is challenging.

In their analysis of the rollout of ODR in Brazil, Vieira de Carvalho Fernandes and others outline a number of challenges which have resonance when it comes to the rollout of ODR more generally.[40] These challenges are as follows. Brazil has a litigation culture. Such a culture may initially be ODR resistant. Brazilians do not generally trust private platform providers. There is a need for a cadre of well-trained, high-quality providers. Enforceability is an issue. There is a lack of common data standards across Brazil. Finding suitably qualified developers is difficult and hardware infrastructure may also present a challenge. Despite these challenges, the authors conclude that Brazil is a promising location for the future rollout of ODR. And, in truth, none of the issues identified seem insurmountable, as follows:

- *Brazil being a litigation culture or ODR-resistant:* ODR aversion could be overcome by awareness campaigns.
- *Brazilians not trusting private platforms*: This could perhaps be overcome by introducing state certification of ODR schemes.

- *The need for a cadre of ODR providers:* The only solution would seem to be to develop state-sponsored training and certification.
- *Enforceability:* This is curable by legislation.
- *A lack of common data standards:* Again, this would seem to be curable by legislation.
- *The difficulty of finding suitably qualified developers:* This would seem resoluble by government acting in tandem with educational institutions.
- *The challenges regarding hardware infrastructure:* The only solution would seem to be to expand the existing digital infrastructure.

Figure 4: Some useful questions to ask regarding proposed courtroom technology

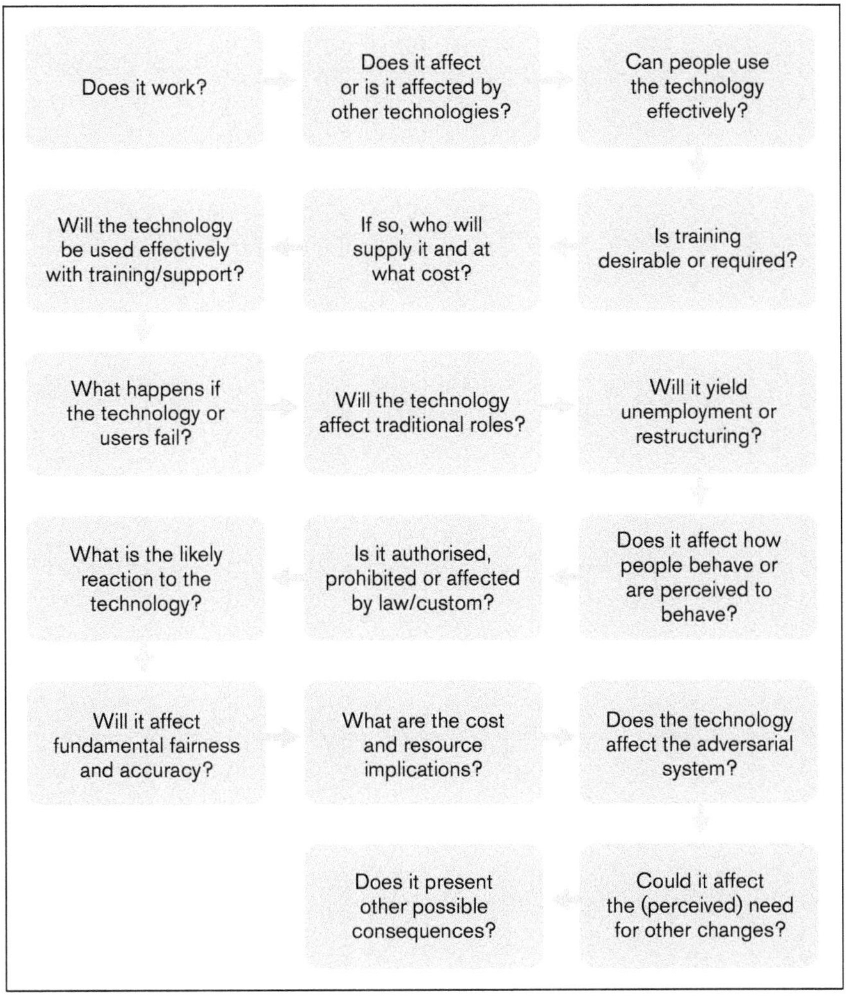

The success of technology in the courtroom depends in part (perhaps even primarily) on its ability to uphold procedural safeguards, a cornerstone of justice. As former US Supreme Court Justice Felix Frankfurter noted in *McNabb v United States* (1943)[41] – and his observation still holds true – "The history of liberty has largely been the history of observance of procedural safeguards."[42] If these safeguards can be preserved or enhanced through digital systems, a bright future for virtual hearings seems assured. In this regard, the procedural safeguards identified by the US Federal Trade Commission (FTC) in *Consumer Protection in the Global Electronic Marketplace* (2000) have stood the test of time remarkably well. The FTC's procedural recommendations included developing a workable international framework for jurisdiction and applicable law; pursuing the partial convergence of national and international consumer protection laws; and encouraging the development of arrangements for cross-border judgment recognition and enforcement.

Key learnings

- *A physical courtroom is no longer invariably essential.* The COVID-19 pandemic demonstrated that physical courtrooms are not a prerequisite for the doing of justice. Remote hearings, document sharing and asynchronous communication have shown that legal processes can thrive in digital spaces. That said, some disputants – especially those without reliable internet access – may struggle to participate fully in an entirely digital process.
- *Technology has a long history in legal reform.* The gradual integration of technology into courts, such as microphones in the 1930s and video evidence in the 1970s, has paved the way for today's digital courtrooms. However, while past innovations have supported legal processes, they have rarely replaced core judicial functions, raising a question about whether ODR can substitute for traditional courts in complex cases.
- *Digital courtrooms improve access to justice.* Online platforms remove geographical and financial barriers, enabling rural populations, foreign witnesses and those with limited mobility to participate in legal proceedings. An ODR platform must prioritise inclusivity to ensure broader access to justice for underserved populations. Of course, some individuals may simply lack the digital skills to navigate ODR platforms and must also be provided for.
- *Efficiency and cost savings are core benefits.* Digital systems streamline case management, reduce bureaucracy and allow remote participation, significantly lowering logistical costs. These efficiencies free up judicial resources for complex cases, making ODR a cost-effective solution for

busy court systems. Cost savings should not come at the expense of procedural fairness. Moreover, the upfront investment required to develop and maintain a secure and effective ODR platform can be substantial, potentially offsetting long-term savings.

- *Technology enhances transparency and accountability.* Digital platforms allow for real-time access to hearings, creating a transparent and open system (though public access remains an issue). That said, the shift to digital records also raises concerns about data security, privacy and the potential for cyberattacks. Moreover, even as transparency increases, the impersonal nature of digital hearings could, paradoxically, reduce perceived accountability.
- *Resistance to change must be addressed with evidence.* Judges, lawyers and legal professionals often resist technological change. Some of this resistance may stem from legitimate concerns about procedural integrity, judicial independence and the safeguarding of disputant rights. Demonstrating the advantages of ODR through pilot projects, data and examples from other jurisdictions may help to overcome irrational scepticism and build trust.
- *Procedural safeguards are paramount.* Upholding procedural fairness is critical for the success of ODR platforms. That said, enforcing procedural safeguards in an online environment presents challenges, particularly as regards the identification of parties, enforcement and the prevention of undue influence. Additionally, reliance on automated processes may inadvertently introduce biases that are hard to detect.
- *Remote systems must be designed to avoid bias.* While digital hearings offer many advantages, studies show that potential drawbacks can present, such as harsher decisions or credibility concerns as regards remote testimony. ODR platforms must be designed with safeguards to counteract these biases, ensuring fair treatment for all participants. That said, eliminating bias in digital systems is complex, as algorithms may inherit biases from their training data.
- *Hybrid models may be the best solution.* A fully online system may not be suitable for all cases. Hybrid models that combine in-person and virtual elements may allow courts to tailor process to needs. Conversely, hybrid models may inadvertently create a two-tiered justice system, where those with greater resources can access in-person proceedings while others are relegated to ODR.
- *Imagination is key to transforming justice.* Embracing technology in the courtroom requires courage, creativity and a willingness to break from tradition. Building an ODR platform is an opportunity to redefine justice, making it more accessible, transparent and user-focused for a

digital age. On the other hand, rushing to implement ODR without fully addressing its limitations could conceivably undermine trust in the justice system.

3. The Susskind and Briggs Reports

Our Group maintains that a primary role of the state in a democratic liberal democracy is to provide an affordable and accessible public dispute resolution service with an independent Judiciary at its core. ... However, this policy position does not preclude the possibility of judges providing this service across the Internet. Nor need it limit the role of the courts to dispute resolution (as opposed to dispute containment and dispute avoidance).

Susskind Report[43]

The ... Online Court has been much the most intensive subject of consultation and debate ... General reactions have ranged from straight condemnation: "it will just be an expensive disaster" (from the Young Bar) to the warmest of welcomes: "I am the happiest man in England" (from Prof Richard Susskind), with every shade of approval, scepticism and disapproval in between ... Very few have rejected the concept out of hand ... Much the largest concern has been about the need to cater for those who would be challenged by the need to communicate with the court by computer.

Briggs (Final Report)[44]

Improving ODR: 10 key lessons

- Prioritise accessibility and affordability.
- Construct a multi-tiered system.
- Ensure that there is procedural fairness and trust.
- Design for digital inclusivity.
- Balance efficiency with user interaction.
- Use technology to reduce costs.
- Retain flexibility in cases that may be brought.
- Deal with concerns about 'second-class' justice.
- Make public legal education part of an ODR scheme.
- Allow for continuous adaptation and improvement.

In 2015, the UK Civil Justice Council published *Online Dispute Resolution for Low-Value Civil Claims*, a groundbreaking report that remains a cornerstone of court and court-connected ODR analysis nearly a decade later. The report was prepared by an advisory group chaired by Professor Richard Susskind, a leading champion of ODR. Advocating for radical change in the UK court system, the report highlighted the need for a new approach to resolving low-value civil claims, one that leverages technology to address the inefficiencies of traditional courts: costliness, slowness and complexity (the last of which particularly affects self-represented disputants).

The Susskind Report suggested that information technology (IT) can be used to support court systems in two very different ways. First, to improve what is already in place – that is, enhancing rather than replacing offline mechanisms. (A criticism of this approach is that it can yield what is known as 'mess for less' – a lower-cost online process that is still not especially streamlined.) Second, to deliver services in entirely new ways – a process that requires court service providers to start afresh, with a blank sheet of paper.

The Susskind Report considers ODR to be a form of dispute resolution that embraces the use of IT and the Internet to help resolve disputes (and not merely to involve the computerisation of court systems). Bringing this notion of ODR to bear, the report notes that when a conflict is addressed using ODR, a traditional courtroom is not required. Instead, the process of resolution is conducted entirely or largely across the Internet – that is, the doing of justice becomes an online service.

The principal recommendation of the Susskind Report was that the United Kingdom should establish a new, internet-based service, to be known as His Majesty's (HM) Online Court and comprising three stages, shown in Figure 5. Although the report was confined to a consideration of claims under the value of £52,000, its authors considered that the online court process could also be extended to suitable family law cases and to other appropriate cases currently dealt with offline.

In terms of the various elements of a successful low-cost small-court regime (though the same points could be made in respect of any ODR process), the Susskind Report identified various key features – namely, that it should be affordable to all, regardless of means; accessible, especially to people with disabilities; intelligible to non-lawyers; appropriate for an increasingly online society; swift (not least so that the period of uncertainty for users is minimised); consistent and predictable; trustworthy; focused (ie, judges used only when needed); structured, so that judges are a last resort; cost efficient (with costs proportionate to the amount in issue); fair; robust (have clear rules and fully implement the law); and provide a final form of relief (not least as users need to get on with life).

The Susskind Report considered that past reformers had succumbed to the

Figure 5: HM Online Court proposed structure

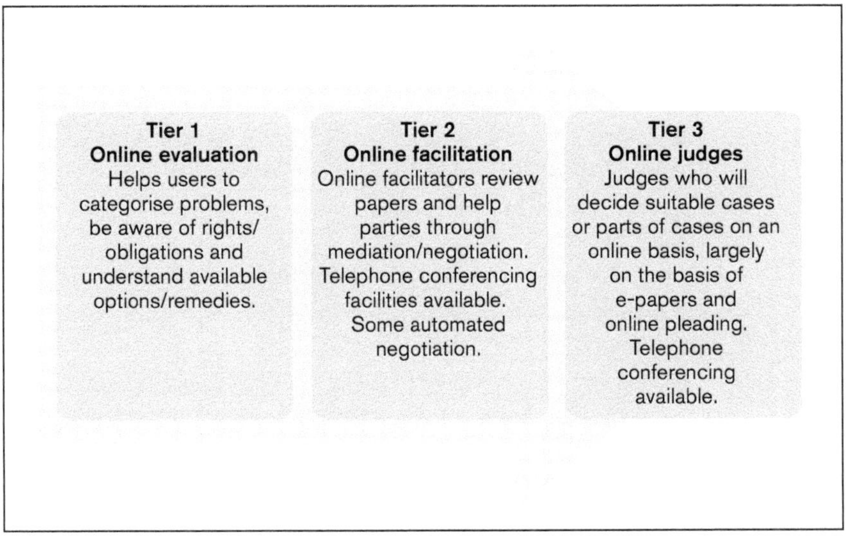

temptation of streamlining existing offline courts, whereas in truth more fundamental change is required in a digital age. Having looked at some existing ODR systems, the Susskind Report moved on to perhaps its most exciting element: reconceiving how justice falls properly to be administered in an increasingly online world and reimagining the role of a national court system in that world.

Cost of new online court

The Susskind Report was particularly interesting when it came to the cost of the proposed online court. The authors of the report were not yet in a position to give fully quantified costs but considered that, even with a bespoke IT system, the cost would be a mere fraction of the then current cost of financing the justice system, observing:

- *It is not yet possible to present a fully articulated business case for HMOC. This can more responsibly be done after some piloting of ODR. But ... two predictions can safely be made.*
- *First, if we are able to take cases out of the conventional court system and into the online environment, then this will reduce both fixed and operating costs ...*
- *Our second prediction is that the introduction of online facilitation (Tier Two) will greatly reduce the number of cases that actually reach judges ...*
- *HMOC will, of course, require robust, secure, and reliable technology on which to run. This need not be costly, because there are already standard ODR platforms that can be licensed and deployed. We expect that the set-up costs of this and ongoing development costs could comfortably be covered by*

the court fees that parties would pay. We further expect that these fees will be lower than conventional court charges ...

- *Even if [Government] ... took the view that a bespoke system should be developed to support HMOC, this would incur development costs that would be modest in comparison to the current expenditure on maintaining and upgrading the current systems. Certainly, it would be a tiny fraction of the £75 million that is being allocated annually for the next five years for the civil justice reform programme.*[45]

One of the most innovative aspects of the Susskind Report is its reconceptualisation of access to justice. It proposed that justice should be structured into three key categories:

- *Dispute avoidance:* Helping individuals to prevent disputes before they arise.
- *Dispute containment:* Resolving disputes early and efficiently to prevent escalation.
- *Dispute resolution:* Providing formal mechanisms to resolve disputes that are not avoided or contained.

The report argues that states currently overemphasise dispute resolution while neglecting avoidance and containment. By shifting priorities, the legal system could reduce the need for costly judicial intervention. The report describes this as a "fluoride moment"[46] for the legal sector: just as the addition of fluoride to Britain's national water supply in the 1950s radically reduced tooth decay for succeeding generations, so a fundamental rethink of access to justice stands to benefit countless millions into the future. Fundamentally, what the report proposes is a preventative approach to justice that would see the report's proposed online court structured and operated in a different way from traditional offline courts.

Susskind proposed a three-tier structure for his envisioned online court (as shown in Figure 6):

- Tier 1 – online evaluation: Users would begin by accessing online tools to assess their legal issues. These tools would guide users through their problems, helping them to resolve minor disputes or recognise when professional assistance is necessary. Fundamentally, this tier would aim to prevent escalation and reduce the need for formal litigation.
- Tier 2 – online facilitation: For a modest fee, trained facilitators would, at this stage, help parties to reach non-binding resolutions using a combination of ADR and early dispute resolution (EDR).* Unlike

* EDR is a form of facilitated ADR. It involves parties at a relatively early stage of proceedings sharing enough knowledge about their respective positions so that they have sufficient knowledge of those positions to arrive at a facilitated settlement.

Figure 6: Present/preferable emphasis of court systems

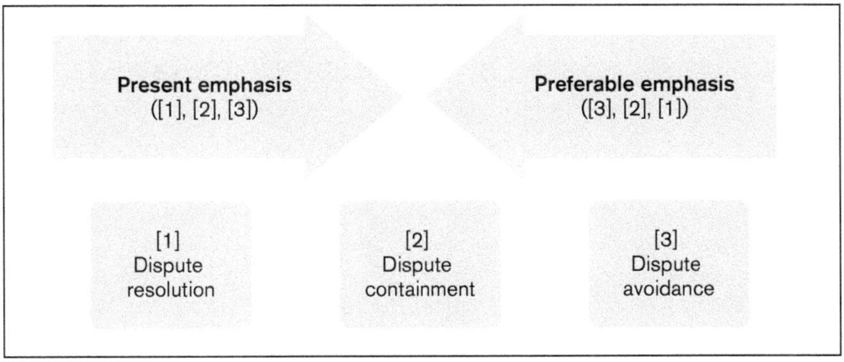

[Paradoxically, what the Susskind Report proposes is that greater, earlier involvement by the state in dispute resolution will lead to lesser, later involvement of judges at the dispute resolution stage – that is, by doing more, states will end up paying less.]

traditional ADR, this process would be integrated into the state-provided system, thereby ensuring accessibility and fairness.* The overall idea is that Tier 1 and Tier 2 would filter out many cases at low cost, and that the cost to the state of Tier 3 would be reduced through its taking place online.

- Tier 3 – online judges: Users could escalate unresolved disputes to this final tier, where online judges would issue binding decisions based on electronic filings, e-pleadings and virtual hearings. Tier 3 fees would be higher than Tier 2 fees but still lower than the costs traditionally associated with going to court. In some cases, judges could refer disputes to offline courts if necessary.

The ideal court system championed by the Susskind Report brings its own challenges, including the following.

Fair trial concerns: Critics argue that ODR may not ensure the same level of fairness as in-person trials. However, it is perhaps worth noting that technology can also enhance procedural fairness – for example, by reducing delays. Additionally, AI-assisted decision-making audits coupled with human oversight and the potential for hybrid hearings (when merited) should ensure that the fairness of ODR proceedings equals or exceeds that of offline proceedings.

---

* Finding adequately trained facilitators can be a challenge. Branting *et al* have suggested three potential computer-aided models of facilitation. The first is an assistive model that would identify or alert a facilitator to significant information, thus lightening the workload of facilitators. The second potential model is a training model that would alert less experienced facilitators to what a more experienced facilitator might have done. The third potential model is autonomous facilitation by a 'bot' in the absence of a human facilitator (Branting *et al*, 467).

Notably, the authors of the Susskind Report were quite robust in their defence of the ability of their proposed online court to offer a fair trial, stating:

> *There is some debate in the ODR community as to whether an online dispute handling process of the sort that we recommend would provide a fair trial ... [W]e see no reason why traditional principles of natural justice (requiring that parties are given an opportunity to plead their cases and that judges are independent) cannot be achieved in using a transparent ODR process that is governed by a clear set of rules. Similarly, we have concluded that well-conceived ODR can provide a fair hearing under Article 6 of the European Convention on Human Rights.*[47]
> (Article 6 is concerned with the right to a fair trial).

Economy class justice: Some fear that ODR could create a two-tier system, with traditional courts offering premier services for wealthier disputants. The Susskind Report rejects this notion, asserting that online courts can deliver high-quality justice for all. It also considers that in time, certain classes of dispute would be required to be heard online, ending any false perception that better services are available offline to a privileged few. (There is a countervailing view to this, which is that mandatory online resolution would remove disputants' ability to choose a format that best suits their needs; whether such an ability is a right is open to question.)

The digital divide: When it comes to the digital divide, the Susskind Report points to the pervasiveness of the Internet and internet usage in British society. And although it accepts that a minority of users might be unable to use the online service, it considers that they should receive special assistance from the online court, rather than have their needs delay the rollout of ODR. This is so important (and in some ways, arguably, a non-politically correct point) that it is worth quoting what the report has to say in this regard:

> *One concern that is commonly raised in connection with ODR is that its compulsory use could greatly disadvantage those who do not use the Internet. This is an important issue ... While it is important that ODR does not create new problems of access to justice, it is also crucial that the current level of Internet usage in England and Wales is grasped. The 2013 edition of The Internet in Britain ... establishes that 78 per cent of the British population are now users (of whom, 65% 'used at least one of a set of government information and service delivery applications in the past year'). While the balance of 22% is certainly a significant proportion, it transpires that only a small fraction of these non-users 'definitely' have no one who could assist them. This suggests that around 5% of the adult population are in fact out of reach today, which is a smaller proportion than is popularly assumed. Nonetheless, we cannot assume that all Internet users will be*

> *able to use ... [the proposed online court] confidently. We suggest that those who are unable to use the service (and this minority group itself is likely to shrink over time) should be given special support by officials ... in the future rather than delay or prevent the introduction of ODR into the court system of England and Wales.*

It is possible that the just-quoted text may paint a somewhat rosy picture of the position presenting. For example, a report published by the House of Commons Library in 2023 indicated that a mere 7% of UK households did not have internet access at home in that year. This was down from around 11% in 2020 and 24% in 2011.[48] However, once age and socio-economic status were factored in, it emerged that 18% of lower-income households did not have internet access, as well as 18% of people aged over 65 years.[49] Ostensibly, the 18% seems an improvement on the 22% referred to in the Susskind Report. However, media coverage suggested that matters were quickly getting worse again, especially for poorer and older people. So, for example, in May 2023, BBC News reported that up to 1 million people had cancelled their broadband access in the previous year because of the high cost of living.[50] In June 2023, *The Guardian* reported on concerns voiced in the House of Lords that millions of citizens were being left out as the world moved online.[51] And in August 2023, *The Guardian* published an editorial expressing concern about the growing digital divide in the United Kingdom, suggesting that, in the pursuit of progress, a technological wall was being erected between the mainstay of society and an older, poorer and more vulnerable category of persons who lived outside England's comparatively wealthy southeast.[52]

Additionally, the point might be made that simply offering assistance to ODR users caught on the wrong side of the digital divide does not fully address structural inequality – that is, those with lower digital proficiency may still struggle with complex legal processes even with support. Moreover, reliance on supplementary measures involves a degree of expectation that users in need of such measures will seek out and effectively utilise assistance, which may not always be the case.

Litigiousness: Some commentators have suggested that the sheer accessibility of ODR could generate litigiousness. The authors of the Susskind Report were unconvinced. They suggested that any uptick in litigation could just as well be the result of persons having a greater opportunity to litigate their disputes than before. Additionally, the report posited that any tendency to litigiousness inherent in an online system could be resolved by pitching the Tier 2 and Tier 3 fees at a level sufficient to deter any such excess.

Ultimately, the Susskind Report remains a visionary blueprint for the future of justice in the United Kingdom and elsewhere. Its emphasis on rethinking the concept of access to justice and the uses to be made of technology, and prioritising efficiency, is compelling. While challenges remain, the report's core argument is clear: ODR is not just an alternative to traditional courts; it is the foundation of a new, more accessible and more equitable judicial system.

In 2015 and 2016, Lord Justice (now Lord) Briggs issued, respectively, his Interim Report and Final Report on the future structure and operation of the UK civil courts.* Nearly a decade later, these reports remain influential, offering a detailed examination of the merits and challenges of, among other matters, ODR and its potential to transform access to justice. The centrepiece of the Interim Report was the proposal for an online court designed to provide access to justice for individuals and small businesses of ordinary means – not simply a digital replica of existing courts but something entirely new. Crucially, this online court would be the first in the United Kingdom designed to be used by disputants without reliance on lawyers. Key features of the proposed online court included the following:

- A focus on simplicity and modest claims: The court would handle relatively straightforward disputes of lower value.
- A three-stage structure:
  - Stage 1: A largely automated triage process to help disputants to identify their claims or defences and provide relevant details.**
  - Stage 2: A mix of conciliation and case management conducted online or by phone. (Briggs' intention was to make conciliation a culturally normal part of the civil court process.)
  - Stage 3: Determination by a lower court judge via phone, video or in-person hearings, with no default traditional trial.
- A separate enforcement stage: This would ensure compliance with judgments.

Briggs argued for a distinct online court with its own rules, separate from existing civil courts. He saw several advantages to this approach.

First, it would keep the online court strictly apart from the existing culture of the civil courts. (That said, isolating an online court entirely may risk creating inconsistencies between online and traditional court procedures. A more integrated approach could perhaps better ensure greater coherence in judicial decision making.)

Second, it would need intensive IT support (so leveraging off an existing court's IT arrangements would not be realistic). (As against that, building a separate system from the ground up requires substantial investment in both

---

* Because only a portion of each report was concerned with the establishment of an online court, both reports are considered here.

** In the medical and nursing professions, 'triage' means the allocation of medical resources by reference to who has the greatest need for immediate attention. In the ODR context, 'triaging' cases involves prioritising legal assistance to the persons assessed to be presenting with the most serious problems.

technology and personnel. A hybrid approach may provide a more cost-effective and sustainable solution.)

Third, well-trained case officers would be required, and it would be better if their sole focus were the online court. (A question perhaps arises as to whether maintaining separate personnel for online and offline courts could lead to duplication of roles and administrative bottlenecks. Training existing court staff to handle both online and in-person cases might ensure better resource allocation and flexibility.)

Fourth, a separate court with separate rules could hopefully avoid perceived convolution in the rules of civil procedure. (It might be observed that while simplifying rules for online disputes is a valid goal, introducing a distinct procedural framework may lead to confusion, particularly for disputants who engage with both online and offline courts. A better approach might be to streamline existing civil procedure rules so that they can accommodate digital processes.)

In terms of jurisdiction – and following consultation that saw suggestions as to the upper limit of online court jurisdiction to range from £2,000–£10,000 – Briggs eventually settled for an initial upper threshold of £25,000 but with the intention that this threshold would increase as the court proved its value. As to the classes of case that should not go before the court, Briggs was of the clear view that claims for possession of dwelling houses, claims for injunctions or other non-monetary relief, class claims (including in personal and corporate insolvencies) and claims by or against minor children or other protected parties were unsuitable for an online court.

Briggs also sensed that, except in very low-value cases (of £5,000 or less), personal injury claims required the levelling influence of lawyers (in cases that would typically be brought against insurers). When it came to disrepair claims by tenants, he considered that such disputants might elect, but would not be compelled, to go to the online court. (The contrary view rested on the claim that such cases are likely to be fact-intensive and involve cross-examination.) As to whether it should be required that cases which came within the jurisdiction of the online court be brought to that court, Briggs considered that it would be unhelpful (and perhaps even unlawful) to make recourse to the online court compulsory until suitable user assistance had been designed, tested and put in place; and that such compulsion should follow only once the online court had proved itself an attractive forum for those using it.

Acknowledging that up to 50% of disputants might face challenges with digital systems (a figure far higher than those considered above), Briggs proposed an 'Assisted Digital' service that would provide help with forms, operate a telephone helpline and offer support for non-English speakers. However, he cautioned against parallel paper-based systems, emphasising the need for robust support services.

Briggs suggested that costs in the online court should be limited to court fees and minor expenses, with no general cost-shifting unless misconduct was involved. As to the need for justice to be done in public, Briggs considered that this presented a technical challenge but not an insuperable obstacle to digitalisation.

Briggs' Final Report addressed feedback to the interim report. Briggs describes the feedback received as having ranged widely from enthusiasm to cautious support, neutrality, scepticism, outright opposition and even a small amount of hostility. Very few people, Briggs found, rejected the concept of an online court out of hand. However, some considered that issues of accessibility could better be met by establishing a more generous free legal aid system. (This perhaps overlooks the point that one reason for moving courts online is not just to increase accessibility but an inevitability in an increasingly digital world.) As touched upon in the introductory quote to this chapter, the issue of most concern to those who responded to Briggs' interim report concerned the digital divide – in particular, the need to cater for those who would be challenged by the need to communicate by computer. (The digital divide is not an issue that Briggs treated with in particular detail in his interim report.)

The principal concerns expressed by those who were critical, sceptical or fearful of the online court concept included the following. The online court would provide second-tier, second-class justice to people wrongly viewed as having second-class claims. A majority of those needing to use the online court would be denied access to justice because of computer literacy issues. The exclusion of lawyers could lead to injustice. The exclusion of lawyers would see the greedy and ill-intentioned prey on vulnerable disputants. The online court would be a rash and unprecedented step in the dark. £25,000 was an unnecessarily high level at which to set the ceiling of the court's jurisdiction. The court would be blighted by government IT failures. The court would not be funded adequately. The proposed Stage 1 was beyond the capacity of IT and would never replace bespoke advice from a lawyer. Determination of disputes about substantive rights other than at a face-to-face hearing would deprive a disputant of "that basic feature of English justice ... a day in court".[53] And finally, online justice threatens a loss of open justice and transparency.

Reading some of these concerns, one would almost imagine that ODR had never previously been trialled in any other jurisdiction. Moreover, they all seem to be informed by a sense of trepidation that the courts would embrace digital technology, rather than seeing it as an evolutionary inevitability and also a transformative opportunity. In any event, Briggs treated as follows with the concerns raised:

- *Second-class justice:* Briggs did not accept that claims below £25,000 were being treated as of secondary importance if they went to the online court. He maintained that it is because claims are so important to ordinary disputants and could not be litigated at proportionate cost or otherwise satisfactorily using lawyers that the online court had been proposed. He also disputed the notion that the processes of the online court would be second-class, emphasising in this regard the preliminary 'triage' process, the fact that cases in need of face-to-face hearings would still get them, the degree of judicial involvement and the potential for appeals. Fundamentally, Briggs thought that the 'second-class justice' point flowed from a hankering for traditional litigation with lawyers engaged on both sides under a full retainer. But that traditional format, he noted, is nowadays so expensive as to render it unaffordable or disproportionately large when compared to any gain that a victorious party might secure in litigation.

- *Digital divide:* Many or most of the persons using the online court would be unrepresented – that is, they would be self-represented 'disputants in person'. The challenges posed for such disputants by having to operate a computer process was continuously raised with Briggs during the consultation process that preceded his final report. For Briggs, the starting point in this regard is that there is no form of litigation process which would not be a challenge to a significant class of disputants. He considered too that the interactive process of Stage 1 triage in the online court would be of real assistance in enabling such disputants to navigate their way through a dispute. And he noted that, over time, there will be an increasing number of younger disputants for whom online communication is easier than using paper. He did not consider it realistic that the issue of computer literacy would be solved by having a computer system and a paper-based system operating in tandem, especially when the end goal was that usage of the online court would be compulsory. He considered the solution to lie in funding, developing and testing services to assist those who found using computers to present a challenge.
- *Exclusion of lawyers:* Briggs indicated that it was not a design objective of the online court to exclude lawyers. Rather, it was intended that the court should be accessible equally to lawyers and disputants in person.
- *A rash leap in the dark:* Briggs acknowledged that at the time of his report, there was no court in operation that completely matched the proposed online court. However, he noted that there were precedents for most of the novel aspects of the proposed court. Thus, online investigative triage (eg, that contemplated for Stage 1) was already in operation in, for example, British Columbia. Conciliation was already a feature of certain UK courts. Paperless hearings were (at the time) on the verge of being trialled in the UK Crown Court. Hearings by telephone and video had long been trialled and tested. The idea of a more investigative, less adversarial court was already being trialled in Europe (and, informally,

by English district judges when dealing with small claims). Additionally, while Briggs accepted that the establishment of the new court would meet with setbacks, troubles and unexpected difficulties, he considered that it was worth stepping a little into the unknown in order to have a civil court that was accessible to individuals and small businesses, providing justice at a modest cost.

The digital divide

The needs of those caught on the 'wrong side' of the digital divide are so common a feature of academic and other commentary on ODR that it is useful to consider the points made in this regard by the final Briggs Report in a little more detail. Thus, Briggs observes:

- *[T]here is no conceivable form of litigation process which will not be a challenge to a significant class of ...* [litigants] *without lawyers.*
- The United Kingdom's *system of advice agencies tries to prioritise such people's needs,* but does not meet them in full.
- Many (in particular current non-users of the civil courts) would find the interactive process of stage 1 triage *of real assistance.*
- *[T]here will over time be an increasing number of younger users for whom online communication is easier than using paper.*
- *Against that, there will be a significant class with specific challenges in using computers, a large enough class to need special assistance, if the Online Court is ... compulsory.*
- Help will also be *needed for those ... challenged by* [both] *computer and paper.*
- *It is not ... realistic ... to seek to solve the problem of the ...* [digitally] *challenged by the permanent retention of a parallel paper-based equivalent ...* [Such a] *hybrid service costs more than either a purely paper-based or purely online service.*
- *The solution lies...in the most intense search for, funding, development and testing of services to assist the ... challenged, sometimes called 'Assisted Digital'.*
- *Designing all ... IT for use on smartphones and tablets ...* [not just] *desk-tops and lap-tops, is widely regarded as ... widening the class of court users likely to benefit from it.*
- *[A]lthough ... existing advice and support agencies ... have the skills best suited to providing face to face assistance,* they need the necessary funding. (Otherwise, the courts would need to *recruit and train ...* [their] *own national force of helpers).*
- *[B]eing challenged by the need to use computers is only one aspect of achieving adequate access to justice with minimal assistance from privately funded lawyers. It needs to be addressed in that wider context.*

The £25,000 ceiling: Briggs remained satisfied that the £25,000 ceiling for online court disputes would not withdraw from the existing civil courts a significant body of cases which could be litigated with legal representation but at proportionate cost and risk. However, he considered that there was a case for a soft launch, with the £25,000 threshold to be reached in stages.

Loss of 'day in court': As Briggs observed, the loss of the traditional 'day in court' is a criticism that can be levelled at any reform which proposes departing from a face-to-face hearing for all aspects of court proceedings. Briggs offered six reasons why he was not persuaded by this criticism:

- All that was proposed to be discarded was the default assumption that there should be a face-to-face hearing.
- If such a hearing were necessary, it would proceed.
- Video hearing offers a (remote) day in court.
- The growth of remote communication means that such communication will likely become a cultural norm.
- The conciliation process offers something akin to a day in court.
- Cost constraints may require some tempering of public expectations as to the feasibility of getting a day in court.

Online justice threatens open justice: Briggs did not accept this proposition. His view was that imaginative use of IT offers a means whereby transparency could be improved rather than merely preserved.

Having considered the various criticisms touched upon above, Briggs moved on to consider some issues that were outstanding since he issued his interim report. First, he noted that the preference within government was for a free-standing online court as the best means of bringing about change from an excessively legalistic culture. Second, as mentioned, Briggs considered that the following types of claim should be *excluded* from the jurisdiction of the online court: non-monetary claims (eg, for an injunction or specific performance); all claims for the possession of homes; certain personal injury claims; professional negligence claims (at least for a time, given their complexity); small IP claims (they already had a user-friendly track via the IP Enterprise Court – this rationale is a little hard to follow if the online court was to be a new, standalone dispute resolution forum); and certain housing disrepair claims. (As will be seen in later chapters, the proposed exclusion of these forms of dispute is more conservative than the approach taken in other jurisdictions – perhaps most notably in China.)

Based on the observations that he had received, Briggs refined the three-stage structure in his interim report to include the following:

- Stage 0: Cautioning users about litigation being a last resort, referring

them to free legal advice and/or providing them with distilled summaries of the law.
- Stage 0.5: Encouraging parties to determine whether a dispute truly requires court intervention. (If so, the full panoply of Stage 1 triage can be avoided.)
- Stage 1: Using online Stage 1 triage software to guide the disputant through an analysis of their grievance in such a way as to produce a document that is capable of being understood by opponents and the court.

As regards Stage 2, Briggs was of the view that the choice of conciliation process for each case should be for an experienced, judicially trained and supervised case officer acting in conjunction with the disputants. As regards Stage 3, by way of supplementary observation to what he had suggested in his interim report, Briggs posited the possibility of specialist experts sitting as judges in some court cases.

Briggs highlighted that it would be wrong to consider that the support needed for prospective online court users would be limited to 'Assisted Digital' and noted that the success of the online court in extending access to justice would depend on parallel progress in public legal education.

The Briggs Reports provide a blueprint for the future of civil justice, emphasising the potential of ODR to deliver cost-effective, accessible and fair outcomes, pointing to the necessity of rethinking traditional court structures to meet the demands of a digital age and highlighting the importance of addressing technological and cultural barriers to the rollout of an ODR platform.

Should justice be completely privatised?

The Hague Institute for Innovation of Law (HiiL) has considered the question of whether courts have a role to play in a world where there is an abundance of private ODR providers.[54] It (rightly) considers that courts continue to have a role to play. The points made by the HiiL include the following:

- No democracy can do without courts, given their critical role in upholding the rule of law. (Online courts ensure continuous, geographically unrestricted access to courts.)
- Courts act as a check on governmental power. (Digital platforms make judicial oversight more accessible.)
- Courts provide fairness and, in criminal law, proportionate retribution. (An online court can enhance timely delivery of these outcomes.)
- Offline court procedures suffer from delay and inflexibility. (Online courts can offer simplified processes.)
- Traditional court proceedings can be complex and slow. (Online courts can make judicial processes less complex and swifter.)
- Traditional procedures tend to remediate past harms. (Online platforms can prioritise future-looking restorative justice.)

- The need for lawyers can restrict access to traditional courts. (Online courts can reduce the need for intermediaries.)
- Specialised courts (eg, dealing with child or drug cases) have been found to work well. (Online courts can support specialisation by directing cases to the right platform.)
- Meaningful system-wide reform of offline courts has proved elusive. (Online solutions can more readily be scaled up.)
- The market for effective legal procedures is inefficient as disputing parties cannot agree on a preferred dispute resolution process. (By contrast, online platforms offer pre-established and readily accessible dispute resolution processes.)
- Leading judges have observed that existing court processes do not adequately meet user needs. (Online courts can be designed to receive continuous user feedback.)

Key learnings

- *Prioritise accessibility and affordability.* An ODR platform should be accessible to all users, regardless of digital literacy or financial standing. Some caution is required: focusing purely on affordability could conceivably compromise investment in robust IT infrastructure.
- *Construct a multi-tiered system.* A good ODR system should include, for example, evaluation, facilitation and adjudication stages. That said, too rigid a structure might yield unnecessary delays as cases are routed through the various steps.
- *Ensure that there is procedural fairness and trust.* Users must trust that an ODR system will provide transparent decision making, fair outcomes, clear rules and an avenue for appeal. Of course, unduly rigorous procedures could compromise the promise of efficiency that ODR entails.
- *Design for digital inclusivity.* An ODR platform should cater for those on the wrong side of the digital divide. The solution lies in the most intense search for, funding, development and testing of services to assist such persons (sometimes called 'Assisted Digital').
- *Balance efficiency with user interaction.* ODR should both streamline dispute resolution and ensure that disputants feel heard and involved.
- *Use technology to reduce costs.* Automation can reduce costs for both government and disputants. Conversely, over-reliance on automation may yield a loss of human judgement and touch in cases requiring deftness and nuance.
- *Retain flexibility in cases that may be brought.* An ODR system should begin with low-value, low-complexity cases but be adaptable to more

complex claims. Using ODR in more complex cases may require careful testing to ensure that confidence in the system is not undermined.

- *Deal with concerns about 'second-class' justice.* An ODR platform must show that online hearings and decisions provide the same level of justice as traditional courts.
- *Make public legal education a part of an ODR scheme.* A good ODR system should include legal guidance tools to help users understand their rights and duties. Self-represented disputants may find complex legal issues challenging, so there will be a need for legal assistance in some cases.
- *Allow for continuous adaptation and improvement.* ODR platforms should evolve based on, for example, technological advances and user feedback. That said, an undue number of changes could conceivably yield confusion and a lack of trust.

4. Two UK examples of ODR in action

Good governance can smooth the pathway to success with an ODR initiative. Poor or non-existent governance will make the path more complicated and difficult, and in extreme instances, ensure that the project fails and the status quo prevails ... In the absence of effective governance, visionary leadership may be sufficient to launch and sustain an ODR initiative of limited scope. As those initiatives begin to succeed, momentum will build and may be a catalyst for more effective governance.

Joint Technology Committee[55]

Since ODR is still in its nascent stages of development ... it is important that the governance framework encourages the growth of innovation both within the Government and in the private sector. To enable this, a balance has to be struck between protecting the rights and interests of its users while ensuring that over-regulation does not stifle innovation.

NITI Aayog[56]

Improving ODR: 10 key lessons

- ODR can significantly improve access to justice.
- User experience should be central to design.
- Digital platforms can resolve most cases without hearings.
- Assisted digital support is essential for inclusivity.
- Transparency enhances trust in the system.
- Automation and AI can improve efficiency.
- Hybrid models offer flexibility for complex cases.
- Public legal education is critical for adoption.
- System flexibility ensures adaptability.
- Small wins build momentum for large reforms.

It has been suggested that there are four phases to ODR development in a nation: the hobbyist phase (when ODR is the plaything of gifted amateurs); the experimental phase (when organisations begin to trial ODR – for example, as a means of resolving customer disputes); the entrepreneurial phase (when private ODR is rolled out on a larger scale); and the institutional phase (when ODR is rolled out at the official level). Among liberal democracies, jurisdictions such as Canada, the United Kingdom and the United States have all entered the institutional phase.* The UK TPT and MCOL offer the clearest examples of successful institutional ODR.

1. The Traffic Penalty Tribunal

The TPT, established in 2000, has steadily evolved into a leading example of online justice. By 2008, its operations began transitioning to an online model and today, over 95% of its appeals are resolved entirely online. This transformation illustrates the potential of technology to streamline dispute resolution while maintaining fairness and accessibility. The TPT's primary function is to adjudicate in motorists' appeals against penalty charge notices (PCNs) issued by local and charging authorities in England and Wales for parking and traffic violations. It operates as a regulatory tribunal established by legislation, independent from local government, with adjudicators serving as impartial judicial officers.

Most cases before the TPT are decided based on uploaded evidence, with telephone and video hearings available if necessary. The TPT's Fast Online Appeals Management System (FOAM) enables users, adjudicators and administrators to view and interact with case details in real time. Parties can communicate, comment on documents and seek administrative assistance through messaging and live chat. TPT statistics from 2021 to 2022 demonstrate its remarkable efficiency: 10% of cases were resolved in 0–1 day, 21% in 2–7 days, 19% in 8–14 days, 31% in 15–28 days and 19% in 29+ days. For appellants who are unable to access the online system, the TPT provides 'Assisted Digital' support, helping them to complete appeals via phone, live chat or post. This commitment aligns with the UK government's Digital Service Standard (on which see later below) and addresses the needs of digitally excluded regions.

FOAM embodies the TPT's 'digital by default' philosophy, which prioritises user experience and customer service over technology alone. Through FOAM, parties gain full visibility of each other's actions and can engage in transparent

* On the four phases, see Ballesteros, 89–90. ODR in China, which is not a liberal democracy, can also be seen to have long entered its institutional phase. There is also a phase prior to the four phases in which – despite jurisdictions such as Canada, the United Kingdom and the United States showing that ODR offers the potential for a great leap forward in terms of effective, efficient and accessible dispute resolution – a state takes no steps to optimise the potential benefits to it of participating in the dispute resolution revolution that ODR is elsewhere bringing about.

communication throughout the appeal process. This system's efficiency means that only 10% of cases require a hearing, conducted via telephone, video or – increasingly rarely – in person. The TPT also emphasises collaboration between legal professionals and systems architects to ensure user-friendly design. Its focus is not just on technology but on delivering accessible, transparent and streamlined justice.

During the COVID-19 pandemic, the TPT enhanced its digital services by moving all hearings to Microsoft Teams; revising communications throughout the appeals process; conducting customer experience surveys post-hearing; and streamlining hearing scheduling for adjudicators. These adjustments, combined with increased public familiarity with online platforms during the pandemic, have solidified the TPT's position as a leader in digital justice in the United Kingdom.

Despite its digital-first approach, the TPT is committed to inclusivity. Proxy (offline) appeals are available for those unable to navigate the online system. (Reviews of postcode data reveal that proxy appellants often come from the United Kingdom's most digitally excluded regions, highlighting the importance of reducing the national digital divide.) The TPT's 'Assisted Digital' service actively engages with these users, ensuring that no one is left behind.

Once a decision has been made by the TPT, appellants and authorities are notified simultaneously and can log in to view the outcome. Reviews of decisions are rare (fewer than 3% of cases) and fewer than 0.2% result in a changed outcome. Exceptional circumstances for review include administrative errors, unavailable evidence or legal errors in the initial decision. After an internal review, appellants may seek judicial review if necessary. So, there is some potential for seepage into offline courts.

In 2021, the TPT outlined key lessons from its digital transformation. These include the following. Processes must complement the digitised approach. Technology should free up time for human customer service. Systems should be well archived to avoid data migration issues. End-to-end processes must be established before launch; refinements follow. Collaboration with stakeholders is essential. Achieving small, connected 'wins' fuels momentum for larger projects. Some observations might be made regarding these learnings. Digitalisation should prompt process redesign, not merely complement existing processes. Digitalisation is about reducing human intervention, not merely freeing up time for some other human action. Excessive archiving may actually cause data migration issues. Over-planning may unduly delay ODR rollout. Excessive collaboration with stakeholders may generate inefficiencies in decision making. Lastly, emphasising incremental successes may unduly distract an ODR provider from effecting bold changes.

The TPT's website exemplifies user-centred design. Upon visiting, users are greeted with a clear summary of its purpose: "Free, fair, and fast appeals.

Decided by expert, independent lawyers." Navigation is intuitive, with buttons such as "How to Appeal", "Submit an Appeal" and "Appeal Sign-In". For Welsh speakers, Welsh-language text is available. Users can watch a two-and-a-half-minute video explaining the TPT's purpose or click through step-by-step guides tailored to their needs. For example, selecting the "Parking" icon initiates a process which enables users to confirm whether their enforcing authority is in England or Wales; access detailed instructions on challenging PCNs before filing an appeal; and begin the appeal process with clear guidance on required documents and FAQs. Throughout, the website employs bold text, large fonts and vibrant colours to create an engaging, accessible experience. The TPT demonstrates how digital transformation can enhance justice delivery. By prioritising user experience, embracing innovative technology and addressing inclusivity, the TPT has set a benchmark for digital justice systems in the United Kingdom and indeed more generally.*

Figure 7: Summary of TPT process

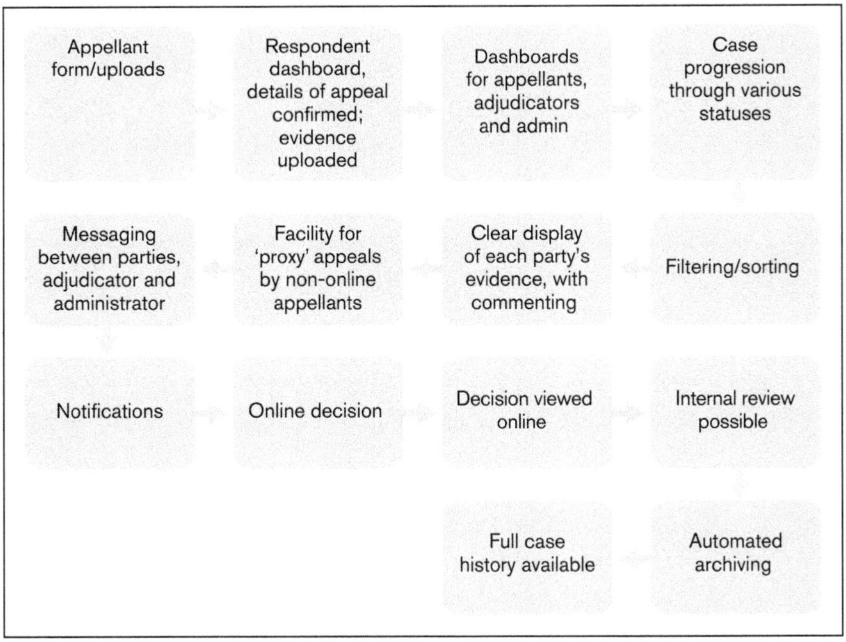

* By way of example, in the United States, Alabama also has an ODR traffic ticket system – Online Traffic Resolution – which operates as follows (see Colee): (1) The person issuing a ticket also provides an information sheet, in English and Spanish. (2) This information sheet directs the recipient to a website that explains how to resolve matters remotely. (3) The person who receives the ticket can plead guilty and either pay in full or seek additional time to make payment. (4) If the ticket is for some form of equipment violation, the system advises how the ticketed person can seek an inspection of their vehicle after the problem presenting has been remedied. (5) Drivers ticketed for failure to show proof of insurance can later upload proof that they are in fact insured. In some instances, there was also the option to make an online request to attend driving school.

The UK government's 14-Point Digital Service Standard[57]

The Digital Service Standard, according to the UK government website, helps teams to create and run great public services. In truth, it reads almost like a guide on how to approach the construction of a successful ODR platform. The 14 points are stated below.

1. ***Understand users and their needs*** *... Develop a deep understanding of users and the problem you're trying to solve ...*
2. ***Solve a whole problem for users*** *... Work towards creating a service that solves a whole problem for users ...*
3. ***Provide a joined-up experience across all channels*** *... Work towards creating a service that meets users' needs across all channels, including online, phone, paper and face to face. [This is sometimes referred to in ODR-related commentary as an 'omni-channel experience'.] ...*
4. ***Make the service simple to use*** *... Build a service that's simple, intuitive and comprehensible ...*
5. ***Make sure everyone can use the service*** *... Provide a service that everyone can use, including disabled people and ... people who do not have access to the internet or lack the skills or confidence to use it ...*
6. ***Have a multidisciplinary team*** *... Put in place a multidisciplinary team that can create and operate the service ...*
7. ***Use agile ways of working*** *... Create the service using agile, iterative user-centred methods ...*
8. ***Iterate and improve frequently*** *... [H]ave the capacity, resources and technical flexibility to iterate and improve the service. [To be avoided are changes that are so frequent as to cause user confusion.]*
9. ***Create a secure service which protects users' privacy*** *... Establish the security risks, threats and legal responsibilities associated with the service ...*
10. ***Define what success looks like and publish performance data*** *... Work out what success looks like for your service and identify metrics which will tell you what's working and what can be improved ...**
11. ***Choose the right tools and technology*** *... Choose tools and technology that let you create a high-quality service in a cost-effective way. Minimise the cost of changing direction in future ...*
12. ***Make new source code open*** *... Make all new source code open and reusable ... Or ... provide a convincing explanation of why this cannot be done ...***

---

* The commentary in this area indicates that the metrics deployed should be both qualitative and quantitative in nature. See, eg, Schmitz, 144–145.

** In a world of oftentimes proprietary software, this is an interesting point. One would perhaps instinctively expect that the government, having expended taxpayer money on coding software, would want

> 13. ***Use and contribute to open standards, common components and patterns** ... Build on open standards and common components and patterns from inside and outside government ...*
> 14. ***Operate a reliable service** ... Minimise service downtime and have a plan ... [for] when it does happen.*

2. Money Claim Online

MCOL is a digital innovation by HM Courts and Tribunals Service, enabling individuals to pursue monetary claims under £10,000 without the need to set foot in a courthouse. MCOL represents a significant step forward in terms of simplifying the civil justice process. However, despite its apparent convenience, the platform's structure, requirements and limitations demand careful navigation by any prospective claimant.

At its core, MCOL is designed for cases that are relatively straightforward: fixed monetary claims involving no more than one claimant and up to two defendants, both of whom must have addresses in England or Wales. This seemingly simple framework belies a host of procedural nuances that users must comprehend to effectively utilise the service.

Not all claims can be processed through MCOL. Those eligible must meet a strict set of criteria. Thus, claims must be for a fixed sum, below £10,000. There can be no more than two defendants involved. Both claimant and defendants must have UK-based addresses. Equally important are the restrictions. For example, MCOL is unavailable to persons under 18 years of age; eligible for legal aid; eligible for 'help with fees'; or making a claim for compensation for an accident or injury. The system is also unsuitable, for example, for claims against a child under 18 years of age; against someone who lacks 'mental capacity' (ie, who is unable to make their own decisions); and against government departments and agencies, such as the revenue commissioners. (As will be seen, some tax disputes can be done via ODR in other jurisdictions, so there seems no reason in principle why such an exclusion should exist in the MCOL system.)

For eligible claims, MCOL breaks down the filing process into eight distinct stages, each structured to ensure clarity and precision:

- *Guidance:* Users are provided with instructions and links to further guidance.
- *Claimant details:* Pre-filled from user's registration; editable if necessary.
- *Correspondence address:* Claimant's address is verified (must be in the United Kingdom).

---

to keep its coding secret. In fact (and for good reason), the opposite applies. Thus, the guidance on the Digital Service Standard explains that because public services are built using public money, "unless there's a good reason not to do so, the code they're based should be made available for people to reuse and build on. Open-source code can be reused by developers working in government, avoiding duplication of work and reducing costs for government as a whole. And publishing source code under an open licence means that you're less likely to get locked in to working with a single supplier ..."

- *Defendant details:* Describes the parties against whom the claim is lodged.
- *Claim particulars:* Claimant must concisely state the nature of the debt and why it is owed. Additional information can be provided if needed.
- *Summary and statement of truth:* Final opportunity to review details. Claims can be saved and submitted within a 28-day period.
- *Payment details:* Court fees paid via credit or debit card.
- *Confirmation:* Once submitted, claims can only be withdrawn via formal filing.

Each stage is essential, underscoring the need for accuracy and attention to detail. Even minor errors at the filing stage can result in delays or complications down the line.

Once a claim is lodged, the procedural landscape broadens. Defendants may respond in various ways, including acknowledgements of service, partial or full admissions, counterclaims or disputes of jurisdiction. If the claimant (and/or counterclaimant) wishes to proceed, the matter goes to court. If the defendant admits the entire claim and the claimant wishes to accept this response, they can request judgment online (or go to court and seek an alternative payment method). There is also provision for informing the court of the settlement or discontinuance of a claim. If a defendant does not respond within the allowed time or makes an admission that is acceptable, the defendant can request judgment with MCOL. A further process needs to be followed when requesting a judgment via MCOL. This involves logging in and selecting the judgment sought; editing claimant details if necessary; editing defendant details if necessary; and choosing a defendant payment option – for example, payment in full/instalments.

3. Conclusion

The TPT and MCOL represent significant advancements in digital dispute resolution in the United Kingdom. While both systems enhance access to justice through digital platforms, their underlying structures and processes vary. The TPT is designed to provide a means of adjudicating on motorist appeals. It functions as an independent tribunal established by legislation and aims to provide fast, accessible and fair adjudication for motorists. MCOL, by contrast, is a civil claims platform that enables individuals and businesses to pursue monetary claims under £10,000 without needing to appear in court. While the TPT is a specialised tribunal dealing exclusively with one form of dispute, MCOL handles a broader range of civil claims, provided that they meet strict eligibility criteria. While both the TPT and MCOL streamline access to justice, their design philosophies, processes and user experiences differ. The TPT prioritises speed, accessibility and user-friendly adjudication, making it an efficient model for regulatory tribunals. MCOL, by contrast, is a structured but more rigid ODR platform, ensuring procedural compliance but requiring claimants to navigate a more formal and document-heavy process.

Key learnings

- *ODR can significantly improve access to justice:* Both the TPT and MCOL demonstrate how digital platforms can streamline dispute resolution.
- *User experience should be central to design:* The TPT's FOAM system emphasises the need for a user-friendly, intuitive interface that allows for seamless case progression. Similarly, MCOL provides a structured, step-by-step claim process. This experience suggests that ODR platforms should prioritise clear navigation and guided workflows to ensure ease of use.
- *Digital platforms can resolve most cases without hearings:* Over 90% of TPT cases are resolved online without requiring a formal hearing, showing that structured ODR processes can significantly reduce court congestion.
- *'Assisted Digital' support is essential for inclusivity:* Both systems recognise the digital divide and offer 'Assisted Digital' services to support users. ODR platforms should include telephone helplines, live chat and proxy (offline) assistance to ensure equal access for all users.
- *Transparency enhances trust:* The TPT publishes appeal outcomes and provides real-time access to case progress. MCOL ensures procedural transparency by adhering to the Civil Procedure Rules. Both systems show that striking the right balance between openness and confidentiality appears essential to maintaining public trust and privacy rights.
- *Automation and AI can improve efficiency:* The structured workflows of FOAM and MCOL automate repetitive tasks, reducing administrative burdens. All ODR platforms should explore AI-driven dispute triage, automated document review and intelligent case allocation to streamline operations.
- *Hybrid models offer flexibility for complex cases:* While the TPT and MCOL primarily resolve disputes online, they allow for video, phone or in-person hearings when necessary.
- *Public legal education is critical for adoption:* The TPT's user-friendly website, with clear explanations and video tutorials, helps users to navigate the appeal process. Of course, even with extensive educational materials, some users may struggle to interpret legal concepts or navigate complex disputes without professional assistance.
- *System flexibility ensures adaptability:* The TPT adapted quickly during

the COVID-19 pandemic by switching all hearings to Microsoft Teams and revising communication strategies. ODR platforms should be designed to evolve to meet user needs in just such way.

- *Small wins build momentum for larger reforms:* The TPT's incremental improvements, from document uploads to real-time messaging and full online case management, illustrate the value of continuous, progressive innovation.

5. ODR in the United States

The use of ODR is expanding rapidly in court settings, with dozens of implementations and pilot projects underway in the United States and abroad ... The following are examples of case types being resolved through ODR ... Small claims ... Traffic and parking ... Property ... Tax assessment appeals ... Low-conflict, low-complexity family court cases.

Joint Technology Committee[58]

ODR is advantageous to the traditional US court system and disputants because it will help mitigate the court docket backlog and streamline the court system. Two key benefits of using ODR platforms are efficiency and accessibility. ... Furthermore, ODR increases accessibility to remedies and justice. An internet-based platform has the potential to reach a larger number of disputants and give those disputants an easier means to resolve disputes.

Wormington[59]

Improving ODR: 10 key lessons

- ODR excels in high-volume, low-complexity cases.
- ODR can improve procedural justice and user engagement.
- Balancing efficiency with procedural integrity is essential.
- Data privacy and security must be prioritised.
- ODR must be designed with accessibility in mind.
- User support and public education are key to adoption.
- ODR should be evaluated using rigorous metrics.
- ODR must be seen as a transformative process.
- Hybrid models may provide the best of both worlds.
- The future of ODR depends on strategic innovation.

Among the world's liberal democracies, the United States is a pioneering leader in the field of court and court-connected ODR. Its relative abundance of ODR programmes offers valuable insights into the challenges and opportunities of digital justice.

Initially (and to this day), ODR seems to have been used in the United States as a form of e-ADR in commercial, family and small claims disputes. However, many American courts have now clambered aboard the ODR "bandwagon",[60] trialling a multiplicity of ODR schemes, with some states (eg, Utah) having commenced ambitious online small claims processes that seek to obviate the need for in-person hearings. Notably, these ventures into ODR do not aim solely for efficiency but also seek to enhance access to justice by providing for meaningful disputant attendance.[61]

The dual promise of accessibility and efficiency has long been touted as ODR's primary strength. Yet, as can be seen even from the first of the introductory quotes above, the focus in the United States has latterly extended to other beneficial aspects of ODR. As one learned commentator has observed, considering ODR solely through the prism of efficiency involves too narrow a view; other important attributes include its potential for increased accountability, equality and fairness because of the manner in which technology constrains discretion, provides a document trail and exposes systematic issues presenting.[62]

Figure 8: Notable ODR rollout in the United States, 2014–2019

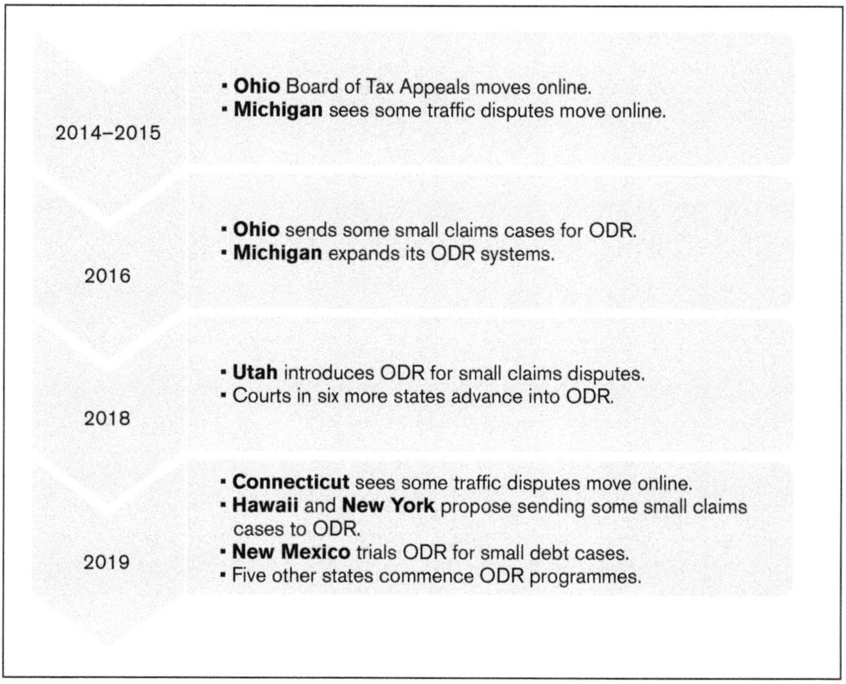

There is also a downside to ODR rollout: there are legitimate concerns over cybersecurity, data privacy and due process – concerns that are only heightened by the intrusion of AI into ODR processes. As one learned commentator has observed in this last regard, among the issues presenting are the transparent usage of algorithms and data; the potential for sensitive data to be accessed and used inappropriately; the wholesale scanning of data by AI-powered technology; and various privacy concerns, such as the giving of consent, the potential for opt-outs and the ability to have data deleted.*

Additionally, the restructuring of traditional court processes to maximise ODR's benefits raises important questions. Can ODR go beyond merely replicating in-person proceedings and deliver outcomes superior to those of offline systems? And what exactly is it that ODR platforms seek or should seek to achieve? Resolving this last question will likely involve some level of government intervention. Historically, privately developed software seems to have placed a premium on redress; however, in court and court-connected ODR, the issue of justice seems more likely to come to the fore. Where the right balance falls to be struck is a matter that only law and policymakers are likely to be able to resolve. As one learned commentator has observed, technology and technologists have provided a means whereby differences in outcomes sought and in design criteria can be accommodated; it is now for policymakers, regulators, institutional decision makers and practitioners to establish appropriate governance for ODR, so that the full potential of the available technology to enhance access to justice can be realised.[63]

Notably, this commentary appears in a journal published in the United States – a jurisdiction where it appears that healthy innovation has outpaced the introduction of necessary regulation. By contrast, as will be seen when it comes to the Council of Europe's well-intentioned, if notably detailed, human rights-based guidance on ODR and AI, this guidance seems to have run ahead of ODR rollout in Council of Europe member states. Arguably, this latter approach risks stifling some level of innovation as the rollout of ODR platforms gathers pace in Europe. As ever with regulation in areas of innovation, there is a challenging balance for law and policymakers to strike; though there is some clarity as to where the present US administration is likely to strike the balance. As US Vice

---

* Thao, 2–3. A good example of the types of issue that AI (and, more particularly, the construction by AI of saleable databases) can present is offered by *Mutnick v Clearview AI, Inc*, 2020 US Dist Lexis 144583. This was a failed application to a US district court for the dismissal of a lawsuit or its transfer to another venue, so it was very much a procedural application. What is of interest is the underlying facts that presented. It was alleged that the defendants had violated privacy rights and used biometric information without the plaintiffs' knowledge and consent. The alleged impugned behaviour involved scraping over 3 billion facial images from the Internet, building a searchable database of the scanned images, providing additional personal and private data and then selling access to the facial recognition database to agencies of the Illinois and federal government. So, the clearest of data confidentiality and privacy issues have the potential to present when it comes to the creation of AI-informed databases (regardless of where the truth of matters lay as regards the allegations made in *Mutnick*).

President JD Vance has latterly observed – specifically of AI, though his comments obviously have resonance when it comes to AI-informed ODR:

> *When conferences … discuss a cutting-edge technology, oftentimes I think our response is to be … too risk-averse. But never have I encountered a breakthrough in tech that so clearly calls us to do precisely the opposite … [O]ur administration … believes that AI will have countless, revolutionary applications … And to restrict its development now would not only unfairly benefit incumbents in the space, it would mean paralyzing one of the most promising technologies we have seen in generations … [W]e believe that excessive regulation of the AI sector could kill a transformative industry just as it's taking off, and we'll make every effort to encourage pro-growth AI policies.*[64]

So, at this time, a low-level or no level of regulation of AI seems to be, to use a colloquialism, the 'order of the day' insofar as the United States is concerned.

A key barrier to comprehensive evaluation of court and court-connected ODR in the United States appears to be the heterogeneity of these schemes, whether in design, implementation or scope.[65] Informal assessments, however, have offered promising findings. For instance, a survey conducted in Ohio revealed that ODR improves disputant participation, reduces court costs, minimises stress and increases voluntary dismissals of suits, while simultaneously improving overall perceptions of fairness and court efficiency.[66]

To ensure that such early successes translate into lasting change, courts must embrace rigorous evaluation methodologies. In their consideration of ODR best practices for court-connected programmes, Acosta and others emphasise the need for both qualitative and quantitative metrics to be applied.[67] On a related note, the guidance on the UK government's Digital Service Standard gives certain insight as to bringing such metrics to bear. Thus, the guidance states as follows of the tenth principle in that standard ("Define what success looks like and publish performance data"). First, defining what good looks like and identifying appropriate metrics mean that service providers can know whether a service is solving the problem it is intended to solve. Second, collecting the right performance data means that service providers will be alerted to potential problems. Third, having such data in hand means that when a service provider makes a change to a service, it will be able to tell whether this has the expected effect. And fourth, by publishing performance data, a provider is transparent

---

* See www.gov.uk/service-manual/service-standard/point-10-define-success-publish-performance-data. By way of more practical insight, the guidance moves on to note that when it comes to applying the tenth principle of the Digital Service Standard, they should "identify metrics which will indicate how well the service is solving the problem it's meant to solve, and track performance against them … [and] use performance data to make decisions about how to fix problems and improve the service". Central government services, the guidance notes, must also publish data on the mandatory key performance indicators.

about the success of services funded by public money.* Without such efforts, the full potential of court and court-connected ODR may remain unrealised.

In 2020, a seminar was convened by the National Institute of Justice, the research, development and evaluation agency of the US Department of Justice. The seminar brought together key stakeholders – including judges, court administrators and ODR programme managers – to discuss best practices for designing and maintaining effective ODR systems. Their insights emphasised the importance of user-centric design, accessibility and engagement.[68] Their observations are too detailed to be considered at length in this book. To give a sense of their (considerable) usefulness, their observations on the design of ODR platforms and programmes are considered below and some associated comment made.

It is testament to the longevity and breadth of American experience in the field of ODR that in 2022, the American Bar Association (ABA) adopted a notably comprehensive set of guidelines to assist ODR system designers, developers, providers (including courts), practitioners and users in arriving at the fair and just resolution of disputes via ODR.[69] The guidance is written for an American audience but has wider resonance. The specific considerations for court and court-connected ODR are considered below.

It will be seen that a lot of the points touched upon in the ABA guidance are separately addressed, for example, in the Susskind and Briggs Reports, the National Institute of Justice seminar and the academic commentary referred to in this book. This suggests a common move among ODR stakeholders towards shared insights that are collectively recognised as being undoubtedly beneficial. Turning to the ABA provisions that are specific to court and court-connected ODR, the guidance observes, among other things, as follows.

Results of National Institute of Justice Seminar (2020): Design of ODR Platforms

Reimagining processes

Issue: Courts could reimagine processes for effective ODR implementation and consider the extent to which ODR should replicate in-court processes.

Possible solution: Develop and disseminate guidance from objective sources about why, when and how to reimagine processes. Provide approaches for courts to develop an understanding of disputant needs.

Comment: This goes back to an issue touched upon in the Susskind Report – namely that one use (and that report's preferred use) of IT in courts "is to enable the delivery of services in entirely new ways. When this is the aim, it encourages new and imaginative thinking and urges reformers to start afresh, with a blank sheet of paper".[70]

Picking the right platform

Issue: Given the array of ODR options offered by private vendors, it can be difficult for court systems to identify a suitable platform.

Possible solution: Provide guidance to help courts identify their technological requirements. Provide guidance for courts on how to effectively communicate requirements for due process and other legal protections.

Comment: As will be seen later below, the ABA guidance* makes a number of helpful observations in this regard, including that "[XI] I. ... Courts should select or develop technology that will address the goals and needs they have identified and be cautious about using technology to perform a function for which it was not designed".

Which case types?

Issue: ODR can be used for a broad variety of case types (eg, criminal, divorce, road traffic and small claims cases). So, to which cases should a proposed ODR platform apply?

Possible solution: Develop documentation that can be shared among courts of which case types have successfully transitioned to ODR. Develop guidance to identify or give examples of case types suitable for initial ODR rollout. Identify channels through which court systems can share information and best practices.

Privacy and security

Issue: Concerns about authentication, data security and privacy can be addressed by improving transparency and trust surrounding information transfer via ODR.

Possible solution: Develop comprehensive guidance on these issues.

Comment: This is such an important area when it comes to any form of online developments that the UK government has developed a 10-point Secure by Design Policy which identifies, among others, the following points:[71] "1. Create responsibility for cyber security risk ... 2. Source secure technology products ... 3. Adopt a risk-driven approach ... 4. Design usable security controls ... 5. Build in detect and respond security ... 6. Design flexible architectures ... 7. Minimise the attack surface ... 8. Defend in depth ... 9. Embed continuous assurance ... 10. Make changes securely."

---

* American Bar Association Section of Dispute Resolution, 241. For an article that gets into minute detail on how to construct an ODR platform, see David Allen Larson (1), 77. Among the key tips offered by Larson when it comes to designing an ODR platform are: (1) to anticipate the conflicts and resistance that will present; (2) to invoke the support and involvement of judges and court administrators from the very beginning; (3) to educate oneself about what is doable before approaching an outside vendor to build the ODR platform; and (4) to exercise care in choosing the type of dispute resolution which it is intended to transpose to the online realm (*id*, 100–101).

Specific ODR features for specific case types
Issue: Some case types might require specific ODR features.
Possible solution: Develop protocols for screening approaches specific to relevant case types.
Comment: This seems especially important in cases that, while they could be treated via ODR, may not be suitable in some instances – for example, cases involving domestic violence and certain child custody cases. As one learned commentator has observed of ODR in the family law context:

- *[S]pecific guidance is important for screening and handling cases of domestic violence and self-represented or limited-resource disputants in ODR ... [For] a victim of domestic violence ... ODR may not provide the remedies and resources necessary ...*
- *Best practice guidance can similarly provide perimeters for considering when ... child custody battles may be improper for ODR: for example, where an in-person hearing is necessary to assess credibility and consider child safety.*
- *Guidance would also be useful on when and how to incorporate a guardian ad litem when using ODR to ensure that the best interests of the child are protected.*[72]

Turning to the ABA guidance, the ABA posits as follows.

Choice of technology: As well as selecting or developing technology that will address identified goals and needs, courts should be cautious about using technology to perform a function for which it was *not* designed. The decisions to be made by courts in this regard include whether to purchase an existing ODR system, build a system in-house or hire a qualified person or firm to build or customise a system. (A risk may present in this regard that looking for perfect technology may result in adequate, if imperfect technology being overlooked.)

Cost-benefit analysis: A cost-benefit analysis should be conducted of any proposed ODR system. That analysis should include consideration of whether access to justice will be improved by ODR and whether the proposed scheme will yield operational efficiencies for the court/s in question. (Care is perhaps required in this regard so as to ensure that the rollout of ODR is not unduly impeded.)

Costs: Any consideration of costs should not be limited to ODR fees but include consideration of other possible savings or expenses (eg, childcare, transportation). Where use of ODR is mandatory, there should be a fee waiver procedure, assuming that such fees have not been prohibited by applicable law. (It is important that the overall efficiencies and attractiveness of an ODR system are not overlooked in the face of some minor costs issue.)

Courts and case types: Specific courts and case types may require different approaches when it comes to the design, development and provision of online versions. (The point might be made that while courts are undoubtedly unique creatures, too rigorous an adherence to existing court culture may stifle ODR innovation.)

Information: Self-represented disputants, the ABA suggests, should be provided with easily understandable information. Other disputants, the ABA posits, will require language and interpretation support and legal or other information.

Legal representation: ODR should processes provide opportunities for disputants to seek advice or assistance from a lawyer or another support person. (There is, of course, a cost dimension to providing such support which requires to be considered as part of the cost-benefit analysis of any proposed ODR platform.)

Mandatory or optional ODR: Whether to mandate ODR is an issue that requires careful consideration and, if implemented, requires continuous evaluation and provision for opting out for people who encounter significant difficulties in navigating the ODR platform. If disputants do opt out, the ABA recommends that they be redirected to court or other dispute resolution processes. (The key risk of making ODR voluntary is that take-up rates may be too low.) It would seem important that any process whereby one can opt into litigation should not be too easy in order not to deter disputants from arriving at a resolution via ODR.

Openness and transparency: Consistent with the practice of offline courts, court and court-connected ODR systems should operate openly and transparently.

Other court processes and support services: Court and court-connected ODR should maintain access to other court processes and support services – that is, an ODR platform should not become a freestanding, siloed venture. (Conversely, requiring ODR platforms to remain too closely tied to traditional court processes may reduce ODR innovation and the potential for an ODR platform to introduce efficiencies into the dispute resolution process.)

Privacy: Privacy is, of course, an important concern. However, unduly rigorous privacy safeguards could make online litigation more cumbersome than its online variant – the very opposite of the end result that ODR seeks to achieve.

Procurement process: A procurement process should refer prospective tenderers to whatever goals a court has identified and also to the ABA guidance on court and court-connected ODR. (A question arises as to whether this may unduly constrain tenderers into offering less innovative tenders than they might otherwise proffer.)

Screening and triaging: The ABA appears to contemplate a hybrid system in which potential users may or may not be routed towards ODR. Screening questions, it suggests, should include questions about, for example, the potential user's comfort with technology, any history of domestic violence (where appropriate), any language issues presenting and whether the potential user has any disabilities that require accommodation. (Conversely, although screening and triaging may be important, they should not be unduly exclusionary.)

Starting small: Courts interested in ODR should begin by identifying a specific problem to be addressed and a manageable starting point. Revision and expansion of the platform can come later. (So cautious an approach could arguably constrain innovation and unduly delay the rollout of a comprehensive ODR system. It might also lead to what one learned commentator describes as the "wheel change dilemma",[73] whereby instead of going for helpful wholesale change, one ends up simply grafting something new onto the old and arriving at an unsatisfactory hodgepodge of the two.)

Understand client wants and needs: Persons designing court and court-connected ODR programmes should have a thorough understanding of current court processes and IT infrastructure, as well as any challenges presenting as regards integrating the proposed ODR platform and, of course, any budgetary constraints arising. Conversely, the ABA suggests that there is also a role for courts in this regard in terms of considering what court processes and rules may need to be adopted or amended and what statutory changes may be needed.

Uniqueness of courts: It is important for court and court-connected ODR system designers, developers and providers to accept that courts have a unique culture, goals, interests and priorities, and to consider how these unique features will be addressed in any proposed ODR system.

Key learnings

- *ODR excels in high-volume, low-complexity cases.* The US experience suggests that ODR is most effective when applied to small claims, traffic violations and other high-volume, straightforward cases. Of course, limiting ODR to low-complexity cases risks underutilising its potential and reinforcing a perception that ODR is somehow a 'second tier' justice system.

- *ODR can improve procedural justice and user engagement.* By offering a structured and transparent digital process, ODR can create a less intimidating and more user-friendly legal experience, particularly for self-represented disputants. Conversely, poorly structured platforms with complex interfaces or limited support may conceivably discourage participation. Additionally, without in-person legal guidance, some users may struggle to use an ODR platform.
- *Balancing efficiency with procedural integrity is essential.* While ODR promises cost and time savings, it must not compromise procedural safeguards – though imposing too many procedural safeguards may undermine the very efficiencies that ODR seeks to achieve.
- *Data privacy and security must be prioritised.* Concerns about data breaches, cybersecurity and confidentiality remain a significant barrier to ODR adoption. Platforms must implement strong encryption, secure authentication and clear data protection policies. Even so, the most secure digital systems are vulnerable to cyberthreats and strict privacy measures require also to be balanced with the need for transparency.
- *ODR must be designed with accessibility in mind.* Accessibility is crucial for successful ODR. This means designing platforms that are mobile-friendly, easy to navigate and inclusive of users with disabilities or who are wary of digital systems.
- *User support and public education are key to adoption.* Courts must actively educate users about their rights and how to navigate the ODR system, albeit that education alone may not be enough to ensure effective participation.
- *ODR should be evaluated using rigorous metrics.* A major challenge in assessing ODR's success is the lack of standardised evaluation methods. Purely quantitative metrics such as case resolution speed and user satisfaction surveys may not capture the full picture. Qualitative assessments, such as fairness perceptions, must be factored into evaluations if efficiency is not to come at the cost of equity.
- *ODR must be seen as a transformative process.* The US experience highlights that ODR should not simply replicate traditional court processes in a digital format. Instead, the proposed adoption of an ODR platform should be treated as an opportunity to rethink dispute resolution.
- *Hybrid models may provide the best of both worlds.* While ODR can resolve most cases online, some disputes may still require in-person or video hearings. That said, maintaining digital and traditional court systems in parallel may introduce significant administrative and financial burdens.
- *The future of ODR depends on strategic innovation.* The US model suggests

that ODR is at a pivotal moment, with its success likely to depend on how well courts adapt to emerging technologies. Technology-driven reform must be carefully managed to avoid impinging on procedural fairness.

6. The US National Center for Technology and Dispute Resolution

Twenty-five years ago, online dispute resolution was envisioned as a natural outgrowth of the Internet going public. With access to new communication channels, it was projected that disputes would emerge in cyberspace. And while this has borne out, it could not have been imagined then the vast breadth and depth of technology's impact on disputing.

National Center for Technology and Dispute Resolution[74]

The economic burden of dispute resolution often turns the process itself into a punishment and thereby hinders access to justice. In this light, ODR offers a cost-effective mode of dispute resolution ... ODR does not require parties to travel long distances ... Further, ODR has the potential to reduce legal costs, by way of reduced time for resolution and by doing away with the need for legal advice in select categories of cases.

NITI Aayog[75]

Improving ODR: 10 key lessons

- Ethical foundations are crucial.
- Standardisation enhances credibility.
- Accessibility is non-negotiable.
- Accountability and oversight matter.
- AI must be transparent and fair.
- Security and confidentiality are legal and ethical imperatives.
- Cultural and legal compliance is essential.
- User empowerment and informed participation are to be aimed for.
- Continuous innovation in the ODR realm is beneficial.
- Future regulation of ODR is inevitable.

Since its founding, the National Center for Technology and Dispute Resolution (NCTDR), based at the University of Massachusetts, Amherst, has played an important role in defining the standards and ethical guidelines that underpin ODR platforms in the United States and further afield. In 2017, it was instrumental in establishing the International Council for Online Dispute Resolution, an organisation dedicated to promoting best practices, ethical guidelines and professional training for ODR practitioners.

Among the more influential contributions of the NCTDR are the Online Dispute Resolution Standards (2022) and the Ethical Principles for Online Dispute Resolution (2016). These provide a comprehensive framework for ensuring fairness, security and transparency in digital dispute resolution.

The ODR Standards serve as a benchmark for ethical and effective dispute resolution. At the heart of the standards is the symbiotic relationship between technology and ethics. The Ethical Principles for ODR (considered later below) assist with the interpretation of the ODR Standards, so as better to ensure that ODR evolves responsibly alongside technological advancements. The fundamental pillars of the standards are accessibility, accountability, confidentiality, equality, fairness, impartiality, competence, legality, security and transparency.

Under the ODR Standards, the following provision is made as regards accessibility. First, ODR must be easy for parties to find. (That said, ease of accessibility has the potential to be a weakness if cases better suited for an offline hearing are nonetheless routed through ODR just because it so accessible. ODR is not, and ought never to be, the only door in a 'multi-door courthouse'.)* Second, it must be easy for parties to participate in ODR. (That said, firm procedural safeguards will likely be necessary to ensure fairness and prevent misuse of the system.) Third, ODR must not limit a party's right to legal representation. (That said, the starting point when it comes to ODR is the proposition that legal representation should not be required, assuming the right level of user-friendliness to the process.) Fourth, ODR should be available in communication channels accessible to all parties. (There may be cost constraints impeding the fullest implementation of this requirement.) Fifth, ODR must minimise costs to participants. (Cost reduction is a key attribute of ODR; however, there is again a challenging balance to be struck between reducing costs and ensuring adequate levels of security and procedural fairness.) Sixth, ODR must be easily accessible by people with different ability types. (Achieving such accessibility across all digital platforms is a

---

* The idea of a multi-door courthouse was conceived in the 1970s by Frank Sander, a onetime Harvard Law School professor. He posited that in the multi-door courthouse, a screening clerk would review each case to determine the most appropriate dispute resolution process for the parties in that case and then direct them down that route. It is the same idea that informs the online screening that takes place in an omnichannel ODR platform (see Cole and Spangler, 477). The type of screening posited by Sander sounds challenging until one realises (as Sander did) that in practically all cases, the best first port of call in terms of dispute resolution is mediation (*id*). Nowadays, it has been suggested that the best first port of call may be virtual mediation (*id*, 478). But there is always the possibility that in any one case, it may not be.

challenging process that seems likely to present practical issues. However, it may be that the answer in this regard lies in accessibility via one key channel: mobile devices. It has been suggested, for example, that[76] ODR should be mobile friendly to help close the digital divide; mobile phones offer new access routes to ODR for low-income people; there is a general expectation that all services will be more available via mobile phone; in a mobile age, it is logical that people should be able to connect with courts through mobile devices; mobile-friendly ODR helps to ease fear of the courts by allowing access through a familiar medium; mobile phones facilitate instantaneous voice and video engagement, expanding access for those with language and literacy barriers; and mobile phones afford lawyers an easier means to coordinate meetings and also enable other third-party professionals to participate.)

Under the ODR Standards, the following provision is made as regards *accountability*. First, ODR systems must be continuously accountable to those they serve. (Again, a careful balance falls to be struck in this regard if oversight mechanisms are not to stifle innovation.) Second, ODR platforms must be auditable and audits should be made available to users. (Audits clearly improve transparency; however, there is a balance to be struck between the frequency of audits and operational efficiency.)

Under the ODR Standards, the following provision is made regarding *competency*. First, ODR providers must have relevant expertise in dispute resolution, legal, technical execution, language and culture. (There is in fact continuing pressure for ODR processes to provide a sufficiently credible service as to win respect and trust for ODR among a diverse and global user base.)[77] This will likely involve a degree of quality certification (the challenge presenting in this regard being to ensure that any certification requirements are not so prescriptive as unduly to limit the number of ODR providers). A second standard concerning competency in service provision is that ODR services must be timely and use participants' time efficiently. (Again, a challenging balance falls to be drawn in this regard so that the speed of an ODR process does not compromise its thoroughness or indeed the ability of parties to present their cases as they wish. This is not a theoretical concern. In a study of ICANN's* Uniform Domain Name Dispute Resolution Policy (UDRP) – considered in Chapter 18 – one learned commentator has concluded that the UDRP has sacrificed a degree of due process in the interests of convenience, efficiency and speed.[78] Perhaps not everyone would agree with this conclusion, but it certainly highlights the difficult task that presents in balancing swift pace and due process in the ODR context.)

* To contact another person on the Internet, one has to insert an address into the computer one is using, be that a name or a number. This address must be unique so that computers can find each other. Formed in 1998, ICANN is a non-profit, public-benefit corporation that helps to coordinate these unique identifiers internationally.

Under the ODR Standards, the following provision is made as regards *confidentiality*. ODR providers must make every effort to maintain the confidentiality of party communications in line with policies that must be disclosed to the parties. (Confidentiality is very important. However, a question perhaps arises as to whether it is fully attainable in "an online world where privacy is, some would argue, an illusion".)[79]

Under the ODR Standards, the following provision is made as regards *equality*:

- ODR providers must treat participants with respect and dignity. (It has been said of dignity – and much the same point might perhaps be made of respect – that it is a normative foundation of dispute resolution,[80] and also a notion that carries moral force without clear content.[81] Respect and dignity are also concepts that may prove to be culture specific. All of this makes application of this standard a challenge.)
- ODR must seek to enable the silenced and marginalised to be heard. (At the general level, as the Susskind Report observes: "One of the great potential benefits of well-designed ODR services is that disputants in person will have access to dispute resolution services that are intelligible and user-friendly for the non-lawyer ... [W]e believe that ODR-based service will be superior to most conventional court service – quicker, less costly, easier to use, and less combative."[82] At the more immediate level, ensuring that someone gets to make their full case *at a hearing* is a challenging standard that offline courts already have to address when treating with disputants in person who are opposed by lawyers for the other side. People need to be heard, but there is only so far that a decisionmaker can go to assist them if the promise and reality of impartiality are to be maintained.)*
- ODR must strive to ensure that offline privileges and disadvantages are not replicated in the ODR process. (A question perhaps arises as to whether this is a sufficiently ambitious standard. As one learned commentator has observed, the continued expansion of ODR has the potential to uncover a rich variety of options that take it beyond the mere online replication of face-to-face dispute resolution processes.)[83]
- ODR providers must strive to ensure that no ODR process/technology provides a party with a technological/informational advantage due to its ODR usage. (It is submitted that, even taking such care, users with more

---

* In her study of the experience of the litigant in person in judicial review cases in England and Wales, Hill touches on precisely this point, observing that when judges seek to provide legitimate assistance to litigants-in-person in a bid to ensure a fair hearing, there is a risk that the judge may be misperceived as helping the litigant-in-person and hence acting partially (see Hill, 259). There is a risk, it might be added, that in some instances a judge may unwittingly cross the line, while seeking to be helpful, and act partially. Under the UDRP, most types of trademark-based domain name disputes fall to be resolved by agreement, court action or arbitration before a domain name will be cancelled, suspended or transferred.

experience in digital environments may navigate ODR platforms more efficiently.)

- Bias must be proactively avoided. (Detecting bias in complex human or AI-informed dispute resolution is a continuing challenge.)
- ODR system design must include proactive efforts to prevent AI from creating, replicating or compounding bias. (A difficult balance falls to be struck in this regard if the potential efficiency benefits of AI-informed ODR are not to be lost.)[84]
- Human oversight is required in ODR design/auditing to identify and eliminate bias and make findings transparent. (Human oversight undoubtedly helps with fairness; however, undue human intervention may reduce the efficiency that ODR otherwise promises because humans are unfailingly flawed and their flaws can contaminate the dispute resolution process.)[85]

Under the ODR Standards, the following provision is made as regards *fairness and impartiality*. First, ODR must treat all parties equitably and with due process, without bias or benefit. When it comes to private ODR platforms, due process issues are a very real concern. Perhaps four key issues present: the privatisation of justice; the potential for private rules to be fixed to produce particular outcomes; the potential for due process rules that exist in a public court and have stood the test of time simply to be disregarded; and a reduction in the power of the state, through its courts, to shape the law. Governments can allow the foregoing to occur, or they can intervene.[86] Second, conflicts must be disclosed before providing ODR services and the obligation to disclose conflicts is a continuing obligation during the ODR process.* (Conflicts of interest exist in professional and private settings, and everyone encounters them occasionally. The solution is to eliminate the conflict or, as a decisionmaker, to recuse oneself from the deliberative process. In theory, it is possible that excessively rigorous disclosure requirements might unduly discourage professionals from involvement in an ODR process, but that is too remote a prospect to counter the need for a conflicts of interest policy.)

Under the ODR Standards, the following provision is made as regards *lawfulness*. First, ODR providers must abide by laws and regulations under which an ODR process falls. Second, ODR providers must uphold laws and regulations under which an ODR process falls. (Clearly, an ODR platform must unfailingly comply with all applicable laws and regulations – albeit that this may prove challenging for a platform operating in a cross-border context.) Third, ODR

---

* The Council of Europe's Guidelines on Online Dispute Resolution Mechanisms in Civil and Administrative Court Proceedings (2021) offer a little more detail as to what may be expected in this regard, stating (at 10) that: "Parties to proceedings involving ODR should be informed about any potential conflicts of interest related to the operation of an ODR mechanism."

providers must disclose to the parties the laws and regulations under which an ODR process falls. (Users may also require guidance on how such laws and regulations may impact on them and their dispute.)

Under the ODR Standards, the following provision is made regarding *security*. First, ODR providers must make every effort to ensure that ODR platforms are secure. (It may prove a challenge in practice to balance security needs with usability.) Second, ODR providers must make every effort to ensure that data collected and communications between those engaged in ODR are not shared with unauthorised persons. And third, disclosures of breaches must be communicated, along with steps taken to prevent reoccurrence. (Data privacy is clearly very important. However, a careful balance falls to be struck in terms of pitching data privacy levels if operational efficiency is not unduly to be affected.) In the European Union, the General Data Protection Regulation (GDPR)[87] will govern the standard of data privacy to be applied. Elsewhere, there is interesting commentary on how to identify what is reasonable data protection. Thus, Draper and Raymond offer a "road map"[88] that seeks to ensure that any ODR solution provides reasonable protection of the parties' data. Elements of this road map include the following:

- Risk associated with outcome = *Probability that outcome will happen* × *Value of outcome.*
- Most protection strategies focus on breach probability, but too much protection makes a system unusable.
- Risk can also be reduced by reducing breach value (eg, by having a data fragmentation strategy, so that breach does not yield full access to data).
- The interrelationship between security, cost and usability yields a golden rule as to when ethics demands further protection:

  Reasonable option for reducing technology risk

  →

  Unethical to maintain current system

Under the ODR Standards, the following provision is made as regards *transparency*. ODR providers must disclose in advance, in a meaningful and accessible manner, the form and enforceability of ODR processes/outcomes and the risks, costs and benefits of participation. ODR data must be gathered, managed and presented in such a way that it is not misrepresented or considered out of context. The sources and methods used to gather any data that influences an AI-informed decision must be disclosed to all parties. ODR which uses AI must publicly affirm compliance with applicable law, regulations and (in their absence) guidelines on transparency and fairness. ODR must disclose the role and magnitude of technology's influence on generating/restricting options and on final decisions or outcomes. Audits of ODR platforms/systems must publicly identify the audit metrics used. Users must be informed in a timely and accessible manner of any data breach and the steps taken to prevent reoccurrence. Ultimately, the potential of ODR to bring transparency to dispute resolution is considerable – and as one learned commentator has observed, the increased transparency which ODR entails over the traditional legal system should boost public trust in the legal system.[89]

As to the Ethical Principles for ODR, these serve as a living document, designed to be able to deal with continuing advancements in technology. The principles inform the ODR Standards and should help to fill gaps in any timelapse between a standard becoming somehow outdated and later being updated. While closely aligned with the ODR Standards, the principles offer a broader approach to dispute resolution in digital environments. The principles are summarised in Figure 9.

The NCTDR frameworks represent a significant step towards ethical, effective and inclusive ODR systems. However, although they are likely to continue to be useful benchmark measures, they also seem likely to be overtaken – at least in Europe – by, for example, the European Ethical Charter on the Use of AI in Judicial Systems and Their Environment (2018) and the Framework Convention on AI and Human Rights (2024) (to which the United States is a party). (These are considered in Chapter 16.)

Figure 9: Ethical principles for ODR (summary)

ODR should be accessible, accountable and confidential

ODR should ensure equality, fairness and honesty

ODR should be operated competently, impartially, neutrally, securely and transparently

ODR should prevent and minimise user harm

ODR should involve informed participation and effective integration [a]

ODR should promote empowerment [b]

ODR should continuously innovate for the good [c]

ODR should always comply with the law

[a] When it comes to integration, what is meant is that ODR processes are integrated within a system and with other entities, networks and systems. The application of ODR is effected within this linked context and should be done (according to the principles) mindful of the need for integration with public entities.
[b] That is, through increased access to justice, enhancement of choice and more effective decision-making.
[c] That is, in such a way as to improve delivery of dispute resolution services and benefits more efficiently, effectively and fairly.

Key learnings

- *Ethical foundations are crucial.* ODR platforms must be built on clear ethical guidelines to ensure fairness, transparency and integrity. Ethical frameworks such as those from the NCTDR provide good blueprints for responsible ODR. That said, an overly rigorous ethical framework may conceivably stifle innovation and adaptability.
- *Standardisation enhances credibility.* Adhering to established ODR standards (eg, accessibility, impartiality, confidentiality) increases trust and acceptance among users, regulators and legal professionals. Conversely, standardisation can create a barrier to entry for new platforms.
- *Accessibility is non-negotiable.* An effective ODR platform must be easy to use, cost-efficient and inclusive. Of course, focusing too heavily on accessibility may compromise other critical factors such as security, efficiency and cost-effectiveness.
- *Accountability and oversight matter.* ODR systems should allow for external audits and user feedback mechanisms to maintain fairness and credibility and ensure that processes are consistently reviewed and improved – though excessive oversight may increase bureaucracy.
- *AI must be transparent and fair.* If AI-informed decision making is involved, platforms must disclose data sources, logic and potential bias – though complete transparency in AI-informed decision making may not always be feasible due, for example, to proprietary algorithms.
- *Security and confidentiality are legal and ethical imperatives.* Robust cybersecurity measures must be implemented to protect user data; of course, unduly rigorous confidentiality may conflict with the need for transparency and accountability.
- *Cultural and legal conformity is essential.* ODR platforms must be designed with sensitivity to cultural differences and comply with local laws. Observing the law is clearly imperative. Respecting cultural norms is also important. Compliance with both, however, could arguably lead to fragmented systems that struggle to scale up internationally.
- *User empowerment and informed participation are critical.* Users must fully understand the ODR process, potential outcomes and their rights before participation. Conversely, providing excessive information may overwhelm a recipient and unduly discourage participation.
- *Continuous innovation is required.* ODR platforms must evolve at pace with technological progress, but unending innovation risks destabilising established processes and creating uncertainty.
- *Future regulation is inevitable.* As ODR becomes more engrained in legal systems, ethical standards may evolve into enforceable regulations. That said, ODR platforms should prioritise innovation over adherence to possible future regulatory developments.

7. The California Access to Justice Commission and the future of legal technology

Legal technology is proliferating. From videoconferencing to web-based applications, legal technology is increasingly pivotal for improving access to justice and expanding the legal safety net. Legal technology serves an important role in a legal system where most people do not have access to legal advice or information, even when they desperately need it.

California Access to Justice Commission[90]

ODR can ... improve access to a variety of dispute resolution processes by addressing major concerns such as lack of access to physical courts or ... [the] cost of dispute resolution as well as the barriers due to disabilities ... Resolving disputes in the comfort of the user's own homes can make the dispute resolution process feel more accessible. This improvement in the overall experience can encourage more parties to opt to resolve their disputes through such formal means as opposed to not agitating their rights at all.

NITI Aayog[91]

Improving ODR: 10 key lessons

- Bridging the digital divide is essential.
- Accessibility must be a core design principle.
- Cost should not be a barrier to justice.
- Ensuring security and confidentiality is critical.
- Judicial and lawyer training is necessary.
- ODR is suitable for a wide range of cases.
- Technology coordinators improve efficiency.
- Rural access must be prioritised.
- There is growing public support for digital justice (at least in California).
- ODR is a permanent evolution, not a temporary fix.

In March 1993, the California State Bar appointed an Access to Justice working group to develop a long-term approach to overcoming existing inequities in the Californian justice system. This initiative led to the subsequent formation of the California Access to Justice Commission. The commission is a leader in advocating for the equitable delivery of justice. In 2020, the commission released two key reports: *Remote Hearings and Access to Justice During Covid-19 and Beyond* and *The Role of Technology in Enhancing Rural Access to Justice*. These reports outline how remote proceedings and digital solutions can reshape legal services, ensuring that justice remains accessible even in the face of global crises.

With courthouses in California closed as a response to the COVID-19 pandemic, Californian judges had to elect which cases to treat as sufficiently urgent to be considered online. What is interesting in this regard is the breadth of cases that they considered were capable of being heard and decided online. Figure 10 shows the case types that were identified by the commission as capable of being heard online. The commission also considered a number of issues that presented as regards online hearings in California, but which have resonance when it comes to ODR more generally. These are considered below.

Figure 10: Cases suitable for online hearing

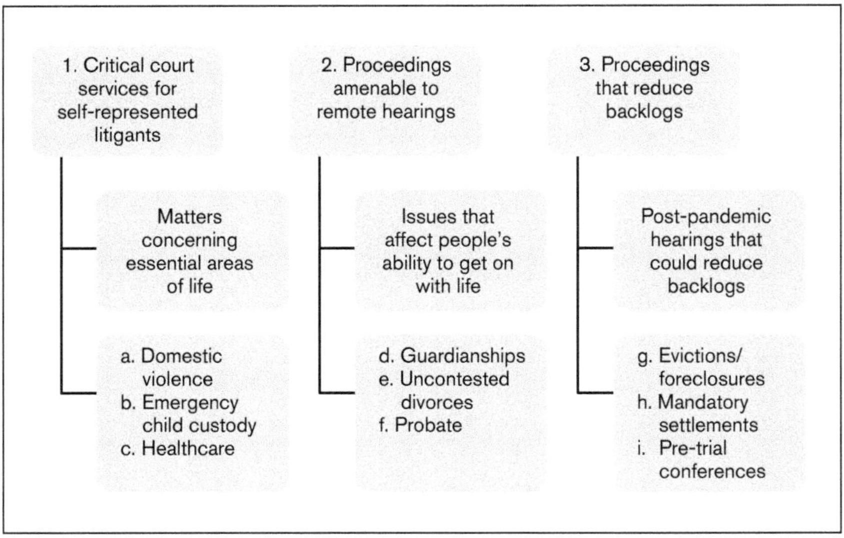

When it comes to selecting and rolling out ODR technology, the commission made a number of points. First, courts should consider allowing voice-only participation accessible via a toll-free telephone number. Second, if 'voice-only' is the sole means of access for one party, a court should consider restricting access for all parties to voice-only so as to avoid disadvantaging the party for whom voice-only is the sole means of access. (A question perhaps arises as to whether this involves reducing an ODR hearing to the lowest common denominator in terms of the technology deployed.) Third, consideration should be given to having self-help hubs where parties can use a computer to access court hearings.

Consistent with the proposition that access to the courts should be free, the commission considers that Californian courts should consider whether a technology platform might be imposing charges inconsistent with this proposition. In its report, the commission gives an example of two platform providers, one of which charges the host for its service and the other of which charges users subject to a refund in the event of eligibility for a fee waiver. (The former would seem a cost that government should bear when it comes to the provision of publicly funded court and court-connected ODR. The latter conceivably risks being potentially exclusionary.)

The issue of accessibility for people with disabilities is not just a matter of technical inaccessibility. Rather, as the commission observes, accessibility is "essential for creating an inclusive justice system operating remotely".* Important accessibility features include automatic transcripts, closed captioning, keyboard accessibility and screen reader support. In this regard, the commission suggests that documents, presentations and similar should comply with the Web Content Accessibility Guidelines and with the US Twenty-First Century Communications and Video Accessibility Act 2010. The guidelines emanate from the World Wide Web Consortium, the body that develops web standards such as HTML and CSS. They deal with an array of issues, including adaptability, distinguishability, input assistance, navigability, operability (including keyboard accessibility), perceivability, readability and steps to counter seizures and physical reactions. The act seeks to ensure that modern telecommunications are accessible to people with disabilities. Although it is US legislation, it arguably provides a useful international *grundnorm* of accessibility features that are desirable in the ODR context. By way of example, the act, among other things, requires the following:

- hearing aid compatibility on newly manufactured and imported telephones;
- telecommunications service providers to make their services and equipment accessible to and usable by people with disabilities;
- real-time text support to be provided so that people with disabilities are able to communicate with others via text;

---

* California Access to Justice Commission (2), 5. One learned commentator has posited the following reasons why it is important to ensure that ODR services are accessible by people with disabilities. First, there are a lot of people with disabilities (16% of the world's population). Second, accessibility is a human right (eg, see the United Nations Convention on the Rights of Persons with Disabilities). Third, universal design (making online services accessible to all) is commercially sensible. Fourth, in the United States, online services inaccessible to people with disabilities may yield liability – for example, under the Americans with Disabilities Act (David Allen Larson (2)).

- Federal Communications Commission inquiries into making communications more disability friendly;
- an enlarged field of devices that must display closed captions;
- devices that receive or display video programming to be fully accessible by people with disabilities; and
- cable and satellite subscription TV services to make their navigational programming guides accessible to people who cannot read the visual display.

Unmentioned by the commission, but also of interest when it comes to designing for people with disabilities, are the Seven Principles of Universal Design, developed in the late 1990s by the Centre for Excellence in Universal Design at North Carolina State University and summarised in the box below.

Seven Principles of Universal Design (summarised)

- *Equitable:* Design should be useful and marketable to people with diverse abilities.
- *Flexible:* Design should accommodate a wide range of preferences and abilities.
- *Simple and intuitive:* Design should be easy to understand, regardless of user experience, knowledge etc.
- *Perceptible information:* Design should communicate information effectively, regardless of, for example, sensory abilities.
- *Tolerance for error:* Design should minimise hazards and adverse consequences of error.
- *Low physical effort:* Design should be usable comfortably, efficiently and with minimum fatigue.
- *Size and space:* Size and space should be provided for and operate regardless of user body mobility or size.

The commission points to the need for users to navigate IT without difficulty, without the need for court personnel to give in-proceeding instructions and without delaying the proceedings. It also suggests that judges and court staff should note regular glitches and problems and report them to the IT vendor. (User feedback should also be sought. Experience suggests that the more stakeholders involved in an ODR system's design and improvement, "the more likely the system is to be sustainable in the long term".)[92]

The commission points (in the context of a primarily English-speaking state) to the importance of catering for people who use other languages. (A remarkable example of language options in operation is a smartphone app trialled in Greece and developed to facilitate the application of ODR in refugee disputes.[93] The basic languages on the app are Greek, Turkish, Italian, Spanish and Arabic;

however, there is potential to add others.[94] A more humdrum but no less remarkable example is the UK TPT, which offers its entire website in both English and Welsh, with the option to choose one's preferred language the moment a user arrives at the homepage.)

The commission notes that just because a person speaks English does not mean that they will be familiar with the terminology of legal English. Thus, care should be taken in terms of using simple language in any written instructions, so as not to disadvantage a party for whom legal English is a challenge. In British Columbia – a global leader in ODR provision – it has been found that public health information needs to be written at the level of a Grade 6 schoolchild, with the suggestion being made that public legal information should be written at the same level.[95] (Grade 6 in a Canadian school is typically for children aged 11–12 years.)

The commission points to a number of control-related questions to which the answer ought to be 'yes' in terms of whether proposed IT is suitable for use in an online hearing. These are summarised in Figure 11.

The commission observes that access to technology is inequitable and there is a persistent socioeconomic digital divide. That said, the commission seeks expressly not to dissuade courts from using remote technologies but merely to point to the need to engage in "creative and inclusive"[96] practices when it comes to ODR.[97] In this regard, the commission highlights the following issues. First, lack of internet access. (If home Internet is inaccessible, for whatever reason, there may be privacy issues with accessing the Internet in public places such as libraries.) Second, limited phone access. (Disputants may have phones with limited minutes/data, impeding access to hearings.) Third, limited email access. (A disputant may not have email, may have email but no internet access, may rarely check their emails or may have a preferred alternative to email.) The commission sees the provision of digital hubs as a solution to these problems. This is one possibility. Other potential means of bridging or reducing the digital divide include[98] increased connectivity; better digital literacy; affordable access to the Internet;[99] investment in digital education; partnerships with the private sector to devise technological solutions; and the development of stronger broadband infrastructure.

Closing the digital divide is not inexpensive: in the United States, research done at Tufts University suggests that the cost of doing so will be above $200 billion.[100] The same research posits the following as useful steps in terms of closing the digital divide in the United States (though arguably they might also be applied elsewhere).[101] First, create a nationwide plan to close the access gap. Second, close the affordability gap through, for example, subventions. Third, invest in digital literacy and skills building. Fourth, raise the high-speed broadband standard to 100 megabits per second. Fifth, tax digital ads to raise the funding to close the digital divide. Sixth, create a competitive internet service provider market. Seventh, clarify gaps presenting and create a national bidding process to elevate the best solutions.

The remaining observations and proposals of the commission regarding open and equal access to the courts are summarised in Figure 12.

Geography, in the sense of people living in isolated areas, can compound the challenges that present in terms of getting legal advice and satisfaction. In 2020, the California Access to Justice Commission published a report on the role of technology in enhancing rural access to justice. Much of the report is California-specific and not of interest to a wider international audience. However, several of the sections consider issues that have resonance when it comes to ODR more generally. By way of overview, the commission notes as follows of legal technology in rural places:

- **Advantages:**
  - *[It] … can play [a] significant role in increasing access …*
  - *[It] can alleviate the need to travel …*
  - *[It] can streamline … [eg,] case management … basic form completion and advice …*
  - *[It] allow[s] lawyers to reach distant clients … enabling more people to receive legal advice*
- **Disadvantages:**
  - *[It] can reproduce barriers it is intended to ameliorate.*[102]

Figure 11: Control-related questions to which the answer should be 'yes'

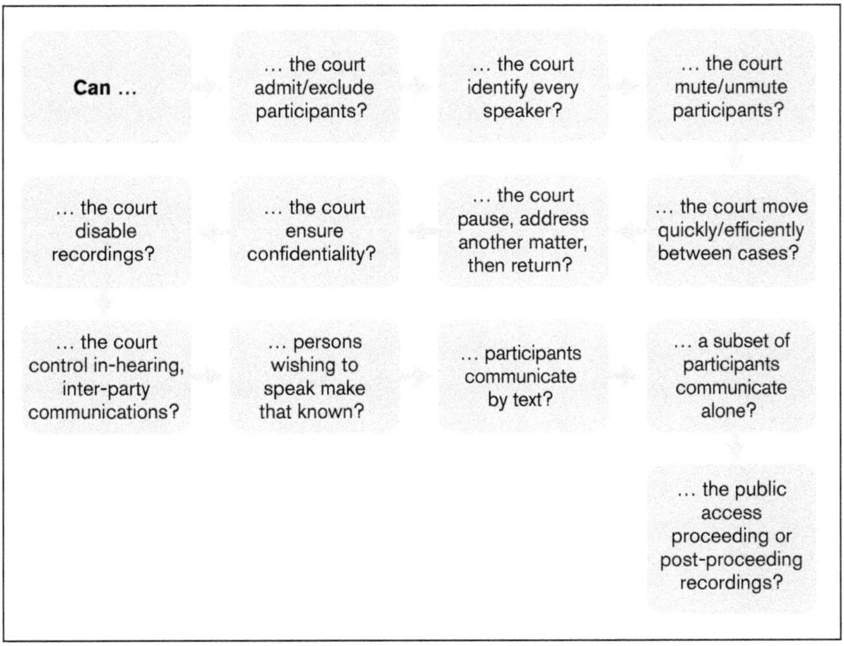

The report notes that online portals, text messages and websites that are simple but dynamic all offer a means whereby, for example, legal aid organisations can broaden their geographic reach and become better connected with clients and other legal service providers. It also notes how courts, legal aid providers and non-profit organisations (charities) are already using new technologies – such as mobile apps, videoconferencing and web-based documents – to overcome access, capacity and resource limitations.

Figure 12: Some proposals regarding open, equal access to courts

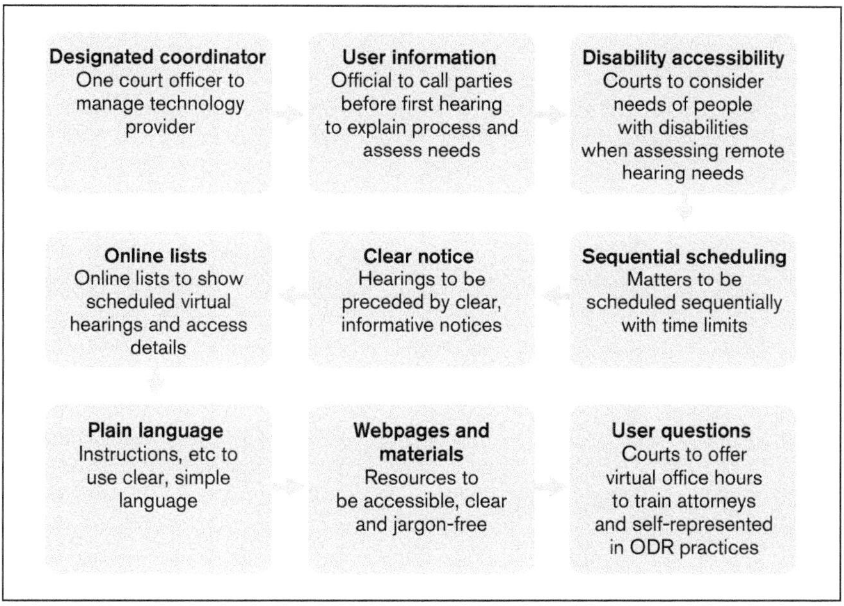

Notably, the commission finds that most Californians are supportive of more online court services and considers that web-based tools have a role to play in terms of increasing access to the civil justice system. The commission points to legal assistance portals and ODR as two key examples of how the legal system might be improved into the future. It sees ODR as having significant potential to assist people in rural California, where the nearest courthouse may be many miles away with poor (or no) public transport options. The key to good ODR systems, the commission posits, is "ensuring that people have the information, knowledge and capacity to access such online systems".[103]

The commission notes the work that had to be done to adapt court practices and processes as the COVID-19 pandemic unfolded. It also recognises that the Internet and mobile applications are a critical domain in terms of the provision of post-disaster legal information. The commission further observes that, in California, rural areas have higher rates of older people and people with disabilities, noting that this presents a particular need as regards the design and implementation of tech fixes in those areas. These include texting diary reminders (this improves appearance rates); developing websites that come up in search results; focusing on how people find services and how results are presented; making web-based tools easy to use; using flowcharts to make information comprehensible; making websites and web tools accessible to those with disabilities; making technological literacy a consideration; providing different language versions; incentivising businesses to increase access to justice for poorer people; remembering that mobile devices are effective communication tools, given the high number of people with mobile access; and bearing in mind the usefulness of AI and biometric security.

The findings of the California Access to Justice Commission highlight four key points that are particular to California but may also have wider international resonance as regards ODR. First, there is an urgent need for continued investment in remote legal services. Second, digital justice is not a temporary response to a crisis but a permanent evolution in legal service delivery. Third, by addressing accessibility challenges, ensuring fairness in digital proceedings and leveraging technology for efficiency, courts can deliver a more inclusive and effective justice system. And fourth, as technology continues to reshape legal services, courts, policymakers and legal professionals must remain committed to ethical innovation, ensuring that digital advancements enhance access to justice for all.

Key learnings

- *Bridging the digital divide is essential.* Many users lack reliable internet or device access, particularly in rural areas. ODR platforms should offer voice-only participation options and establish digital hubs to provide equitable access. That said, creating and maintaining these alternatives could strain available state resources.
- *Accessibility must be a core design principle.* ODR systems should incorporate features such as closed captioning, screen reader support and multilingual functionality to ensure inclusivity for people with disabilities and non-native speakers. Accessibility is clearly critical but may be costly and complex, potentially delaying the deployment of ODR platforms.
- *Cost should not be a barrier to justice.* Access to dispute resolution should be free or affordable. ODR platforms must avoid hidden costs that could disadvantage lower-income users and obstruct their ability to participate. A careful balance falls to be struck in this regard; charging reasonable fees to all but the poorest may conceivably ensure a better quality service.*

- *Ensuring security and confidentiality is critical.* Robust cybersecurity measures, clear policies on data protection and immediate breach notifications are necessary to maintain user trust and comply with legal standards. Conversely, unduly rigorous security measures may conflict with usability and accessibility requirements.
- *Judicial and lawyer training is necessary.* Judges and attorneys must be trained to navigate ODR platforms. That said, intuitive design and user-friendly platforms may reduce the need for extensive training.
- *ODR is suitable for a wide range of cases.* The California model demonstrates that cases involving people who may not presently have meaningful access to offline courts can be handled online in an effective manner.
- *Technology coordinators improve efficiency.* Designating a court technology coordinator should ensure better system operation and help to resolve technical challenges. Arguably, ODR platforms should be user-friendly enough to minimise the need for specialised personnel.
- *Rural access must be prioritised.* ODR platforms should incorporate mobile apps, videoconferencing and remote *pro bono* programmes to bridge the gap in legal service accessibility. That said, limited broadband infrastructure and digital literacy challenges may persist; and in-person legal services may still be necessary for individuals who struggle with technology.
- *Public support for digital justice is growing.* Surveys done in California indicate strong public backing for expanding ODR. It may be that this desire also exists elsewhere.
- *ODR is a permanent evolution, not a temporary fix.* Remote justice is not merely a pandemic response – it represents the future of legal service delivery. However, while ODR has long-term potential, its expansion should not take place at the expense of legal and ethical concerns.

---

* The HiiL has made some interesting comment on meeting the costs of ODR, observing: "[1] ODR procedures ... can be self-financing through user contributions ... [2] Charging users for court procedures ... is somewhat controversial. Courts often prefer to be financed from the general state budget. But only a few countries (such as Norway) succeed in securing sufficient budget to give their citizens free access to courts ... [3] Some ODR procedures ... would still require subsidies ... [For example,] refugees or low skilled criminal defendants cannot pay court and lawyer fees. [4] Costs of adjudication can be allocated to parties according to their resources ... [5] Prices ... should be controlled ... because a court may be seen as a monopolist. [6] Online procedures require substantial investments ... These costs have to be added to the court fees ... [7] Online dispute resolution ... can open the door for a court system where courts would be responsible for the design of procedures and also ... able to charge ... users ... the full costs ... [8] ODR ... lowers the costs of providing access to justice and makes it more easy to set and charge fees for different problems and user groups ... [9] ... ODR can reduce the costs of each additional case to a level where courts can welcome each additional client ... The quality of access to justice can therefore be increased, and court delays ... reduced to zero. The laws of economics predict more citizens will then be willing to pay for use of procedures. [10] The proportion of fees to be paid by each party can be finetuned in such a way that both parties have sufficient incentives to settle" (HiiL, *ODR and the Courts: The Promise of 100% Access to Justice* (HiiL, 2016), 53–54, 56, 93–94).

8. Two US examples of ODR in action

Individuals who use ODR are not identified by gender, race/ethnicity, religion, socio-economic status, age, or other characteristic irrelevant to the dispute that might be casually observed through in-person interactions. As such, ODR can help address some of the issues associated with explicit or implicit bias – an issue known to impact the fairness of outcomes. Technology does not discriminate, except against those who do not have access to technology.
Joint Technology Committee[104]

With the increased awareness regarding racial, caste and gender justice, there have been some concerns regarding the impact of biases, prejudice, and stereotype on decision-making processes and outcomes ... ODR processes can lessen the unconscious bias of the Neutral ... ODR Platforms, especially those based on texts and emails, detach audio-visual cues relating to ... gender, social status, ethnicity, race etc and help in resolving disputes based on the claims and information submitted by the disputing parties, rather than who these parties are.
NITI Aayog[105]

Improving ODR: 10 key lessons

- Tailor ODR to user expectations.
- Choose between centralised and decentralised models.
- Technology selection matters.
- Adoption hinges on awareness and training.
- Hybrid models increase access and efficiency.
- Clear and intuitive user interfaces are critical.
- ODR must address the digital divide.
- Legal safeguards must be maintained.
- Funding and resource allocation require long-term planning.
- Stakeholder engagement drives success.

1. Michigan

In the United States, Michigan is a national ODR leader. As a result, when Michigan entered lockdown during the COVID-19 pandemic, its justice system was better positioned than most to implement and expand ODR services. Shortly before the pandemic, the Michigan State Court's Office of Dispute Resolution introduced two key forms of virtual dispute resolution:

- Zoom dispute resolution: This involved trained volunteers from the Community Dispute Resolution Program (CDRP) providing synchronous mediation via Zoom, a platform that became widely used during the pandemic.*
- MI-Resolve: This is a state-funded ODR platform accessible via computers or mobile devices, enabling asynchronous negotiation either directly between parties or with the assistance of trained CDRP mediators. Despite its potential, MI-Resolve saw limited adoption initially, with only a few CDRP centres using it extensively. While MI-Resolve is funded by the state, it relies heavily on volunteer mediators, making it a cost-effective solution for both Michigan courts and residents.

In 2022, Michigan commissioned an evaluation of its two ODR approaches (Zoom and MI-Resolve) to assess their performance before and during the pandemic.[106] The report provided insights into ODR usage, public perceptions and the future of these platforms.

The evaluation identified several key lessons regarding the use of Zoom in dispute resolution. Thus, centres that adapted quickly integrated Zoom into their workloads with creativity and efficiency. Without Zoom, CDRP centres would have struggled to continue operations. In terms of factors that affected this impromptu transition from in-person dispute resolution to Zoom dispute resolution, the report identified the following, among others:

- *Data access:* Ensuring that workers could access office material online was a challenge.
- *Digital divide:* Zoom was a challenge for users without IT equipment or good internet access.
- *Executive leadership:* There was pressure on centre directors to formulate how virtual dispute resolutiom would operate and take related administrative steps.
- *Funding:* Funding proved difficult because of, for example, the cancellation of fundraising events.
- *Phones:* Enabling users to phone in when centres were shut was

* CDRP offers in-person ADR to aid Michiganders to resolve disputes in a fair and timely manner without having to go to court. Services are offered through a number of CDRP centres across Michigan. The centres rely on trained volunteer mediators/facilitators to meet with disputants and provide low-cost dispute resolution assistance.

challenging. Some centres had voice over internet phone systems, which eased matters. Others set office phones to forward to personal phones.

- *Referrals:* New ways of receiving referrals – for example, from courts – had to be designed.
- *Signatures:* Some centres used DocuSign for immediate signing. Others opted for verbal agreements followed by signing.
- *Software/hardware:* Each centre started with one Zoom licence. Many found that they needed additional licences, as well as hardware (eg, new monitors), despite limited funding.
- *Staffing/volunteers:* Some staff left rather than use Zoom. Conversely, some centres took on new employees who, for example, were willing to mediate from home or worked from home and had flexibility to do some CDRP volunteer work.
- *Technology:* When COVID-19 struck, centres had to get an online system up and running from remote locations.
- *Training:* Training was a real but not insurmountable challenge.

MI-Resolve is a bespoke ODR platform that has the following features. It is an ODR system with enabling prompts. It gives access to a virtual messaging platform. It is open on a 24/7/365 basis. Parties can liaise directly or with mediator assistance. It is asynchronous. To use MI-Resolve, a party must reside, work or have a dispute in Michigan; have internet access; have a current email address; agree to the "Agreement to Mediate" terms; and be over 18 years old. The relevant CRDP centre gets a daily update on progress. If there is no pending court date and no resolution after seven days, a mediator joins the conversation to assist. (If there is a pending court date, a mediator immediately joins.) When parties reach a settlement agreement, it is filed in the local court. The process is entirely confidential. Only in exceptional circumstances – for example, threats of harm – can MI-Resolve messages be used in court. It is used for contract law disputes, child law disputes, guardianship disputes, landlord/tenant disputes, money disputes, neighbourhood disputes, probate disputes and school disputes. (This is a notably wide range of disputes and showcases the potential breadth of cases to which ODR can be applied.) And it allows attorneys to join represented parties on the platform and to participate in the mediation.

Training on the use of the software is provided by the software provider. However, more bespoke training on special CDRP practices and processes is provided by the Michigan State Court Administrative Office. In terms of factors that eased the transition from in-person dispute resolution to MI-Resolve, the report identified the following, among others:[107] ease of access for those disputants with IT equipment and Internet; regular system updates; comprehensive training; community funding support; executive flexibility/leadership/vision; outreach to potential referrers; and a systemic willingness to have citizens with disputes use MI-Resolve.

Figure 13: Factors that helped/hindered the rollout of MI-Resolve

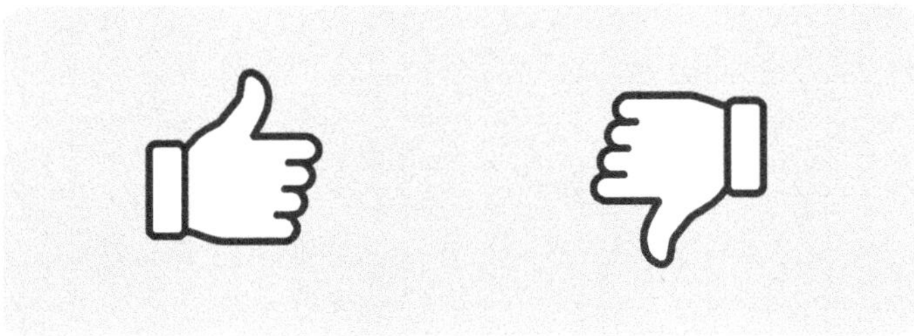

Helped

- Having the right equipment
- Internet access
- Promotion by courts and others
- Community support
- Hubs to aid access

Hindered

- Problems finding respondents
- Some courts' disinterest
- Unwillingness to try new processes

The experience of stakeholders with Zoom and MI-Resolve systems was gauged by way of a comprehensive stakeholder survey that engaged with attorneys, CDRP centre board members, court administrators, judges and other referrers. The results make for interesting reading. When it came to Zoom, most stakeholders agreed that Zoom had increased public access to mediation by removing the barriers to entry posed by in-person mediation; that Zoom is as effective (or even more effective) than in-person mediation; and that (post-pandemic) in-person and Zoom mediation should be promoted equally.

By contrast, there were divergent views on the effectiveness of MI-Resolve as a means of settling disputes. Half of the CDRP centre members who were surveyed suggested that it should only be used for certain types of disputes. (Most found it optimally effective for debt collection and small claims.) Contact was found to present a challenge if a user had incorrect contact details for the other party. And traditional mediators did not see MI-Resolve as 'real' mediation because it involves asynchronous emails and no audio or visual contact.

Despite this relatively cool response, the report concludes MI-Resolve has shown positive potential and the capacity to develop more fully in the near future. In this regard, the report makes particular reference to the following features. First, because it is provided online and free of charge to Michiganders, it increases access to dispute resolution services. Second, if successfully used, MI-Resolve should reduce the need to go to court (hence reducing demand on the judicial system). Third, even if using MI-Resolve does not produce an immediate agreement, it can be a useful first step in dispute resolution. Fourth, CDRP centres and courts found that using MI-Resolve helps users to gather needed documentation and organise their arguments so that subsequent hearings or mediation sessions were faster and more productive. (This could also be seen as a failure of

MI-Resolve.) Fifth, there is a sense that multi-party functionality can only improve MI-Resolve. Sixth, the authors of the report considered that once more training was provided and operating issues were identified and addressed through use, MI-Resolve had the potential to prevent more types of disputes from going to court. Seventh, other planned enhancements – such as a system dashboard and an interface allowing data to be uploaded to the CDRP case management system – would, the report posited, greatly enhance the ability of the Michigan State Court Administrative Office and CDRP centres to monitor MI-Resolve utilisation and outcomes. Eighth, the positive opinions of MI-Resolve held by directors whose centres had used it the most suggested to the authors of the report that other centres might also find it to be a useful tool once they had more experience with it. Ninth, the report concluded that it was important that CDRP centres continue actively to promote MI-Resolve for it to become more widely adopted.

Figure 14: Some positive features of MI-Resolve

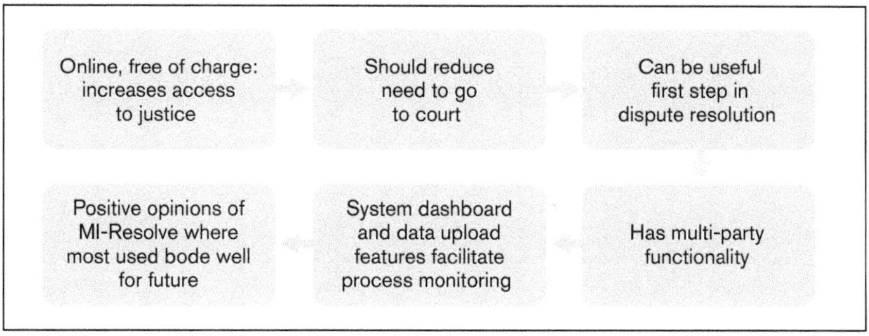

Figure 15: Comparing in-person versus Zoom dispute resolution

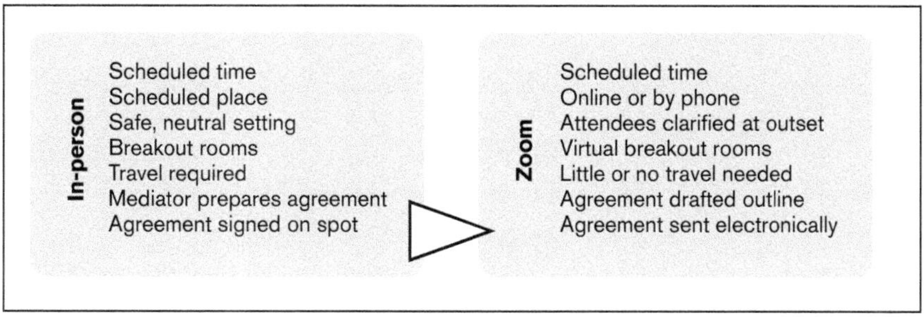

Michigan's experience with ODR demonstrates both the challenges and the opportunities of virtual dispute resolution. The pandemic cemented Zoom as a standard mediation tool, while MI-Resolve shows significant potential for growth. Moving forward, Michigan's CDRP centres face key decisions about, for example, case selection, referral strategies and volunteer recruitment. As ODR continues to evolve, Michigan's approach will likely serve as a model for other jurisdictions in the United States and elsewhere that are seeking to balance efficiency, accessibility and effectiveness in the ODR context.

2. Utah

In 2016, Utah's Judicial Council proposed ODR as a means of enhancing access to justice while improving the efficiency of the state's court processes. Council members recognised that newer generations of court users have different expectations regarding online access to legal services. Utah's ODR initiative has therefore sought to create a user-centred process that aligns with evolving public preferences. Small claims cases (disputes under $11,000) were selected as the initial focus of ODR, as they are relatively straightforward and frequently involve self-represented disputants. The success of the project hinged on three key principles: utilising familiar and accessible technology for users; adapting court processes to function efficiently online; and ensuring that user legal rights and interests remain protected. The goal was clear: to make ODR easier, faster and cheaper, while preserving the safeguards and advantages of traditional court proceedings.

The Utah judiciary played an active role in the development of ODR. This has been credited as a factor in the success of Utah's ODR scheme, with one learned commentator observing that Utah offers a good example of how ODR innovations can run more smoothly when high-level judges (in Utah's case, then-state supreme court judge Deno Himonas) are involved in the change process.[108]

In June 2016, Utah's Judicial Council established an ODR steering committee, chaired by Justice Himonas. This committee comprised attorneys, court employees, users and judges. At its first meeting, the committee formed a 'disruptive innovation' subcommittee tasked with designing a new court process that prioritised user needs over traditional judicial structures. The committee's objectives were to promote access to justice for small claims disputants; reduce litigation costs; encourage dispute resolution and settlement; create a simple, inexpensive, efficient system for parties and courts; ensure ease of use and understanding; provide individualised assistance; maintain procedural justice safeguards for fairness and transparency; and ensure alignment with Utah's judicial mission and core values.

There are five distinct stages in Utah's ODR process.

First, *education and evaluation*. This stage informs users about their claims and potential defences. The plaintiffs initiate their case via a court website and access MyCase, an online portal that allows them to track case progress, view documents and utilise chat, document preparation and negotiation features. The defendants enter the system upon receiving a summons, guiding them through a structured response process.

Second, *communication*. During the communication stage, parties are encouraged to use the chat function to discuss the case and attempt to find a resolution to the dispute. A facilitator is also available once both parties have accessed the ODR web portal. Parties are told that shared information is confidential. In effect, the communication stage operates as a chat board. If the parties agree to settle, the facilitator assists them to generate a settlement agreement to be signed and filed online. If a settlement agreement is not filed and the case is not resolved within 35 days, the facilitator sets the case for online or offline trial, depending on the case's complexity.

Third, *facilitation and trial preparation*. The job of the ODR facilitator is to help parties who cannot resolve their dispute to create a trial preparation document that outlines the claim, defence, facts and evidence on which the parties agree and disagree. The facilitator and parties must complete this document within 35 days of joining ODR or a trial is scheduled.

Fourth, *adjudication*. Once parties are scheduled for trial, they no longer have access to the online chat functions used during the communication stage. Instead, they progress to an 'on the record' chat area, where the trial is held (if held online). Once the judge reaches a decision, their order is explained on the chat platform prior to being posted.

Fifth, *post-judgment*. Once an order issues, additional information/tools (eg, concerning appeals, motions to enforce) are available in the ODR portal's post-judgment section.

Utah began trialling its ODR platform in three court districts in 2018. Unlike other states, which used private service providers, Utah's Administrative Office of the Courts designed and built the platform in-house, making this the first bespoke judicial ODR platform in the United States. It is strikingly easy to use. For example, if one goes to the page dealing with small claims, there is a section entitled "I am suing someone" and another entitled "I am being sued". The sections can be accessed by scrolling down or by pressing the relevant button on the page. The two sections are then broken down into the following key issues (which themselves link through to still more pages of interest):

Figure 16: Examples of links and hyperlinks in Utah ODR platform

Information for people suing someone (plaintiffs)

Follow the steps below to sue someone in small claims. Click on one of the headings for details.

Step 1. Know the limits in Small Claims Court.
Step 2. Decide where to file.
Step 3. Fill out forms and file.
Step 4. Serve the papers.

Next steps

Information for people being sued (defendants)

If you received an affidavit and summons for a small claims case, read it carefully to know what to do. What does your summons say?

It says to register for ODR.
It says I have to go to trial.
What are my other options?

Next steps

There is also a "Related Information" section where it is possible to obtain comprehensive but easily understandable information under an array of headings.

The Utah website is slightly more sombre in its presentation than, for example, the UK TPT and does not have the same (engaging) use of colour or even the same pleasantness of font type and size. Additionally, as the University of Arizona's Innovation for Justice (I4J) Program was later to suggest (in a review done after the site and process were trialled), the site could benefit from having some video information for those who find reading a challenge. However, these are minor observations regarding what is a readily navigable and understandable site that does a remarkably good job at conveying a lot of necessary information in a manner that is not at all overwhelming. Moreover, its muted text and tones manage to suggest that, for all the ease of access and easiness of language, one has entered a court website and there is a certain seriousness of purpose that goes with that.

As mentioned, after Utah's ODR site was initially launched and trialled, the University of Arizona's I4J Program conducted an independent evaluation, leading to several key recommendations, all of which have more general resonance when it comes to ODR platform design.

Recommendation 1 – "Ease the transition from paper to platform":[109] The report recommends that the platform use best practices when it comes to URL formation (ie, the website address), website naming and the user interface design. In particular, the report suggests the following changes, among others. First, there should be a short, simple URL with a familiar domain name (eg, utahcourts.gov/ODR). Second, the URL should not be case sensitive; if it has to be case sensitive, any summonses should indicate this to be so. Third, the URL should appear on each summons with a QR code by which the ODR platform can be accessed. Fourth, each summons should display the web address by which the ODR platform can be accessed. Fifth, the terms 'online dispute resolution' and 'OR' should appear on the website homepage. Sixth, on paper documents, key information that will be sought/necessary online should be highlighted. Seventh, best practices in user interface design should be used – for example, by adopting high-contrast colours, using a clear information hierarchy in the site and not placing text on images.

Recommendation 2 – "Streamline the registration process":[110] The report found that the registration and login process on the platform required repeated cross-referencing between the paper summons/affidavit and the ODR website. It also lacked, for example, sufficient error prevention mechanisms. In particular, the report suggests the following changes, among others. First, the number of required steps should be reduced. Second, a progress bar should be added that tells users how far they have gone before completion. Third, the system's password requirements should be stated and the user provided with an option to see their password being entered so as to avoid mistakes. Fourth, there should be error prevention feedback to prevent users from entering incorrect data. Fifth, the verification process should be improved by including text advising that a verification message is on the way and may take a minute to arrive. Sixth, there should be 'tooltips' that flash up, for example, a picture of the paper document that a user holds and show where the information to be inputted is to be found on that document.

Recommendation 3 – "Simplify document sharing and review":[111] The report found that users considered previewing, sharing, signing and uploading documents to be very difficult. Seven out of eight participants experienced a critical error and half of participants were unable to complete the task even with a facilitator's help. Identifying how to upload documents was not intuitive: many users struggled even to locate files on their phone. In particular, the report suggests the following changes, among others. Users should be able to share documents in the chat feature. The upload process should be simplified through a combination of icons and text. Feedback on upload status should be provided. A simplified review process should be added that allows users to review and confirm settlement details. Error prevention measures should be implemented. And users should be allowed to print documents before and after signing them.

Recommendation 4 – "Improve ODR information and help":[112] The report recommends that, for example, the Utah platform should anticipate and address questions about ODR during the user experience and apply best practices in terms of FAQ design, user onboarding and visual hierarchy. In particular, the report suggests the following changes, among others. Information should be structured so that it is clear and easy to find. A homepage welcome message should be added. There should be a FAQ button on the homepage and in the main navigation menu. The FAQs should sit within the ODR platform, not on a separate website. The information provided should be clear and scannable and address higher-priority issues first. An overview guide should appear the first time and be skippable on a second or later visit. And there should be a welcome overview video that is captioned/subtitled in several languages.

Recommendation 5 – "Clarify legal information and user options":[113] The report recommends that, for example, the platform should use best practices for visual information hierarchy, define keywords and simplify the response experience for defendants. These recommendations arise from concerns expressed by users as to a lack of access to, or comprehension of, legal information. In particular, the report suggests the following changes, among others. Necessary information should be clear and readily accessible. A visual hierarchy should clearly flag user options. Pop-up definitions of key terms should be provided. A claim response tool should enable defendants to draft bespoke responses. The use of the ODR facilitator should be clearly explained. And the ODR facilitator should commence each chat with a brief explanation of their role and user options.

General recommendations: The report also makes a number of more general recommendations (which have resonance that reaches beyond the Utah ODR platform). These include the following. First, an ODR platform should provide equal access/opportunity to all users, regardless of cognitive, hearing, movement and sight ability. Second, an AI chatbot should offer relevant assistance as words are keyed in. If the chatbot cannot help, this should prompt a facilitator to join and assist. Third, there should be a bank of standard responses that users might use. Fourth, there should be a "Help" button on each page that provides help relevant to the point from which the help is accessed. Fifth, there should be an on-platform calculator on which calculations can be done and supplied to the facilitator and/or the other side. Sixth, the Spanish-language portion of the ODR platform could be improved. Seventh, there should be an option to have a private conversation with the facilitator. Eighth, a paper guide to the ODR process should be delivered to defendants along with the initial summons and affidavit. Ninth, an ODR platform should adapt to the screen size of the device from which it is being viewed. Tenth, an ODR platform should allow for synchronous contact if desired. Eleventh, there should be a short, simple exit survey for users to rate their overall experience by choosing from three emoji faces. Twelfth, videoconferencing should be included on the ODR platform to allow for remote hearings/trials. Thirteenth, the ODR platform should contain informational videos with captions and subtitling.

3. A comparison between the two initiatives

Utah's ODR programme represents a bold reimagining of court accessibility and efficiency. By focusing on user needs and leveraging technology, Utah has created a system that is not only functional but also scalable. The findings of the I4J evaluation provide valuable insights into common challenges and best practices for ODR implementation. As more states, both in the United States and worldwide, consider ODR, Utah's approach will likely serve as a blueprint for the future of digital dispute resolution.

Michigan and Utah have each established themselves as pioneers in ODR, though their approaches reflect different strategies. While both states have aimed to enhance access to justice and modernise court processes, Michigan's focus was on adapting existing community-based dispute resolution programmes; while Utah pursued a court-integrated, purpose-built ODR system designed from the ground up.

Michigan used Zoom dispute resolution and MI-Resolve to transition to online mediation. By contrast, Utah's initiative emerged from a judicial policy shift that sought to address declining court usage and evolving public expectations. Utah's system was built in-house by the court administration, making it the first fully customised state-run ODR platform in the United States.

Utah's approach is centralised and structured, with a well-defined five-stage process: education, communication, facilitation, adjudication and post-judgment (all integrated directly into the state's small claims court system). Michigan relied on existing non-profit mediation centres spread across 83 counties, allowing each centre a degree of flexibility in its implementation of ODR.

Both states faced challenges in adoption, but the rates of integration differed significantly. Michigan's Zoom dispute resolution was widely embraced during the pandemic and seamlessly incorporated into hybrid mediation models post-pandemic. MI-Resolve saw a slower rollout. Utah, by contrast, ensured that every disputant within the system was directed towards ODR. This mandatory participation led to higher engagement.

Utah placed strong emphasis on user experience design. Its MyCase portal offered structured pathways for plaintiffs and defendants, complete with chat functions, document sharing and trial preparation assistance. Michigan's MI-Resolve lacked an equivalent level of structured guidance.

Michigan's volunteer-based model significantly reduced costs, as MI-Resolve relied on unpaid mediators rather than court-appointed facilitators. Utah's system, while designed for efficiency, required a greater initial investment in software development, judicial training and process redesign. However, its streamlined case handling has reduced court backlogs, offering long-term cost savings.

Both states faced technical barriers in their transition to ODR. Michigan's challenges stemmed from a lack of centralised oversight, leading to inconsistencies in MI-Resolve adoption. Utah's hurdles were more technology-centric, with users struggling with, for example, document uploads and registration steps.

Michigan and Utah's ODR initiatives showcase two distinct yet complementary approaches to digital justice. Michigan's community-based, cost-effective model is adaptable and scalable for states with strong mediation programmes. Utah's court-integrated, structured platform sets a precedent for jurisdictions seeking a mandatory ODR process.

Key learnings

- *Tailor ODR to user expectations.* ODR should be designed to provide a seamless digital experience that meets evolving public preferences. (It might be observed that while adapting to user expectations is important, ensuring due process and legal safeguards should take precedence).
- *Choose between centralised and decentralised models.* Whereas Michigan's ODR relies on a volunteer-based, community-driven approach, Utah has developed a court-integrated, centralised system. While a centralised system may offer consistency, it may also be inflexible. Conversely, a decentralised, community-driven model risks inconsistency and unequal access.
- *Technology selection matters.* Utah's custom-built system ensured tailored functionality, while Michigan used off-the-shelf solutions. Custom-built systems provide tailored solutions. Off-the-shelf technology allows for swift implementation and easier updates without undue financial cost.
- *Adoption hinges on awareness and training.* Mandating ODR participation, as Utah did, may ensure high engagement but could also reduce user autonomy. That said, voluntary participation respects user choice but may result in lower usage rates.
- *Hybrid models increase access and efficiency.* Michigan's hybrid approach of Zoom for synchronous mediation and MI-Resolve for asynchronous negotiation provides flexibility. However, a single, well-structured ODR system may be more effective than offering numerous options to users.
- *Clear and intuitive user interfaces are critical.* Utah's structured navigation, chat functions and document-sharing features enhance user experience. ODR platforms must prioritise user-friendly design and accessibility. But while user-friendly interfaces are essential, oversimplifying ODR systems may lead to legal nuances being overlooked.
- *ODR must address the digital divide.* Limited internet access and low technology literacy hinder participation in ODR. However, providing extensive digital access initiatives may not fully resolve participation issues: in-person legal support may remain necessary for some people.
- *Legal safeguards must be maintained.* The experience of both states shows that ODR must preserve procedural justice, ensure fairness and protect confidentiality. That said, legal safeguards, if excessive, may slow dispute resolution and make the process overly complex.
- *Funding and resource allocation require long-term planning.* Utah's successful court-managed system required significant upfront

investment. However, high initial investment in ODR infrastructure may be unsustainable for some jurisdictions.

- *Stakeholder engagement drives success.* The most successful ODR programmes appear to have involved many stakeholders in the design process. However, involving too many stakeholders may lead to prolonged decision making, conflicting priorities and delays in implementation.

9. Three Canadian examples of ODR in action

ODR can expand access by helping eliminate a wide variety of obstacles that prevent individuals from understanding and exercising their rights. Financial barriers are an obvious challenge, but access issues also include physical barriers as well as barriers of language and literacy. People with family responsibilities, work-travel requirements, limited mobility, health issues, challenges related to language or literacy, immigration status, those who live in remote areas, and members of the armed forces who are deployed can engage with the justice system more conveniently, inexpensively, and simply through ODR.
Joint Technology Committee[114]

[B]y virtue of being cost effective, convenient and quick, ODR provides parties an opportunity to exercise their rights and explore avenues, that they might have otherwise not pursued given the lengthy and expensive nature of litigation ... As a result, it can be one of the mechanisms to increase access to justice. By introducing mechanisms that can ensure greater procedural fairness ... ODR can attempt to level the bargaining powers of parties ... That said, given the prerequisite requirements of technological infrastructure and digital literary, it will be long journey for ODR to be able to provide access to justice for all.
NITI Aayog[115]

Improving ODR: 10 key lessons

- Enhance accessibility.
- Prioritise speed.
- Ensure cost efficiency.
- Offer guided self-representation.
- Promote transparency.
- Foster early resolution.
- Leverage digital communication.
- Cater for specialisation.
- Maintain confidentiality.
- Provide for continuous feedback.

In this chapter, I consider the operation of British Columbia's Civil Resolution Tribunal (CRT), Ontario's Condominium Authority Tribunal (CAT) and PARLe, a dispute resolution process operated by Quebec's Consumer Protection Agency.

1. The Civil Resolution Tribunal

The establishment of the CRT marked a transformative step in the provision of public justice in British Columbia. The CRT is an independent, quasi-judicial body that provides an accessible and affordable means of resolving civil disputes without the need for lawyers or court appearances. Instead of adopting the traditional courtroom model, the CRT encourages a collaborative, problem-solving approach and offers self-help tools to guide users toward resolution. It actively promotes self-representation – although legal representation can be permitted. To ensure transparency, all CRT default and final decisions are publicly accessible. In fulfilling its mandate, the role of the CRT is to encourage the resolution of disputes by agreement between the parties and, if resolution by agreement is not reached, to resolve the dispute by deciding the claims brought to the tribunal by the parties. The CRT may also provide the public with information on dispute resolution and make its ODR services available to the public generally.

The CRT was established under the Civil Resolution Tribunal Act 2012, which sets out its mandate and operational framework. The tribunal is required to function in a manner that prioritises the following features.

First, *accessibility/informality*. Service users can access online services wherever and whenever they choose. They can also access CRT services by email, mail, telephone, videoconference or in person at any of 65 service locations in British Columbia. (That said, in 2022/23, over 99% of service users chose to use the CRT's online services.) The CRT also works with community legal advocates around British Columbia who represent people with barriers to accessing the justice system, getting them to test anything they develop that will be used by the public.

Second, *speed*. Long legal disputes can tax the financial, mental and physical wellbeing of participants. This is why the CRT seeks to help disputants to resolve claims as early as possible. In this regard, the CRT's platform offers a 'Solution Explorer' (bespoke software) that, through a series of questions, helps people to better understand their legal issue and options before they spend time and money on making a claim. In the year to 31 March 2023, the Solution Explorer was used over 30,000 times.

Third, *economy/efficiency*. Use of the Solution Explorer is free. The CRT charges for its services but its fees are staggered so that users only pay for the services used. It also offers a discount for use of online services. If parties reach agreement during the negotiation stage, the application fee is refunded. Because most services are provided remotely, its expectation is that most users will not incur any travel costs. Efficiency is achieved by automating business processes, actively case managing files and making improvements based on internal data and public feedback.

Fourth, *flexibility*. The CRT offers a range of tools and services aimed at helping disputants to resolve their disputes. These include the Solution Explorer (available on a 24/7 basis), searchable access to CRT decisions, an online negotiation tool, the services of a case manager and the potential for a binding CRT decision in the absence of disputant agreement.

In addition, the CRT applies principles of law and fairness; recognises any relationships between parties to a dispute that will likely continue after the tribunal proceeding is concluded; uses electronic communication tools to facilitate the resolution of disputes brought to the CRT; and accommodates, so far as the CRT considers reasonably practicable, the diversity of circumstances of the persons using the services of the tribunal.

The CRT adjudicates on a range of disputes, including small claims disputes (up to C$5,000); strata property (ie, condominium) disputes; disputes with cooperatives and societies; intimate image protection claims; and motor vehicle accident disputes.*

In essence, a CRT proceeding has two phases: the case management phase and the tribunal hearing phase. In the case management phase, resolution by agreement between the parties is facilitated and preparations are made for the tribunal hearing should one be required. In the tribunal hearing phase, the dispute is heard and the tribunal gives a final decision to resolve the dispute if it is not resolved in the case management phase. In general, parties must represent themselves in a tribunal proceeding.

- *Case management phase:* The role of a case manager is to assist in the resolution of disputes, including by aiding the parties in reaching resolution by agreement; assisting the parties in identifying the facts relevant to resolving the dispute; determining the evidence or other information that will assist in resolving a dispute; and making a recommendation to the tribunal as to the process to be used in hearing the dispute, if the tribunal has jurisdiction to hear it.

* The CRT's role as regards road traffic accident claims was the subject of challenge in *Trial Lawyers Association of British Columbia v British Columbia (Attorney General),* 2022 BCCA 163. There, British Columbia's Court of Appeal heard an appeal against a British Columbia Supreme Court decision declaring parts of the CRT's vehicle accident claims jurisdiction unconstitutional and of no effect. The Supreme Court's decision struck down the CRT's jurisdiction to decide whether injuries as a result of a motor vehicle accident are minor and to adjudicate claims about liability and damages of up to C$50,000. The British Columbia Supreme Court held that these areas of jurisdiction were the responsibility of the superior courts at the time of confederation, and that granting the CRT the authority to determine such claims was essentially taking that authority from the superior courts. The British Columbia Court of Appeal allowed the appeal, finding the legislation to be constitutional having regard to the historical character of superior courts and the policy objectives of the legislation. The court found that the jurisdiction of the superior courts was unaffected, with the British Columbia Supreme Court retaining significant involvement in personal injury and motor vehicle accident claims.

- *Tribunal hearing phase:* Among other matters, in resolving a dispute, the CRT may conduct a hearing in writing; by telephone, videoconferencing or email; through the use of other electronic communication tools; or by any combination of those means. It is not necessary for the means of communication to allow all parties to the dispute to take part at the same time. The CRT may hold an in-person hearing if it considers that the nature of the dispute or some extraordinary circumstance makes an in-person hearing necessary in the interests of justice. The default position is that an in-person hearing must be open to the public.

In April 2022, the CRT launched a new website, designed with information accessibility in mind. The revamped website contains a balance of text and visuals, built-in Google Translate functionality and design elements such as varying font sizes and colours. The service design goals of the new site were to make key information easy to find, present information in plain/accessible language and manage participant/public expectations about different aspects of the CRT process. A visit to the revamped CRT website is a notably seamless, even enjoyable, experience. The opening page immediately offers the user the chance of proceeding in a variety of languages. On the English-language page, there are two prominent questions and response buttons:

Want to make a CRT claim?

Apply now

Did someone make a CRT claim against you?

Respond now

A brief description of the CRT and its website follows. The words "Neutral, fair, and convenient" are highlighted in large bold text. Five different-coloured boxes invite the visitor to learn more about various claim types ("Intimate images", "Motor vehicle accidents", "Small claims", "Strata property"* and "Societies and cooperatives"). For users who want information delivered by video technology, there is a two-minute video that shows how the CRT works by tracking an imaginary claim. Going back to the coloured buttons and clicking on the one marked "Intimate images", one is brought to the following series of screens:

* Strata housing includes, for example, apartment-style condominiums, duplexes, townhouses, fractional vacation properties and even single-family homes in bare land strata corporations. There are different types of strata developments including, for example, commercial, industrial and residential. Strata corporations are self-governed. The strata corporation is made up of all the strata lot owners. Strata lot owner responsibilities include approving an annual budget and electing a strata council. It is up to the strata council, owners and residents to ensure compliance with strata legislation, bylaws and rules.

- This page explains that in British Columbia, it is against the law to share or threaten to share an intimate image of someone without their consent. It also points to the potential to make a claim for an intimate image protection order, a claim for damages and a claim for a penalty (where a person does not comply with an intimate image protection order). There is also a quick exit button that brings the reader straight to the Google homepage (possibly in the event that the reader is disturbed while reading). Under the heading "Make a claim", the reader can access the CRT's "Solution Explorer", which is flagged as being free to use and anonymous, comprising a series of questions that will yield customised legal information and options based on the answers given. By clicking on the "Explore and apply: intimate images" button, the visitor is brought to the next screen. If the user chooses instead to scroll down, they are given various organisations that can provide emotional and other support. There is also a FAQ section where the visitor can link through to the answers to various questions concerning intimate images; the CRT; safety and privacy; whether and how the CRT can assist people under the age of 19; the making of a claim; parental questions; adviser questions; the CRT process; the use of evidence and technology; what happens after one gets a CRT order; and respondent questions.

  Because there are many questions posed in the Solutions Explorer, each potentially bringing one to a different limb of the tool, it is necessary to proceed by reference to an imagined scenario. In this imagined scenario, Mandy – a 25-year-old woman – had a personal relationship with Don and allowed him to take intimate images of her that showed her in a state of nakedness. Sometime afterward, Mandy ended her relationship with Don. Minded to have revenge on Mandy, Don circulated some of the intimate images to Mandy's parents, without Mandy's permission. Extremely upset, Mandy accesses the CRT website to see what she can do. Mandy accesses the opening page and clicks on the button marked "Explore and apply: intimate images".
- Having clicked on the just-mentioned button, Mandy is not brought immediately to the Solution Explorer. Instead, she is brought to the Solution Explorer terms of use and asked to indicate her assent to same. There is a very brief account as to how she can make a claim; what the disclaimers and terms of use are; a hyperlink to the full terms of use (which are not an especially user-friendly read); and (back on the initial page) an opt-in box, whereby the reader agrees to the Solution Explorer terms of use.
- By clicking on the "Next" button, Mandy is brought to the question: "What would you like to learn more about?" There are three options. The first concerns what Mandy can do if someone has shared or threatened to share an intimate image without her consent.

- By clicking on the just-mentioned question, Mandy is brought to a readable one-page document about intimate images and the law of British Columbia. Colour, spacing, icons and varying font sizes make for an easy read; as do boxes squaring off the different segments of text.
- By clicking "Next", Mandy is brought to a page with two options. The first offers the possibility to learn more about the CRT and possibly make a claim.
- By clicking on the just-mentioned option, Mandy is brought to a readable one-page document about intimate images and the role of the CRT.
- By clicking "Next", Mandy is brought to a readable one-page document about what constitutes an intimate image.
- By clicking "Next", Mandy is brought to a question about the nature of the image about which she is concerned – for example, whether it contains nakedness.
- By clicking "Yes" to the just-mentioned question, Mandy is brought to another question asking whether someone has shared or threatened to share an intimate image of her without her consent.
- By clicking "Yes" to the just-mentioned question, Mandy is brought to a readable one-page document about what constitutes a reasonable expectation of privacy.
- By clicking "Next", Mandy is brought to a question about what she now wants to do. (This is followed by a six-sentence description of what she can do.) The first of two options presented is to ask the CRT for an intimate image protection order to stop or prevent the image being shared.
- By clicking on the just-mentioned option, Mandy is brought to a readable one-page document about CRT intimate image protection orders.
- By clicking "Next", Mandy is brought to a question about her age (or, if she is exploring on behalf of someone else, their age). A two-sentence explanation follows as to why this question is being asked (because there are things to be advised if Mandy or the subject of the search is under 19 years of age).
- By clicking the answer "19 or older" to the just-mentioned question, Mandy is again asked what she wants to do. The first option is to ask the CRT for a protection order to have the image of her taken down – that is, to make a CRT claim.
- By clicking on the just-mentioned option, Mandy is brought to a readable one-page document about applying for a CRT intimate image protection order.
- The next screen (headed "Make a CRT Claim") tells Mandy that she has

reached the end of her exploration and invites her to access a screen that will show a summary of her exploration and all the resources that she has seen thus far, and identifying her next steps.

- The next screen (headed "Make a CRT Claim") thanks Mandy for answering questions about her scenario, reassures her that her answers were anonymous and invites her to click "Apply" to make a claim with the CRT. It tells Mandy that she will be brought to the correct form for what she wants to do, asked to provide her contact details and told that she will need to answer some questions about what she wants to claim. Mandy clicks on "Apply".
- Mandy is brought to a screen headed "Dispute Application". Helpful detail as to the process now to be followed is provided under the sub-headings "What you need to do", "What the CRT will do" and "What you need to know before you start". The last of these headings provides some new information – for example, the application takes about 10 minutes to complete; a draft can be saved and submitted at any time within 30 days; and there is no application fee. A private mail address will be needed – if Mandy does not have one, she is encouraged to contact the CRT for other options. Mandy is also told that there are paper forms which she can fill out and post in.
- Mandy clicks on the "Start Application" button and is then brought to a "Sign up" screen, where she is invited to create an account and progress her application. (The process that follows the commencement of her application has been described previously above.)

The CRT represented (and represents) a paradigm shift in dispute resolution, demonstrating how technology can enhance access to justice. By prioritising user experience, flexibility and cost efficiency, the CRT has created a scalable model for digital dispute resolution worldwide.

The CAT was Canada's first online tribunal. Its objective is to help condominium owners and corporations to resolve disputes affordably, conveniently and quickly. (A condominium is a building or group of buildings that contains a number of individually owned apartments or houses.) The CAT helps to resolve disputes on a whole variety of issues, including those relating to noise, parking, pets, smells and a broad gamut of issues that can arise for condominium owners and tenants.

2. The Condominium Authority Tribunal

The CAT was established under Ontario's Condominium Act 1998 and derives its authority from that act and the CAT Regulation 2017. It uses an ODR system (the CAT-ODR System) to assist users to resolve condominium-related disputes. The process is notably easy to use. The best way to describe it is by reference to the CAT's downloadable online guide, *Filing an Application: A User Guide*. This is a short (13-page) but notably comprehensive handbook to the mechanics of bringing a claim before the CAT. The process that the CAT follows is considered later below.

The CAT recommends in its user guide that before filing an application with the CAT, prospective disputants should consult the Condominium Authority's *Guided Steps to Common Issues*. This is essentially an online guide to resolving disputes before they escalate to the point that parties need to have recourse to the CAT. Proceeding on the basis that most issues can be resolved collaboratively, the authority (in its guide) provides information on applicable rights and responsibilities, identifies guided steps to help resolve different common issues and offers sample letter templates that can be used. In terms of issues that the authority can help with, it identifies the 15 key categories shown in Figure 17. Space constraints mean that it is not possible to examine how the guide treats with each of these categories. It will suffice by way of example to show how one of the issues ("Pets and animals") is addressed; this is because each of the categories is treated with in a roughly similar manner.

The *Guided Steps to Common Issues* break down disputes into a four-step process, with a structured, intuitive online navigation system. Consider the example of a condominium owner (Della) experiencing issues related to pets and animals.

Step 1: If Della clicks on the "Pets and Animals" hyperlink, she is brought to a new page. Under the heading "Step 1. Identify the Issue", this page indicates that it is one of four screens that can be accessed regarding pet and animal issues. (The others are "Legal Considerations", "Find Solutions" and "Escalate Your Issue".) As regards identifying the issue, the authority, for example, notes that many boards have requirements in their governing documents that are intended to regulate the keeping of pets. Most such disputes, the authority observes, will be resolved by reference to, and enforcement of, the governing document.

Scrolling down, Della is given the option of proceeding to the next step or reading up further on her rights. If Della clicks, for example, on the "Pet and Animal Issues" button, she is given a few (briefly stated) examples of the kinds of disputes it is referring to – for example, "Keeping pets that are not allowed by the condo". The text is easy to read and very brief, but also useful and informative. Different font sizes and icons are strategically used and particular terminology ("governing documents") highlighted and hyperlinked to a definition. A "Did You Find This Helpful?" question appears at the bottom (so the authority is continuously monitoring user satisfaction), and Della is asked whether she wants to sign up for news and updates from the authority.

Step 2: If Della clicks to continue to the next step, she is brought to a new

Figure 17: Issues that the CAT assists with

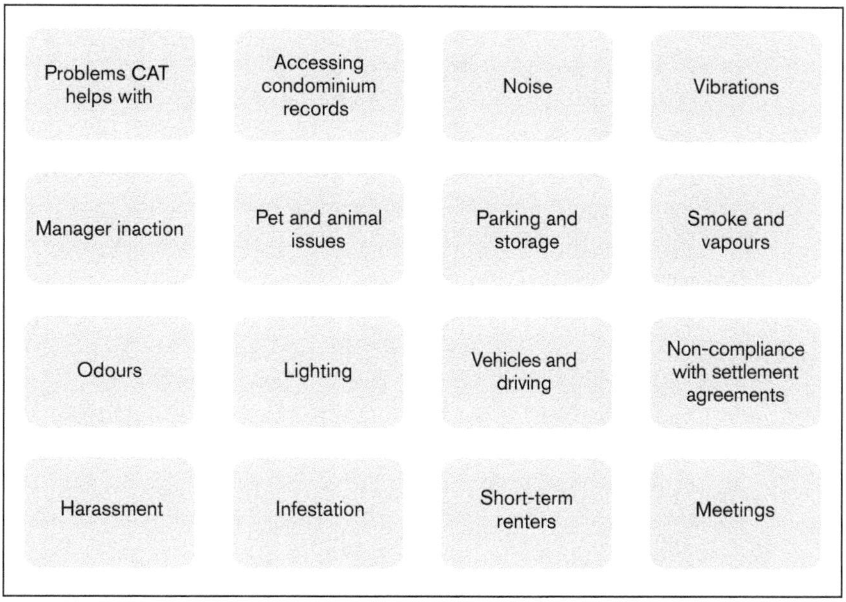

screen/step. This is headed "Step 2: Legal Considerations" and briefly states its purpose: "There may be municipal bylaws regarding pets, depending on where you live." Scrolling down, Della is given brief but helpful guidance on pet and animal provisions in governing documents, the rules concerning service animals and what may be stated in municipal bylaws. The guidance suggests some useful first steps that the reader might take. Notably, under the heading "What Does the Condo Act Say?" (using the colloquial name by which the governing legislation is known), the screen refers to a trio of relevant legislative provisions and, in notably simple English, explains what they provide. A hyperlink to a consolidated version of the Condo Act is provided. Scrolling down, Della finds that Section 119(1) provides as follows, in the careful but not always very user-friendly language that is so often to be found in statute:

> *A corporation, the directors, officers and employees of a corporation, a declarant, the lessor of a leasehold condominium corporation, an owner, an occupier of a unit and a person having an encumbrance against a unit and its appurtenant common interest shall comply with this Act, the declaration, the by-laws and the rules.*

Once again, Della is given the opportunity of accessing related topics or continuing to the next page. As with the first page, a "Did You Find This Helpful?" question appears at the bottom and Della is asked whether she wants to sign up for news and updates from the authority.

Step 3: If Della clicks to continue to the next page, she is brought to a new screen/step. This is headed "Step 3", with a by now familiar icon indicating that this is the third of four screens (and reiterating what each of the four screens treats with). This page is essentially an interim page that flags a number of key issues that might be troubling Della and takes her to a final screen that will address her particular issue. This interim page contains no links to related topics (though it does have a "Did You Find This Helpful?" question at the bottom, along with the option to sign up for news and updates from the authority). The issues are grouped under two headings: "For Condo Owners" and "For Condo Boards and Managers".

If Della is a 'condo owner' and clicks on the first issue ("Another resident is causing a pet or animal issue"), she is brought to another screen (still a part of Step 3). Here, Della must click on a list of possible variations of the problem affecting her. She is then given succinctly stated practical advice as to the next steps to be taken; given guidance on the fact that condominiums must maintain a list of owners and mortgagees; told to contact those responsible and given template letters to send, depending on who Della believes is causing the issue; given guidance on the fact that condominium owners must ensure that occupants comply with the law and with the governing documents; and advised to contact the authority if she has any questions about pet issues. As with every page thus far encountered on the website, at the bottom of the page there is a "Did You Find This Helpful?" question at the bottom, along with the option to sign up for news and updates from the authority).

Step 4: If Della clicks to continue to the next page, she is brought to a new screen/step. This is headed "Step 4: Condominium Authority Tribunal" and briefly states its purpose in the following terms:

> *You may be able to file an application with the Tribunal if you tried the previous steps and it did not work. The Tribunal provides an online dispute resolution system that helps condo communities resolve condo disputes conveniently, quickly and affordably.*

This screen again contains the icon indicating that this is the fourth of four screens (and reiterating what each of the four screens treats with). Scrolling down, Della is given brief but helpful guidance on the CAT and on previous CAT cases concerning pet and animal disputes (with a hyperlink to the decisions). The potential that Della might wish to obtain legal advice is also highlighted and a hyperlink is provided to a legal resources page that gives more information on affordable legal advice, free legal information and the potential to avail of legal expense insurance. As with every page thus far encountered on the website, at the bottom of the page there is a "Did You Find This Helpful?"

Figure 18: CAT's formal dispute resolution process

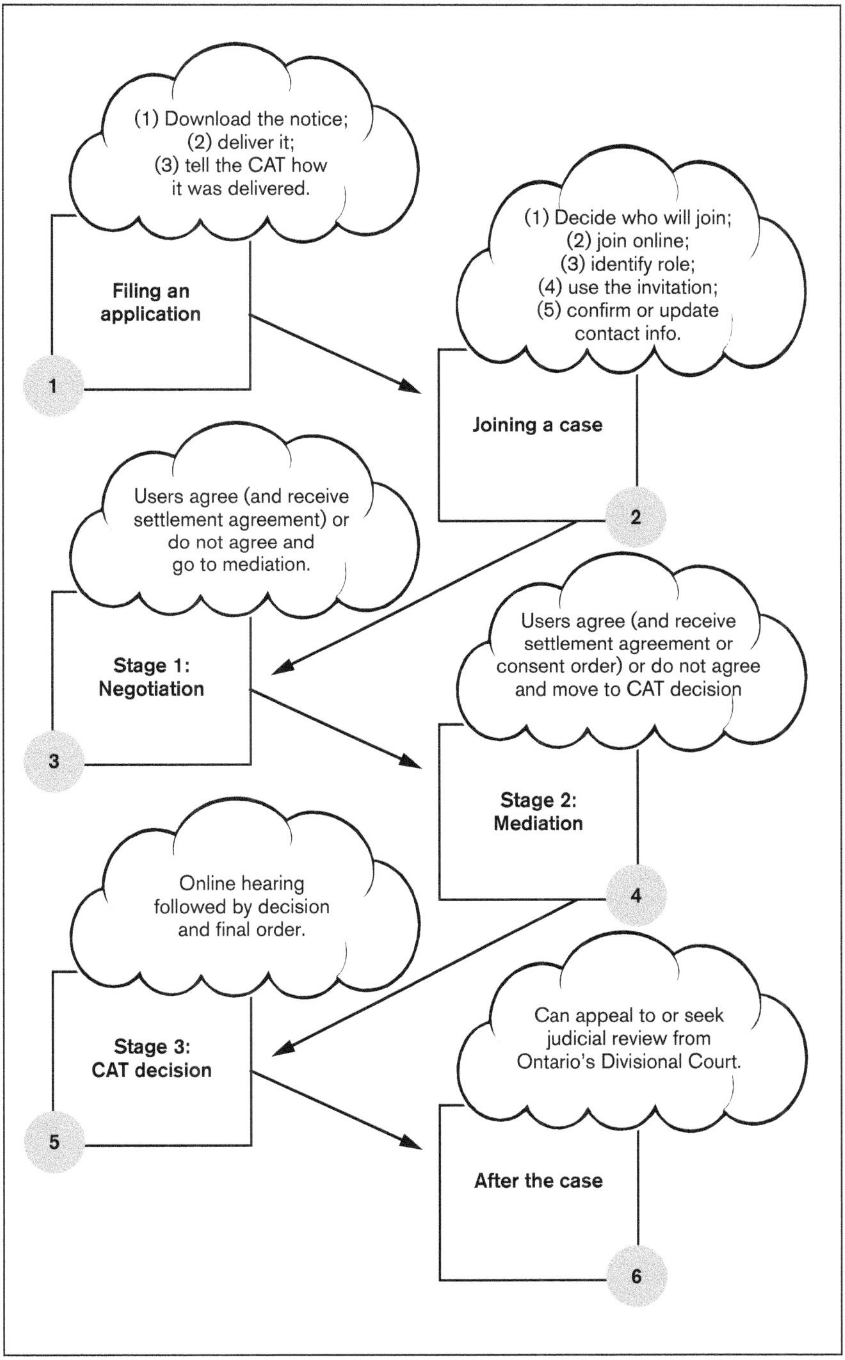

question at the bottom, along with the option to sign up for news and updates from the authority). At the end of the page Della is given the option to click on a "File a Tribunal Application", which brings her through to the formal process of commencing a complaint. In terms of the steps involved in the process, these essentially comprise a negotiation stage (in which the parties seek to resolve their dispute directly); a mediation stage (in which efforts at resolution take place with the online assistance of a mediator); and the decision stage (at which point an online hearing is conducted by a CAT member).

Throughout the authority/CAT website, there is skilful use of large writing, bold text and different font sizes to make the experience informative and interesting; and simple language accompanied by hyperlinks to more elaborate (yet still simply worded) explanations. Every step on the website is both intuitive and logical. As a lawyer, one is left with the impression that if a professional had given Della the advice and guidance that she receives as she progresses through the screens described above, she would have been offered competent, informative, sensible and useful advice on her legal rights and on her next steps (and the end result to which those steps might lead).

The CAT represents a progressive shift in legal dispute resolution, offering a scalable model for all specialised tribunals. By prioritising early resolution, user-friendly digital navigation and efficient online adjudication, it demonstrates how technology can transform legal accessibility without compromising procedural fairness.

3. PARLe

Quebec's Consumer Protection Agency has pioneered a free, impartial ODR platform to resolve conflicts between consumers and traders efficiently. Since 2016, the agency has utilised PARLe to fulfil its commitment to affordable, accessible and efficient consumer dispute resolution. (It is no coincidence that the verb 'to speak' in French is '*parler*'.)

Consumers who wish to initiate the dispute resolution process via PARLe must first contact the Consumer Protection Agency. If they meet the eligibility criteria, an agency officer provides access via email, along with guidance on how to proceed.

The agency highlights four key benefits of the PARLe platform. It is a neutral, private and secure environment for resolving disputes. It can provide mediation services, if required. It offers a cost-free, practical solution to disputes, irrespective of the value of the disputed good or service value. And it is a highly effective process (disputes are typically resolved within 25 working days).

To use PARLe, consumers must satisfy two conditions: the dispute must be a civil dispute, and the other party must be a participating merchant. Once these criteria are met, consumers can register, create a file and submit a proposal to the merchant via the platform. A user guide and summaries of recent judgments are available to help consumers formulate a well-supported claim. Merchants may accept the proposal or counteroffer. If negotiation stalls, a certified mediator can assist in reaching an agreement. If a dispute is settled, the platform enables parties to download the agreement for formal filing and enforcement.

The Consumer Protection Agency does not have access to dispute files, ensuring complete confidentiality. However, consumers who are unfamiliar with online platforms or those encountering difficulties may seek assistance from a third party (excluding lawyers). To authorise this, consumers must complete an assistance mandate, a document included in the agency's initial email.

A growing number of Quebec merchants have embraced PARLe. Participating sectors include appliance and furniture retailers, automobile dealers, department stores, home renovation firms and swimming pool builders. A publicly available, regularly updated list of registered traders is accessible via the agency's website.

Traders must meet several eligibility criteria. If their industry requires an agency-issued licence, they must maintain a valid licence at all times; they must not be subject to ongoing punitive action by the agency; they must not have been the subject of multiple criminal proceedings initiated by the agency within the previous five years; and they must not engage in activities harmful to the public interest. Failure to comply with these requirements may result in suspension or exclusion from the PARLe scheme.

For traders, the agency promotes PARLe as offering various key benefits. First, a swift and simple resolution to consumer disputes. Second, a free, highly effective system. Third, avoidance of litigation. Fourth, negotiations conducted in a neutral, secure environment. Fifth, optional mediation services available when needed.

The CRT, CAT and PARLe are three distinct ODR systems, each of which is designed to enhance access to justice and streamline dispute resolution processes. While they share a digital-first approach, their jurisdictions, operational structures and dispute resolution mechanisms reflect the diverse legal landscapes they serve.

The CRT has the broadest jurisdiction, handling small claims (up to C$5,000), strata property disputes, cooperatives and societies disputes, intimate image protection claims and motor vehicle accident disputes. This wide scope makes it a generalist tribunal covering multiple legal domains.

By contrast, the CAT is a specialised tribunal dealing exclusively with condominium-related conflicts. These disputes commonly involve noise, pets, parking, bylaw enforcement and shared property issues. The CAT's focus reflects the complexity of condominium governance and the necessity for specialised expertise in this area.

The PARLe platform is unique in that it facilitates consumer-trader dispute resolution. Unlike the CRT and the CAT, which adjudicate disputes through legally binding tribunal decisions, PARLe emphasises negotiation and mediation between consumers and businesses, thereby avoiding litigation.

All three platforms rely on a structured, multi-stage ODR process; however, their approaches differ in emphasis and flexibility. A key distinction is that the CRT and the CAT provide binding legal decisions, whereas PARLe primarily seeks to facilitate amicable resolutions between consumers and traders. This makes PARLe more akin to an ombudsman service, while the CRT and the CAT function as adjudicatory bodies.

Each platform is designed to be user-friendly, intuitive and accessible, but their approaches to legal guidance and support vary. The CRT provides a guided software tool, the Solution Explorer, which assists users in understanding legal

Figure 19: The PARLe process

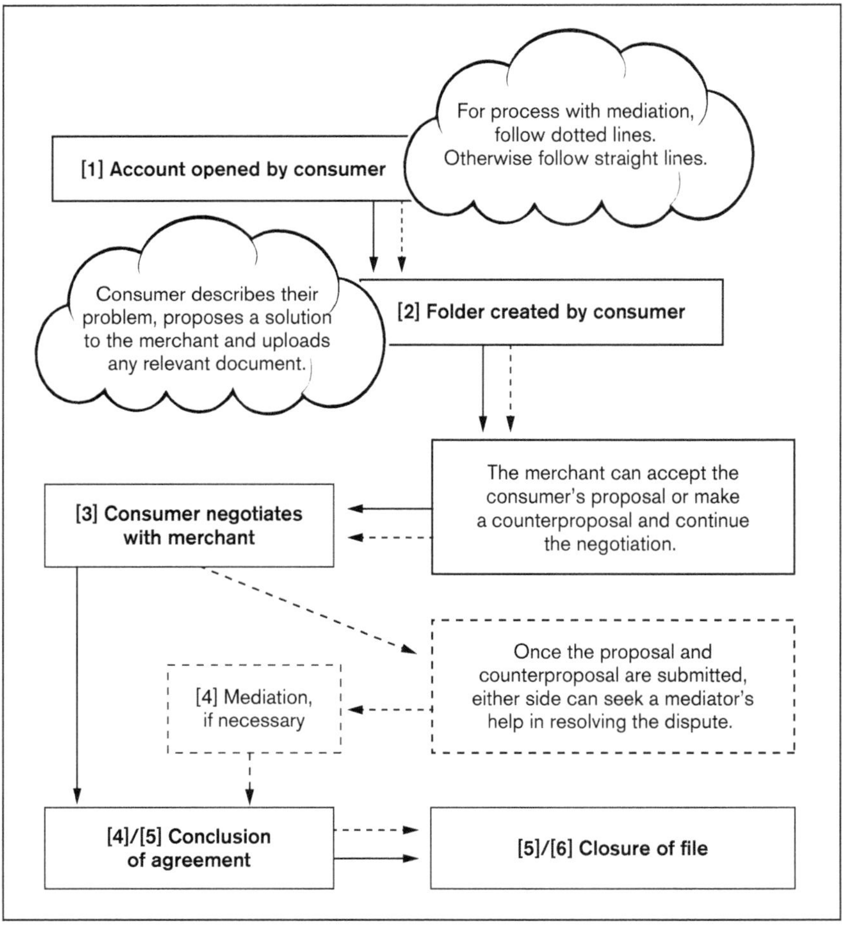

options before filing a claim. This tool is central to the CRT's commitment to self-representation and ensures that users explore ADR before entering the tribunal process. The CAT offers a step-by-step guided interface that is designed to help users identify issues, explore legal considerations, review possible solutions and escalate disputes if needed.

Before users formally file claims, PARLe offers a consumer-friendly digital environment with a user guide, legal summaries and FAQs to help consumers frame their claims.

While all three platforms ensure secure case management, PARLe differs in its confidentiality provisions. CRT and CAT decisions are public, promoting transparency. PARLe cases remain entirely confidential, as the Consumer Protection Agency cannot access user files. This confidentiality is beneficial for consumers and traders who prefer to settle disputes without reputational risks.

Another key contrast lies in who can participate in the ODR process. The CRT and the CAT have mandatory jurisdiction over relevant cases, meaning that parties must engage with the tribunal if their dispute falls within its scope. PARLe is voluntary, requiring traders to opt in. Participating traders benefit from an expedited, litigation-free resolution process. However, traders must meet eligibility requirements, including maintaining valid licensing and compliance with consumer protection laws.

Key learnings

- *Enhance accessibility.* An ODR provider should build an intuitive, multi-channel interface that overcomes, for example, physical and linguistic barriers. That said, overreliance on ODR may exclude those with limited internet access or competence.
- *Prioritise speed.* An ODR provider should design processes that expedite dispute resolution. Caution is required in order to ensure that speed does not compromise the depth of analysis.
- *Ensure cost efficiency.* An ODR provider should seek to keep services affordable and accessible. It must also ensure that in doing so, it does not diminish the quality of the ODR platform.
- *Offer guided self-representation.* An ODR platform should empower users to understand their legal options by themselves. However, excessive automation may miss the nuance that would be brought to bear by legal professionals.
- *Promote transparency.* ODR providers should seek to ensure that decision making is transparent. (It is necessary to balance such openness with the need for data privacy and confidentiality.)
- *Foster early resolution.* ODR should encourage pre-litigation negotiation. That said, such an approach may not be effective for every dispute.

- *Use digital communication.* ODR platforms should utilise varied digital channels – such as email, online forms and video – to cater fully to diverse user needs. However, it must also ensure that robust cybersecurity and infrastructure are in place to maintain reliability and privacy.
- *Cater for specialisation.* ODR platforms should have focused modules for particular dispute types. That said, overspecialisation is to be avoided, as it could lead to inflexibility as regards cases outside the specialised categories.
- *Maintain confidentiality.* An ODR platform should have strong privacy measures. However, it is important to maintain enough transparency to facilitate accountability.
- *Provide for continuous feedback.* An ODR platform should allow for real-time user feedback. Such feedback needs to be weighed against regulatory and operational constraints.

10. ODR and the European Union

Improving ODR: 10 key lessons

- Ensure that the platform adapts to market changes.
- Ensure trader participation.
- Prioritise user engagement.
- Simplify processes and make them clear.
- Assess private sector alternatives first.
- Ensure that costs are justifiable.
- Use governance or incentives to compel or encourage participation.
- Align the platform with consumer needs.
- Test and improve the platform continuously.
- Promote awareness and trust.

1. The ODR Regulation

In 2013, the European Union adopted the ODR Regulation.[116] Its purpose was to create an EU-wide ODR platform – an interactive website serving as a single access point for consumers and traders seeking out-of-court resolution of disputes arising from online transactions. The platform would be designed to provide general information about resolving such disputes and allow users to submit complaints via an electronic form, attach supporting documents and transmit cases to a competent ADR entity. Additionally, it would offer ADR entities a free, electronic case management tool, enabling them to conduct dispute resolution entirely through the platform.

Several key considerations informed the adoption of the regulation. The lack of simple, efficient, fast and low-cost mechanisms for resolving consumer disputes across the European Union was seen as a barrier to the internal market. This was perceived to undermine confidence among both consumers and traders in cross-border online transactions. The digital economy was growing in importance, making it essential that consumers and traders felt secure in online transactions. A reliable and effective ODR mechanism was seen as instrumental in fostering such confidence. Consumers and traders often struggled to find viable out-of-court solutions for cross-border online disputes. As a result, many such disputes simply remained unresolved. While ODR was recognised as a potentially effective solution, the European Union lacked mechanisms to facilitate online dispute resolution. This deficiency was seen as detrimental to consumers, a hindrance to cross-border commerce and a distortion of competition among traders – all of which impeded the growth of online markets.

Figure 20 illustrates the envisioned ODR process under the regulation. In theory, it appeared to be a well-conceived framework for fostering trust in the online marketplace. However, despite its promise, the ODR Regulation ultimately failed to deliver on its objectives, falling victim to rapid changes in the digital space. By October 2023, the European Commission had proposed its repeal,[117] and at the time of writing the ODR process under the regulation is being phased out.

The European Commission offered several reasons for the repeal of the regulation Thus, although adopted in 2013, the regulation had remained unchanged despite remarkable transformations in the digital consumer market. Additionally, since its launch in 2016, the platform had attracted a high number of visitors. However, only 200 cases were resolved per year across an EU-wide market of 440 million consumers, a figure that could not justify the costs of maintaining the platform or the compliance burden on businesses. (Closing the platform was expected to save €500,000 annually.) Moreover, when the regulation was first proposed in 2011, digital markets were still emerging and there were no guarantees that adequate private or public tools would develop to assist traders in engaging with ADR entities. With the evolution of online complaint-handling mechanisms, this concern became obsolete. Beneficially, the platform did serve a role in identifying ADR entities accredited under the ADR Directive. However, since the obligation to maintain such a list under that directive remained extant, the European Commission proposed repurposing what was once the ODR platform for this function instead. Also, the commission had received advice indicating that the platform required a very substantial overhaul to meet contemporary ODR standards. Given its underperformance, the cost of such an upgrade was deemed unjustifiable.

The commission's repeal proposal also included an analysis of how the ODR platform was used. The platform, it seems, received between 2–3 million visitors annually. Only 2% of visitors opted to contact the trader to initiate an ADR process. Most visitors left the platform after a few seconds. Of the traders contacted, only 2% agreed to commence ADR (there was no obligation on them to do so). Around 40% of traders reached out to consumers outside the platform to resolve disputes directly, while 58% took no action at all. Even after improving the homepage with better information and an interactive Q&A system, the number of ADR requests declined – suggesting that when consumers better understood the platform's function, fewer saw it as a viable solution.

Ultimately, the commission concluded that the platform's poor performance

Figure 20: Establishment and operation of ODR regime

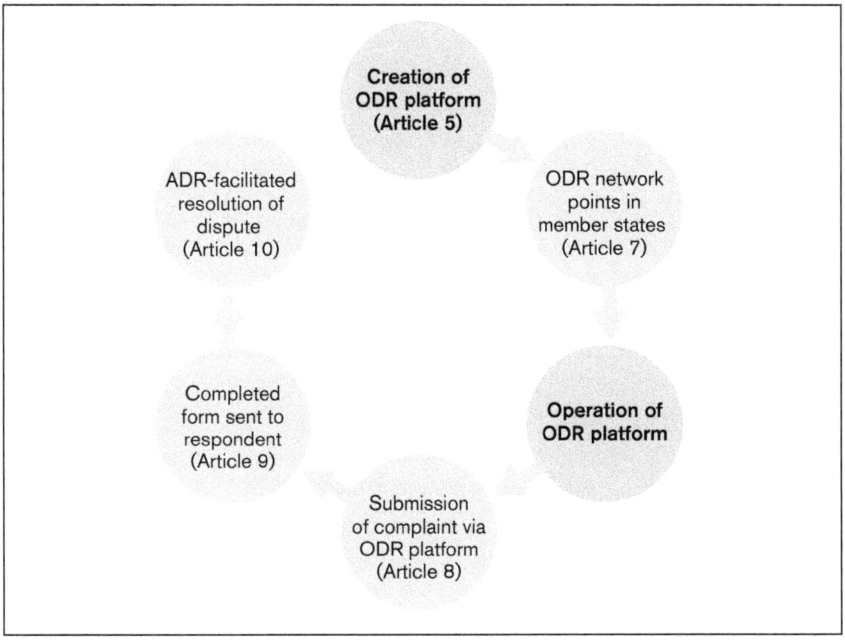

resulted from several factors: a lack of prior information on the part of users; limited trader interest; and difficulties that consumers faced in aligning their disputes with the eligibility criteria of different ADR entities. The closure of the EU ODR platform represents a relatively rare disappointment in the ODR field; though one can expect that, as in any market, there will be successes and failures – here a well-intentioned failure.

Given that each member state has its own self-governing national judiciary, it seems unlikely that much will be achieved at the EU level in terms of ODR rollout within member states. This is unfortunate given the likely advantages that would accrue from a pooling of national expertise under the auspices of the European Union.

What key learnings might be taken from the above analysis of the ODR Regulation? First, the EU ODR platform did not evolve along with the digital economy, eventually making it outdated. (A possible solution to this weakness would be to build flexibility into an ODR system, allowing for occasional technological changes.) Second, the EU ODR platform relied on voluntary trader participation, but only 2% of contacted traders engaged with the system. (A possible solution to such a weakness would be to secure trader engagement through incentives or legal requirements.) Third, millions of persons visited the EU ODR platform annually. Yet most left within seconds and only a tiny fraction initiated dispute resolution. (A possible solution to such a weakness would be to improve user experience with an intuitive interface that encouraged deeper engagement.) Fourth, many consumers abandoned the process after learning how the platform actually worked. (A possible solution to such a weakness would be to streamline ODR process and provide clarity on eligibility, timelines, etc.) Fifth, one of the driving assumptions of the platform – that traders lacked online complaint handling mechanisms – ultimately became outdated. (A possible solution to such a weakness would be to evaluate thoroughly, before launching a public platform, whether private sector solutions already address the problem more efficiently. That said, it seems that public-private sector solutions were unsatisfactory when the platform came into being and then evolved to become more satisfactory after platform was established.) Sixth, resolving only 200 cases per year at a cost of €500,000 to the EU taxpayer was unsustainable. (This result points to the need for continuing cost-benefit analyses to ensure that a platform delivers measurable value for money – as well as a hardheaded willingness to admit failure when it does not.) Seventh, a particular weakness of the EU ODR platform was that traders were under no obligation to use it, leading (perhaps inevitably) to a low level of trader engagement. (A possible solution to such a weakness would be to consider regulatory mechanisms or incentives that would incentivise or require active participation by stakeholders.) Eighth, the eligibility requirements and ADR options of the EU ODR platform did not align with the form of many consumer disputes. Ninth, the platform appears to have remained relatively static in form, despite evidence of declining effectiveness or increasing ineffectiveness. (A possible solution to such a weakness would be to implement ongoing monitoring, data analysis and user feedback arrangements.) Tenth, many consumers and traders were unaware of the existence of the EU ODR platform or were sceptical as to its effectiveness. (A possible solution to such a weakness would be to invest in widespread awareness campaigns.)

2. The e-Codex Regulation

One new measure that touches (tangentially) upon the dispute resolution arena is the recent adoption of the e-CODEX Regulation.[118] The term 'e-CODEX' is shorthand for 'e-justice communication via online data exchange'.[119] The regulation provides for secure electronic communication in some cross-border civil and criminal proceedings between citizens and courts, and between member state administrations. It does this by means of various access points in member states. These access points can securely exchange electronic messages with each other directly over the Internet using a set of common IT standards or protocols. The system also allows for the exchange of documents using standard digital forms.

Prior to the adoption of the e-CODEX Regulation, the e-Codex system had been used by at least 10 member states in a range of pilot programmes. The e-CODEX regulation moved the governance and management of the e-CODEX system from this *ad hoc* consortium to eu-LISA.* Additionally, it sets out the composition of the e-CODEX system and the responsibilities of the European Commission, member states, eu-LISA and national entities which may be managing access points.

3. The ADR Directive

Various jurisdictions have established legislative frameworks to ensure the quality, fairness and efficiency of conciliation bodies and ombudsman schemes. In the European Union, a key measure of this type is the ADR Directive.[120] It has been suggested that the directive was, at least in part, a reaction to an awareness that ADR was not being adequately used in the European Union.[121]

The ADR Directive does not expressly define what it means by 'ADR' – perhaps deliberately so as to avoid unduly constraining the ambit of the directive. As good a definition as any is provided in the dictionary of terms on Utah's small claims ODR website: "Methods of resolving disputes outside of official court proceedings. These methods include mediation arbitration, and conciliation." A close reading of the ADR Directive suggests that, for its purposes, there are four core elements to an ADR procedure.[122] First, it involves 'out-of-court' resolution. Second, it requires an ADR entity that proposes or imposes a solution or facilitates amicable resolution. Third, it applies to contractual obligations stemming from sales and service contracts. Fourth, it encompasses domestic disputes and cross-border disputes within the European Union. So, the ADR Directive applies to all disputes between consumers and traders regarding sales or service contracts, whether concluded online or offline, both domestic and cross-frontier.

Four key principles underpin the ADR Directive. First, preventing market fragmentation. (A fragmented internal market weakens competition, economic growth and job creation.) Second, enhancing public trust. (Eliminating direct and indirect barriers to the internal market is vital to consumer and trader confidence.) Third, ensuring access to effective dispute resolution. (A robust ADR framework benefits consumers and enhances their trust in market transactions.) And fourth, ensuring that online and offline transactions are regulated. (Effective ADR access is particularly critical for cross-border shopping within the European Union.)

As regards subject matter, the directive aims to enhance consumer protection and facilitate the internal market's proper functioning by ensuring that consumers can voluntarily submit complaints to independent, impartial, transparent, effective, swift and fair ADR entities.[123] The ADR Directive does not

---

* That is, the European Union Agency for the Operational Management of Large-Scale IT Systems in the Area of Freedom, Security and Justice.

preclude national laws that mandate ADR participation, provided that such laws do not restrict access to judicial remedies.[124]

In terms of scope, the ADR Directive applies to out-of-court resolution procedures for domestic and cross-border disputes concerning contractual obligations stemming from sales or service contracts between EU-based traders and EU-resident consumers, through the intervention of an ADR entity that either proposes/imposes a solution or facilitates an amicable agreement.[125]

As to access to ADR entities and procedures, EU member states must facilitate consumer access to ADR procedures; ensure that disputes involving traders established in their jurisdiction can be submitted to an ADR entity that complies with the directive's requirements; ensure that ADR entities maintain up-to-date websites providing clear information about ADR procedures, online complaint submission, document upload functionalities and (where applicable) offline complaint submission options.[126] Member states must also ensure that ADR decision-makers possess the requisite expertise and maintain independence and impartiality.[127]

In terms of transparency, ADR entities must publicly disclose, via their websites and upon request, clear and easily comprehensible information about their services and procedures.[128]

The directive imposes procedural safeguards to ensure fairness in ADR processes. Parties must engage in ADR procedures freely and with full knowledge of their rights.[129] ADR procedures must not deprive consumers of mandatory legal protections.[130] Participation in ADR must not preclude parties from seeking judicial remedies due to expired legal time limits.[131]

Member states must promote awareness of ADR mechanisms and facilitate cooperation between ADR entities to ensure consistent quality and accessibility.[132] They must also oversee ADR entities to verify compliance with the directive's quality standards.[133] This is clearly a bid to ensure the quality of ADR procedures.

The ODR Regulation and the ADR Directive represent two contrasting approaches to consumer dispute resolution within the European Union. While both have sought to improve access to fair and efficient dispute resolution, their methods diverge significantly. The ODR Regulation sought to create an endogenous, self-contained system by establishing an EU-wide digital platform for resolving disputes arising from online transactions. In contrast, the ADR Directive took an exogenous approach, setting legal standards for ADR entities while leaving implementation and oversight to national authorities.

The ODR Regulation, adopted in 2013, was designed to provide a single-entry point through which consumers could submit complaints electronically and have them forwarded to an accredited ADR entity. However, despite its promise, it failed due to low engagement and lack of trader participation. Additionally, the platform proved rigid and costly, leading the European Commission to propose its repeal by 2025. (The platform fully closed on 20 July

2025.) By contrast, the ADR Directive was more flexible and sustainable. Rather than creating a centralised system, it required member states to oversee ADR entities and ensure they met EU-wide standards of independence, transparency, fairness and accessibility. Unlike the ODR Regulation, which applied only to online transactions, the ADR Directive covers both online and offline disputes, making it broader in scope and more adaptable.

The failure of the ODR Regulation underscores the risks of an overly centralised, digital-first model without strong enforcement. The success of the ADR Directive, on the other hand, highlights the advantages of leveraging national legal systems while maintaining common EU-wide standards.

4. The Platform-to-Business Regulation

The Platform-to-Business (P2B) Regulation[134] lays down rules to ensure that business users of online intermediation services and corporate website users of online search engines enjoy appropriate transparency, fairness and effective redress. It is the last element (redress) that is of interest when it comes to this book.

Under the regulation, providers of online intermediation services (other than relatively small providers) must establish an internal system for handling the complaints of business users. (Each EU member state must ensure adequate and effective enforcement of the regulation in its territory.) The internal complaint-handling system must satisfy the criteria shown in Figure 21. As well as the necessary features shown in that figure, an internal complaint-handling system must allow business users to lodge complaints directly with a provider regarding alleged non-compliance with the regulation, technological issues which relate directly to the provision of online intermediation services (and which affect the complainant), and measures taken by (or behaviour of) that provider which relate directly to the provision of the online intermediation services and (again) which affect the complainant.

In terms of the detailed operation of the internal complaint-handling system, providers must undertake certain tasks, as follows.[135] First, duly consider complaints lodged. Second, duly consider the follow-up which may be needed to adequately address the issue. Third, process complaints swiftly and effectively. Fourth, communicate to the complainant the outcome in an individualised manner and in plain and intelligible language. Fifth, give (in the terms and conditions) all relevant information relating to the access to and functioning of their internal complaint-handling system. Sixth, establish and make easily available to the public information on the functioning and effectiveness of their internal complaint-handling system. Seventh, verify that information at least annually and, where significant changes are needed, update that information. (The information must include the total number of complaints lodged, the main types of complaints, the average time period needed to process the

Figure 21: Necessary features of internal complaint-handling system

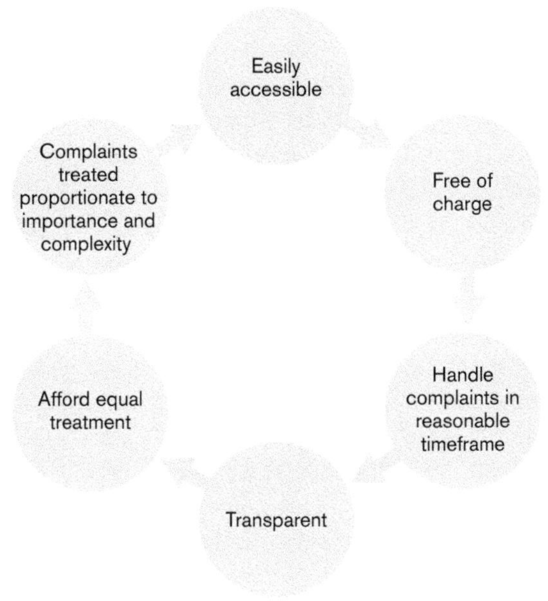

complaints and aggregated information regarding the outcome of the complaints.)

Providers of online intermediation services must also identify in their terms and conditions two or more mediators with whom they are willing to engage to attempt to reach an out-of-court settlement agreement.[136] In something of an impingement on the voluntariness of mediation, the regulation requires that, notwithstanding the voluntary nature of mediation, providers and users must engage in good faith throughout any such mediation.[137] Mediation also comes at something of a cost to providers: they must bear a reasonable proportion of the total costs of mediation in each case.[138]

The P2B Regulation establishes rules to ensure fairness, transparency and redress mechanisms for business users of online intermediation services (eg, marketplaces, app stores and social media platforms) and corporate website users of online search engines. In the context of ODR, the key element of interest is redress – particularly how platforms must provide internal complaint-handling systems and engage in mediation.

As mentioned, the regulation mandates providers of online intermediation services (except small providers) to set up an internal system for handling complaints. This aligns with ODR's focus on procedural justice, ensuring that businesses have structured, transparent and accessible mechanisms to resolve disputes efficiently.

Key features required of the internal complaints-handling system include allowing business users to lodge certain complaints; ensuring that complaints are duly considered, processed and communicated; and maintaining transparent reporting. These obligations reinforce the broader principles of ODR – such as accessibility, efficiency and fairness – by embedding structured dispute resolution mechanisms within digital platforms.

A notable element of the P2B Regulation is the requirement for platforms to identify at least two mediators in their terms and conditions with whom providers are willing to engage. The regulation compels both providers and users to participate in mediation, even though mediation is typically voluntary. Additionally, platforms must cover a reasonable proportion of the costs, regardless of the mediation outcome. This approach resonates with ODR's emphasis on balancing automation with human oversight by ensuring that disputes unresolved through internal mechanisms have a structured pathway to out-of-court resolution. However, it also raises concerns about the burden placed on platforms.

ODR is not merely digitised ADR but a broader reimagination of dispute resolution, leveraging technology to enhance efficiency and accessibility. The P2B Regulation, by embedding structured redress systems within platforms, represents a step towards integrating ODR into the online marketplace. The requirement for internal complaint mechanisms and mediation aligns with the general thrust of ODR as regards procedural fairness and user accessibility.

5. The European Bank for Reconstruction and Development

Before moving on from the European experience, it is worth briefly mentioning some recent work done by the EBRD. Founded in 1991, the EBRD is an international financial institution that was established to foster the transition of states towards open market-oriented economies, largely by providing project financing in countries which are committed to and apply democratic principles. EBRD membership comprises 66 governments, the European Union and the European Investment Bank.

In 2023, the EBRD published a document entitled *Are You Ready for Online Courts?* The document outlines the preparedness of 17 countries in the EBRD's regions of activity for ODR.[139] The document is of interest for a number of reasons. It shows how the wider world is faring as regards the rollout of ODR. It shows the types of factors that a reputable international body considers to be of relevance when it comes to the rollout of court-annexed ODR. And it shows what issues the EBRD considers ought to be addressed so that successful rollout can be achieved.

The report notes that to some extent, ODR is a concept whose time has already come, pointing in this regard to ICAAN's UDRP, private successes such as the eBay and PayPal dispute resolution processes, the EU ODR platform,

UNCITRAL's Technical Rules and national developments such as British Columbia's CRT and the UK MCOL scheme.

Proceeding on the basis that online courts should be a part of national justice systems, the EBRD seeks in its report to identify the preconditions and laws required for the construction of an effective e-justice system. Because of the type of banking business in which the EBRD is engaged, it pays special attention to e-justice in the business context. The principal building blocks of online courts, as identified by the EBRD, are shown in Figure 22.

Figure 22: Four key building blocks of ODR

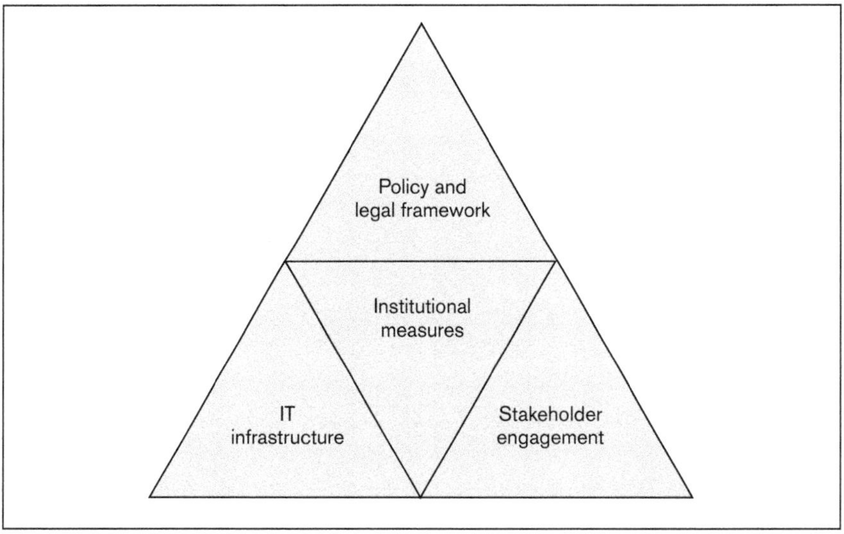

When it comes to digital improvements to the justice system, the EBRD considers that states should set clear, measurable, verifiable objectives; treat technology as a means to an end rather than an end in itself; and ensure that the legal framework is conducive to the doing of e-justice.

Positing that certain areas of the law are more fitted to ODR than others, the EBRD suggests that such areas include business-to-business (B2B) disputes, certain forms of ADR, the enforcement of uncontested claims and small claims disputes. The real-life experience of the various jurisdictions considered so far in this book shows that the usefulness of ODR extends beyond the limited categories of dispute identified by the EBRD.

The EBRD considers that public investment in modernised, reliable IT infrastructure is essential for e-justice reforms. Additionally, the EBRD considers it important to the development of a robust e-justice system for states to prioritise stakeholder engagement (involving all interested parties in the development and improvement of e-justice systems), capacity building (ensuring that stakeholders are empowered to use e-justice effectively), accessible court procedures (so as to better ensure openness and inclusivity for all) and transparency (in order to promote public confidence and trust in the justice system).

Though the EBRD considers online courts to be in their nascency, it also considers that online justice offers the promise of bridging a justice gap that affects many worldwide. That said, the EBRD does not favour an internationalist model of ODR but a bespoke version tailored to each jurisdiction's individual needs and levels of development.

It is perhaps the appendix to the EBRD guide that is most useful for any state minded to construct an ODR scheme. It identifies the building blocks necessary for the establishment of such a scheme and then identifies essential measures, significant measures and useful measures that will assist in constructing the relevant building block. (An 'essential measure' is a core and indispensable step on the path towards a successful online court; a 'significant measure' is an important such step; and a 'useful measure' is a 'nice to have' but non-essential step.) In terms of the requisite building blocks in the construction of an ODR scheme, the EBRD suggests the following:

- E-governance and e-justice policies should include comprehensive strategies and operational roadmaps with targets and key performance indicators. (That said, an overly rigorous focus on pre-defined strategies and key performance indicators may conceivably stifle adaptability in a digital landscape that is constantly evolving.)
- An ODR system should include recognition of e-signatures and e-documents. (Without harmonisation, the establishment of cross-border ODR may be hindered by legal incompatibilities in such recognition rules among different jurisdictions.)
- States should legalise the e-filing of e-documents, prescribe security/technical requirements and require compliance with data protection laws. (While e-filing is beneficial, excessive security and compliance requirements could create barriers for smaller firms and the self-represented.)
- Provisions should be adopted concerning, for example, what documents may be e-served and how, proof of delivery and the protection of personal data. (That said, digital service of documents raises concerns about reliability and fairness, as email and online notifications can be ignored or perhaps lost.)
- States should identify what proceedings may be the subject of online hearings, how documents are to be accessed and the applicable rules and procedures. (That said, while online hearings will likely improve efficiency, they may disadvantage disputants without good internet access or those unfamiliar with the digital environment.)
- Provision should be made, for example, for the creation, documentation

and registration of such documents, their legal status and issues such as enforceability and transferability. (That said, reliance on electronic documents raises cybersecurity concerns that may be costly to address.)

- States should establish expert commercial courts. (This could arguably risk creating a two-tier system of justice. It is arguable that standardised technology upgrades across all courts are to be preferred.)
- States should include provision for court-annexed mediation and how mediators are to be accredited/registered. (That said, mandatory ADR is best avoided as it may not align with the best interests of disputants.)
- Provision should be made for simplified e-filing, lower fees than for contested claims and short timelines for pronouncement. (That said, such fast tracking may arguably lead to 'rubber-stamping' without adequate judicial scrutiny.
- Provision should be made, for example, for various infrastructure upgrades. (That said, such upgrades take time. In the meantime, those in areas with poor access to the Internet would be subject to some level of exclusion from any revamped ODR process.)
- Provision should be made for e-filing and document management, access and security controls, accessible design, adaptability, scalability, cross-system integration, change management and ongoing user support and training. (Of course, a highly integrated system may reduce flexibility in the face of technological change.)
- States should favour user-focused design. (It might, however, be posited that while a user-friendly digital interface seems beneficial, reliance on online portals may risk alienating those with low digital literacy.)
- Provision should be made for participatory/iterative design, stakeholder feedback, comprehensive and useful information portals, and user guides and support. (That said, unduly extensive stakeholder consultations may needlessly impede timely implementation of an ODR scheme.)
- States should provide for obligatory or incentivised digital activities, full user guidance and deadlines for a transition to use of e-tools. (That said, requiring use of e-tools may disadvantage older or less technologically adept users.)
- States should include assessment of training needs, identification of knowledge gaps, tailored and blended training, and mandatory training in required topics. (This requires sustained and potentially costly investment, for which states need to be prepared.)
- States should include the possibility for self-representation, simplified court procedures, standardised filings, accessible forms and affordable, reasonable and transparently identified fees. (It is possible that ensuring due process while also facilitating accessibility may be a difficult balance to attain.)

- A commitment to transparency should include, for example, comprehensive publication of decisions/judgments, (paradoxically) anonymised versions of court judgments, an online registry of arbitrators/mediators and a user-friendly online court system portal. (While publishing judgments should promote accountability, needless anonymisation may reduce their value as legal precedents and as builders of confidence in the fairness of an ODR scheme.)

In terms of commercial dispute resolution, the EBRD suggests that understanding the workings of commercial dispute resolution is vital to designing online courts. (This is because the EBRD considers that ODR ought not merely to reflect existing processes in electronic form but should seek to improve and transform such processes.)

Key learnings

- *Define clear objectives but maintain flexibility.* ODR initiatives should set clear, measurable and verifiable objectives to ensure progress and accountability. Some caution is likely required in this regard: overly rigid targets and performance indicators may stifle adaptability to evolving technology.
- *Recognise ODR's broader applicability.* While ODR is particularly suited to B2B disputes, small claims and ADR, its potential extends beyond these categories. However, expanding ODR too broadly without a phased rollout may lead to inefficiencies, especially in complex disputes requiring human judgement.
- *Prioritise strong IT infrastructure investment.* Modern, reliable IT infrastructure is a fundamental requirement for an effective ODR system. Of course, infrastructure upgrades require significant investment and time, potentially leaving certain jurisdictions at a disadvantage.
- *Ensure that legal frameworks facilitate ODR, not hinder it.* ODR-related laws and regulations should be comprehensive, clear and aligned with existing legal principles. That said, overly complex or restrictive legal requirements may impede ODR rollout.
- *Promote stakeholder engagement without delaying implementation.* Engaging all relevant stakeholders better ensures that ODR systems will meet user needs and should also build trust in digital justice. However, excessively in-depth consultation may delay necessary reforms.
- *Balance transparency with privacy concerns.* Transparency in ODR should foster trust and consistency in an ODR system. While such openness is essential, there is also a possibility that excessive transparency could lead to data privacy concerns.

- *Develop a scalable and adaptive case management system.* Integrated case management systems should be designed for scalability. Conversely, unduly rigid or centralised systems may struggle to adapt to technological advances.
- *Balance efficiency with procedural safeguards.* Simplified procedures should reduce costs and improve access to justice, though oversimplification may compromise procedural fairness.
- *Mandate digital competency without creating barriers.* Lawyers, judges and court staff should be required to develop digital competency. That said, requiring digital proficiency may disadvantage older professionals or those from less technologically developed regions.
- *Ensure that technology serves justice, not the other way around.* ODR should be seen as a tool to enhance justice and should not be allowed to compromise the fundamental principles of justice.

11. ODR and China

Though the digital divide is real, it is shrinking. The proliferation of smartphones over the last few years has narrowed the divide significantly. Internet access is primarily an issue if websites can only be used from desktop or laptop computers ... Individuals who do not have Internet access at home may have access through a family member or at a public library or local Wi-Fi hotspot ... "It may be that in the future public libraries, providing access to public computers, will become more central to dispute resolution than courts."

Joint Technology Committee[140]

A pre-condition to ODR integration is robust technology infrastructure across the country. This includes access to computers, smart phones and medium to high bandwidth internet connection for at least the length of time it takes to conduct meaningful hearings. The lack of such requirements is likely to disadvantage those that have limited access to digital infrastructure.

NITI Aayog[141]

Improving ODR: 10 key lessons

- Government leadership and investment assist in ODR rollout.
- Develop a comprehensive digital infrastructure.
- Create a unified ODR ecosystem.
- Leverage AI and automation for efficiency.
- Aim for full digital case progression.
- Establish clear regulatory frameworks.
- Address due process and ID verification issues.
- Ensure procedural fairness and accessibility.
- Encourage international compatibility and interoperability.
- Continuously refine and evolve the system.

1. China leads the way

ODR developments in liberal democracies such as the United States and the United Kingdom will naturally be of the greatest interest to judges and lawyers in sister democracies, given that many of the same legal issues are likely to present in all democracies when it comes to rolling out a full-service ODR platform. Even so, it is impossible to write a book on ODR without mentioning developments in China, a pioneer in ODR.[142]

China launched its 'Smart Justice' campaign in 2016. In the same year, the construction of smart courts became part of China's national development strategy. By 2019, a rudimentary smart court system was in place; but, as for western countries, it was really the COVID-19 pandemic which created a sudden need for ODR. A lockdown was imposed on Wuhan (other places followed) in February 2020. In September 2020, the Supreme People's Court issued a notice requiring all courts in China to deploy ODR, online mediation and ADR.

2. China's ambitions for its court system

Meanwhile, at a seminar in March 2020, the then-president of the Supreme People's Court gave an address revealing the sheer breadth of China's ambitions for its court system.[143] He spoke of various matters, including the following. First, constructing a one-stop diversified dispute resolution mechanism system. (A diversified dispute resolution mechanism offers various types of ADR and ultimately litigation.) Second, improving the work being done regarding online appeals. Third, making full use of integrated mediation platforms to improve dispute settlement efficiency and promote one-stop dispute settlement. Fourth, integrating services such as litigation guiding (essentially, hand-holding users through the process so as to optimise their online experience) and self-service triage. Fifth, ensuring the synchronous generation of electronic judgments (ie, issuance of judgments at case-end). Sixth, promoting remote trials to overcome inconvenience caused by location. Seventh, encouraging courts to improve big data analysis.* Eighth, having online case filing, mediation and judgment delivery. And ninth, ensuring that all courts made full use of the mediation platform.

In 2023, Justice Yinqiang, another senior member of the Chinese judiciary, delivered a speech about ODR in China that gives a good idea of the progress made over the intervening three-year period.[144] He noted that the Chinese courts had actively and innovatively promoted ODR. As a result, the entirety of

* The European Ethical Charter on the Use of Artificial Intelligence in Judicial Systems and Their Environment (2018), which is considered at some length in Chapter 16, contains a glossary which defines 'big data' as referring to "large sets of data from mixed sources (eg, open data, proprietary data and commercially purchased data.) For data derived from judicial activity, big data could be the combination of statistical data, records of business software connections (application logs), court decisions' databases, etc".

the case procedure, from filing a case to enforcement, could be conducted online. To achieve this goal, China refined the rules regarding ODR; improved its ODR system; created an ODR system that integrated litigation, arbitration and mediation; and optimised its online dispute resolution mechanisms so that they worked well. As regards the future of ODR in China, Yinqiang suggested, among other things, that the future would involve promoting digitalised justice; further strengthening the integration of technology; coordinating development and security; deepening digital judicial innovation; enhancing the application of technology in the judicial system; improving information access inclusiveness, "so that all types of parties to a case can enjoy inclusive, equal and non-discriminatory digital judicial services"; and bringing online dispute resolution to the next level.

What is particularly interesting about this speech is that it might almost have been delivered by a judge from any of the other jurisdictions considered in this book in terms of the issues to which it refers.

3. China's practical implementation of its ODR innovations

The implementation of court and connected ODR in China has benefited from major investment by the Chinese government. Notably, strong leadership has also been shown by the courts in the rollout of ODR. (It will be recalled that strong judicial leadership has been credited for the success of the Utah ODR system.) The effect of all of this is that the Chinese judiciary has been "radically transformed"[145] by online processes. As one learned commentator has observed, in terms of the level of AI usage in the court process, China may be unparalleled – not to mention its use of blockchain as a security tool, voice recognition software to create court records and technology that can provide an informed first draft of proposed judgments.[146]

That said, in China – as in other countries – internet courts are not perfect.[147] Among the impacting factors are IT quality, the education level of users, the degree of IT understanding among legal professionals and the IT abilities of judges and court personnel.[148] For persons without internet access, the potential for exclusion is a concern.[149] Those with internet access and savvy must determine how best to navigate the system, as with the advent of widespread ODR in China, the etiquette of and strategies for litigation are all changing.[150]

A notable Chinese innovation was the establishment in 2017 of the Hangzhou Internet Court – a court with jurisdiction solely over internet-related disputes. Notable features of that court include the ability to do all steps from application filing through to enforcement via the Internet; the automatic generation of documents and records; the fact that video recordings of hearings constitute the trial record; the use of AI technology to draft judgments; and the absence of any need for court clerks during hearings.

More internet courts (in Beijing and Guangzhou) were launched in 2018.

One commentator has described how, in internet courtrooms around China, disputants enter modern buildings with large video walls, encounter voice-enabled technology and attend to paperwork assisted by automated prompts. Judges sit in cutting-edge courtrooms where they conduct video conferences and parties appear online through the medium of video technology. The Beijing Court even has an AI 'judge' with a human image and voice and facial expressions. The role of this 'judge' is to assist human judges by completing repetitive basic work, thus freeing them to focus on the challenges of trial work. The court, it appears, has "high hopes"[151] for the AI judge (which is programmed to participate in question-and-answer sessions and meaningful communications with users).[152] All that said, there seems to be little publicly available information about whether the Beijing Court is achieving its stated goals as regards judicial efficiency and transparency.[153] There is, however, suggestion that its operations have been marred by some degree of bureaucratic slowness;[154] and also that lawyers sometimes find that cases involving politically well-connected parties are often missing from online case databases.* Moreover, the depth of China's overall commitment to transparency seems, with respect, to fluctuate. Thus, following the establishment by the Supreme People's Court in 2014 of the China Judgments Online website, a mind-blowing 141 million judgments were placed online,[155] tens of thousands of cases were added daily and the site was visited by tens of millions people each day.[156] However, from 2021 onwards, the pace of uploads seemed to slow[157] – possibly due to a general retreat by the Chinese state more generally from the perception of transparency as a virtue.[158]

4. China's online operation and litigation rules

The Online Operation Rules of the People's Courts (2021) lay the foundation for a fully digitalised judicial system in China. These rules formalise the use of advanced technologies such as artificial intelligence, blockchain, big data and cloud computing to enhance litigation, mediation, trial management and enforcement. The goal is to make legal processes more efficient, accessible and transparent by allowing parties to engage in court proceedings remotely while ensuring strict security and procedural integrity. The rules identify five guiding principles. First, making processes convenient and efficient – that is, providing diversified dispute resolution and litigation services on one website, at one place and with one account to relieve the burden of litigation on disputants. Second, focusing on effectiveness – that is, comprehensively

* See Tahura and Selvadurai, 16. There does seem, however, to be a desire to do right in this regard. Thus, in January 2025, the Supreme People's Court announced that a new case search platform (available at http://dyjfalk.court.gov.cn) now allows users to access cases and learn about resolutions through mediation or arbitration. One year previously, the Supreme People's Court had launched an online case archive aimed, among other matters, at promoting standardised verdicts and enhanced judicial transparency (Anon (6)).

supporting online trial and enforcement activities of the people's courts to ensure the progress of judicial work and improve judicial efficiency. Third, strengthening overall coordination and planning – that is, giving priority to building and using a unified information system for courts nationwide, and continuing to promote compatibility and sharing of information infrastructure, application systems and data resources. Fourth, keeping abreast of the times – that is, keeping business processes, litigation rules and trial models up to date. Fifth, protecting security and reliability – that is, collecting, storing, processing and using data in accordance with the law; protecting state secrets, trade secrets, personal privacy and personal information; and ensuring information security.

At the core of this transformation are smart court information systems, comprising a comprehensive digital infrastructure designed to support all aspects of judicial work. (Of note is the fact that under the rules, the people's courts at all levels must cooperate with enterprises and universities in accordance with the law to promote the construction, operation and maintenance of the smart court information system.) Smart services facilitate online case filing, mediation and legal consultations, allowing disputants to initiate proceedings and interact with the courts remotely. The smart trial system facilitates virtual court hearings, AI-assisted adjudication and standardised sentencing. The smart enforcement system streamlines case tracking, enforcement measures and asset recovery. Judicial personnel also benefit from a smart management system which provides digital tools for trial supervision, personnel management and administrative tasks. These systems work in concert to create an interconnected digital judiciary, enhancing both the speed and the quality of legal proceedings.

Beijing Internet Court

In 2019, the Beijing Internet Court produced a White Paper on the Application of Internet Technology in Judicial Practice. The White Paper identifies a number of innovations undertaken by the court to that time, including the establishment of:

- an Internet Technology Judicial Application Centre to carry out studies on the basic theory of the smart court, platform construction, core technology, innovation and development;
- processes to address problems such as poor communication, information transmission distortion and disappointing user experiences;
- an 'intelligent case push function' which seeks to provide judges with guidance on standard process and identify the key elements of cases;
- a system that can generate five types of judgment with one click;
- an 'Online Litigation Experience Area' to give the public a sense of the deep integration of technology into the judicial process;

- an 'Online Smart Litigation Service Centre', featuring one-click submission and one-stop service;
- a 'Mobile Micro Court', through which (by way of app) parties can file online, submit case queries and avail of online mediation, online litigation and various other functions;
- a cybersecurity system that includes the use of blockchain so as to better ensure the safety of information and data; and
- an 'AI virtual judge' (a chatbot-like function) that can simultaneously provide voice and text answers.

China's Online Litigation Rules (2021) are also of interest. Among other things, they provide that online litigation has the same legal effect as offline litigation. They also contemplate a wide array of proceedings as suitable for ODR, including civil and administrative cases; certain criminal cases; certain civil proceedings, such as debt recovery and bankruptcy proceedings; civil, administrative and certain enforcement cases; and other cases appropriate to be tried online. The rules identify five guiding principles for the conduct of online litigation. First, the principle of impartiality and efficiency – that is, courts must conduct online litigation in accordance with the relevant laws, streamline trial process, improve working mechanisms and provide technical support to enhance judicial efficiency and ensure judicial fairness. Second, the principle of legality and voluntariness, whereby the right of the parties and other participants in an action to choose the method of litigation must be respected and protected. Third, the principle of protecting parties' rights – that is, courts must fully protect the procedural rights of parties. Fourth, the principle of providing convenience to the people – that is, courts must optimise online litigation services, while also taking into account the needs of different groups in litigation, providing more guidance and convenience to vulnerable groups such as minors, the elderly and people with disabilities. Fifth, the principle of security and reliability, whereby the courts must, in accordance with relevant laws, safeguard national security; protect state secrets, trade secrets, personal privacy and personal information; and ensure the security of online litigation data. The people's courts must also regulate the application of technology so as to ensure technology neutrality and platform neutrality.

The rules then proceed to make detailed provision regarding the operation of online trial processes. For example, there is extensive provision on blockchain evidence; a requirement that those who appear in online courts respect judicial etiquette and comply with court rules; provision that online proceedings should be as open to the public as their offline counterparts; and provision for the synchronous generation of transcripts during proceedings.

5. Some practical challenges

As one would instinctively expect in any jurisdiction, the rollout of ODR in China has encountered some practical challenges. For example, it is difficult to define the kinds of cases that are especially suitable for ODR when (as is the case in China) all case types are ostensibly open to the application of ODR mechanisms. Second, issues of due process present – for example, even as regards a matter as simple as how to identify the parties. Conspiracy to violate the rights of third parties has also been pointed to as a real risk in China as ODR continues to expand there.[159]

Third, when it comes to using ODR between businesses and consumers in the United States and their counterparts in China, some concerns have been expressed. Among them are cultural differences and the related need to tailor a dispute resolution method to minimise cultural differences. There is also the political culture in China as pertains to the Internet – what, for example, if (after due consideration) a person wishes to 'click and settle' on a website only to find on returning to that site that it has been blocked by the authorities?

6. China v United States

Comparing the ODR systems of the United States and China provides good insight into how different governance structures can shape legal technology. The United States has approached ODR with an emphasis on user autonomy, procedural fairness and decentralised implementation. China has built a state-controlled, technology-driven judicial ecosystem, using AI, big data and automation to enhance efficiency – though also extending state oversight.

Among the world's democracies, the United States has been a global leader in ODR adoption, integrating it into court systems, commercial platforms and consumer protection frameworks. The primary motivations for expanding ODR have been to improve access to justice, reduce court congestion and streamline dispute resolution. Key features of the approach adopted in the United States include the following. First, a general focus on high-volume, low-complexity cases. (ODR has been adopted for small claims, traffic violations, consumer disputes, tax assessment appeals and low-conflict family court cases.) Second, hybrid and voluntary participation models. (ODR in the United States is typically voluntary, allowing users to opt in. That said, some states – such as Utah – have tried mandatory ODR. In fact, this may account in part for the success of court and court-connected ODR in Utah.) Third, public and private sector collaboration. (The United States has seen significant private sector involvement in ODR development. Platforms such as eBay and PayPal pioneered online mediation, while court-connected ODR systems often partner with legal technology providers. And the National Center for Technology and Dispute Resolution has played a key role in standard-setting and ethical guidance for ODR implementation.) Fourth, emphasis on procedural fairness and user engagement. (ODR in the United States is typically designed to enhance disputant engagement, reduce default rates and improve perceptions of justice.) Challenges, of course, remain. For example, the decentralised nature of ODR in the United States has led to inconsistencies in design and implementation across different jurisdictions. Moreover, data security and privacy concerns remain a significant issue in a world where debates are ongoing about AI fairness, algorithmic bias and cybersecurity.

China has taken a different approach to ODR rollout from that of the United States, aggressively digitising its judicial system and, in the process, creating a highly centralised, AI-supported dispute resolution infrastructure. Key features of China's ODR model include the following:

- *State-mandated ODR:* Since 2020, China's Supreme People's Court has required all courts to deploy ODR, online mediation and ADR mechanisms.
- *State integration of AI and big data:* China's ODR system incorporates AI-assisted adjudication, automated legal document generation and blockchain-secured evidence. AI is used to assist in drafting judgments, reducing human involvement in early-stage dispute resolution.
- *Seamless digital case progression:* From case filing to judgment enforcement, all stages of dispute resolution can be conducted within a single online ecosystem. This streamlines legal processes but may also raise concerns over due process and judicial independence.
- *Government oversight and potential risks:* The use of big data analytics enables state monitoring of dispute resolution trends. This level of state control could conceivably undermine judicial impartiality and privacy rights, particularly in politically sensitive cases.

Fundamentally, the United States and China represent two opposing paradigms of ODR implementation. The United States approach prioritises voluntariness, user engagement, procedural fairness and privacy, making it more adaptable to liberal democratic legal structures. China's ODR model, by contrast, demonstrates the power of a unified, government-driven strategy. The integration of AI, big data and automation allows for unparalleled efficiency. Yet so centralised a system may yield concerns about judicial independence, state surveillance and due process limitations. Conversely, it may also simply represent a bid at quality control. Thus, it has been suggested that arguably the interest of the Supreme People's Court in Al and big data is driven in part by a desire to strengthen oversight and to address concerns about patronage, corruption and even incompetence.[160]

Key learnings

- *Government leadership and investment assist in ODR rollout.* A well-funded, government-backed ODR initiative such as that of China can accelerate adoption and integration across the judicial system. Government leadership ensures widespread implementation and uniformity. However, over-reliance on state-driven initiatives may reduce innovation.
- *Develop a comprehensive digital infrastructure.* A robust technological framework – including high-speed internet, secure digital platforms and AI capabilities – is essential for effective ODR implementation. China's 'smart courts' illustrate the benefits of seamless digital integration. That said, in jurisdictions with weaker digital infrastructure or rural connectivity issues, such a model may exclude those without reliable internet access.
- *Create a unified ODR ecosystem.* Integrating arbitration, mediation and litigation into a single ODR platform increases efficiency and streamlines dispute resolution, as can be seen in China's courts. Conversely, decentralised models may allow for greater user choice and adaptability in resolving disputes.
- *Leverage AI and automation for efficiency.* AI-driven tools can enhance judicial efficiency and reduce case backlog, as demonstrated by China's internet courts. Potential overuse of AI in judicial decisions raises concerns about transparency, fairness and accountability.
- *Facilitate full digital case progression.* China's system enables cases to be filed, mediated, tried and enforced entirely via online processes, reducing costs and increasing accessibility. That said, digital-only processes may exclude vulnerable populations unfamiliar with online systems.
- *Establish clear regulatory frameworks.* China's Online Litigation Rules (2021) provide clear guidelines on, for example, procedural fairness and online security, ensuring greater consistency across digital courts.
- *Address due process and identity verification issues.* Robust identity verification measures are crucial for maintaining the integrity of ODR systems – albeit that digital identity verification remains a challenge as impersonation and fraud risks persist.
- *Ensure procedural fairness and accessibility.* China's focus on accessibility should better ensure broader user engagement. However, this is a challenging area: digital literacy varies across populations and complementary education and support programmes are generally necessary to ensure greater fairness and accessibility.
- *Encourage international compatibility and interoperability.* An effective

ODR system should align with international legal standards to facilitate cross-border dispute resolution. Obviously, differences in political and legal systems create challenges in terms of harmonising international ODR mechanisms.

- *Continuously refine and evolve the system.* China's iterative improvements to its online services highlight the need for ongoing ODR refinement. Regular evaluations and stakeholder consultations should better ensure balanced, responsible innovation.

12. ODR and artificial intelligence

[W]e affirmed the following key priorities … Promoting AI accessibility to reduce the digital divide … Ensur[ing] that AI is open to all, inclusive, transparent, ethical, safe, secure and trustworthy … Enabling innovation … by creating the conditions conducive to its development and avoiding market concentration … Encourag[ing] the deployment of AI that positively impacts the future of work and labour markets and opens up prospects for sustainable growth … Making AI sustainable …

Paris AI Summit Declaration (2025)

The judge is an essential part of our legal system, it is true. But consider the lamplighter: a man … who would go around in the dusk, lighting the gas lamps in a town or city. An essential task; a needed task; before the advent of electrical circuits … Will the judge join their company? It is true that the judge is at the centre of our system. But this is more a consequence of circumstance, than of a priori logic.

Abdullah[161]

Improving ODR: 10 key lessons

- Be careful to have human oversight.
- Audit predictive models continuously.
- Carefully curate data.
- Be ethical but flexible in usage of AI.
- AI usage should be explainable.
- Optimise human oversight to better ensure fairness.
- Proactively mitigate bias.
- Conduct human rights assessments.
- Engage with stakeholders.
- Promote AI literacy.

1. Introduction

In Frank Riley's science fiction story, "The Cyber and Justice Holmes" (1955),[162] Judge Anderson is an old-fashioned American judge in a world where the state attorney has been campaigning to have judges replaced by computer machines (cybers) – a proposal to which Anderson instinctively takes objection. But Anderson's eyes are opened to the potential usefulness of cybers at a hearing in which a university professor demonstrates the limits to computer-thinking by asking a cyber a question that it cannot answer: "What are the magnitudes of a dream?" The professor suggests that in fact, what he has demonstrated is that cybers should be seen not as a threat but as an invention with limits. Anderson, as he watches on, realises that judges have nothing to fear: cybers will do humdrum court work and judges will be freed to undertake what they do best: the multi-faceted and nuanced task of human judgement.

Seventy years later, we live in a world in which AI can act as a crutch to human judges in the way that Riley presciently envisioned, undertaking humdrum tasks and freeing them to undertake the challenging task of bringing their human experience and critical thinking to bear when exercising judgement. At remarkable speed, the fiction of the past has become the reality of today. It has even been suggested that technology is now a fourth party in ODR disputes.[163] The others are the decision maker and a presumed two disputants. As a fourth party, this latest technology can administer the dispute resolution process, schedule meetings and facilitate communication.[164]

2. Use of AI in court systems

AI is a complex and growing field which has, as one of its primary objectives, the replication through technology of human cognitive and decision-making capacities so as to enhance problem solving. As mentioned previously, the European Ethical Charter on the Use of AI in Judicial Systems and Their Environment (2018) offers a useful definition of 'AI', defining it as "[a] set of scientific methods, theories and techniques whose aim is to reproduce, by a machine, the cognitive abilities of human beings. Current developments seek to have machines perform complex tasks previously carried out by humans".*

There is already extensive use of AI systems in many jurisdictions around the world.[165] Recently published guidance to UK judicial office holders identifies certain potential risks in the uses of generative AI by UK courts and tribunals.[166] Thus, the guidance draws a distinction between potentially useful

* Malik (at 3310–3311) expands on the concept of AI in the following helpful terms. First, it is the emulation of human intelligence in machines. Second, it involves creating algorithms and computational models that enable computers to perform tasks that need human-like intelligence. Third, it involves various technologies, such as ML and natural language processing. Fourth, it can assist with repetitive and mundane tasks, freeing human actors to undertake more complex and creative work. Fifth, it can analyse large datasets with high accuracy. Sixth, it can improve overall efficiencies in business and, it is submitted, in dispute resolution.

tasks, tasks that are not recommended and indications that work may have been produced by AI. Among the potentially useful tasks are summarising large bodies of text, drafting presentations and completing administrative tasks such as composing emails and memoranda. Tasks not recommended to be done by AI include legal research and analysis. Indications that work may have been produced by AI include references to cases that do not sound familiar or have unfamiliar citations; parties citing different bodies of case law in relation to the same legal issues; submissions that do not accord with a judge's general understanding of the law in the area; submissions that use US spelling or refer to non-UK cases; and content that (superficially at least) appears to be highly persuasive and well written, but on closer inspection contains obvious substantive errors.

Whatever about the potential drawbacks of AI, all commentators seem broadly in agreement that the objective of every right-thinking judicial system is to serve justice and enhance the welfare of all. The US Federal Judicial Center has recently identified nine AI takeaways for judges. These comprise a series of pointers concerning AI which the centre considers that judges ought to be aware of when it comes to the deployment of AI.[167] First, there are many different methodologies – a court should satisfy itself that a specific AI application, its design and its specific use meet the foundational requirements for the purpose for which it is to be used by a court. Second, AI/ML* learns as it proceeds, so AI systems need to be tested and validated on an ongoing basis. Third, humans are always involved: behind each AI application there are, for example, human choices, values – and bias. Fourth, AI predicts; it does not conclude. Fifth, the accuracy of AI depends on the quality and volume of data. Sixth, the 'heart' of AI is the algorithm; the accuracy of an AI application depends on the algorithm applied to that data. Seventh, narrow AI is brittle – that is, not particularly good (yet) at situational awareness. Eighth, AI is nimble – it can see cumulative anomalies, links and patterns in data that humans cannot. (Humans, of course, can spot contextual nuance that AI cannot.) Ninth, AI has biases.

In the context of ODR, by doing repetitive and predictable tasks, AI frees human judges to concentrate on more complex and nuanced issues. Additionally, AI can analyse vast amounts of data to identify patterns and trends, thereby providing valuable insights that can inform decision making

* As mentioned previously, ML, per the glossary to the European Ethical Charter on the Use of Artificial Intelligence in Judicial Systems and Their Environment (2018), "makes it possible to construct a mathematical model from data, incorporating a large number of variables that are not known in advance. The parameters are configured gradually during the learning phase, which uses training data sets to find and classify links. The different methods of machine learning are chosen by the designers depending on the nature of the tasks to be completed (grouping.) These methods are usually classified into three categories: (human) supervised learning, unsupervised learning and reinforcement learning. These three categories group together different methods including neural networks, deep learning, etc".

within dispute resolution processes. The implementation of AI in ODR entails three principal challenges (summarised in Figure 24).[168] First, maintaining privacy and data security. (ODR platforms often handle personal data, so AI-informed ODR systems must be designed to preserve privacy and confidentiality.) Second, striking the right balance between automation and human intervention. (Overreliance on AI could lead to nuances in argument being missed; however, under-reliance could mean that the full efficiencies of AI go missed.) Third, ethics. Usage of AI-informed ODR may yield concerns as to bias, fairness and the digital divide.

Figure 23: Usefulness of AI in court systems[169]

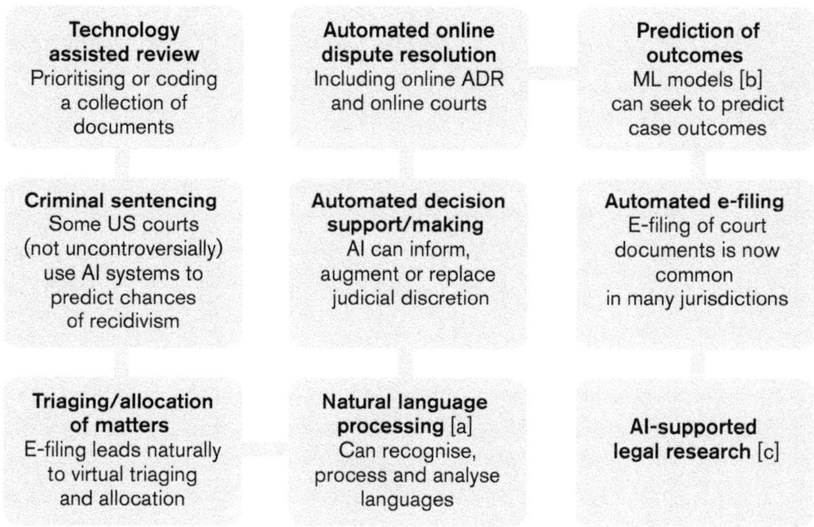

[a] Natural language processing (NLP) can analyse large amounts of text, distilling information of relevance from the often abundant folders of information provided to the busy trial judge. It can be used to identify relevant information and assist in creating coherent and precise legal documents. Also known as 'tone analysing software', NLP can discern emotions in submitted text.[170]
[b] ML uses data and algorithms to imitate the way that humans learn, gradually improving accuracy. Through the use of statistical methods algorithms are trained, for example, to make classifications or predictions. In this sense, all algorithms are predictive. ML models can identify patterns in legal data, predict case outcomes and suggest relevant legal precedents.
[c] Legal research tools automate the search for precedent, statute and case law. By quickly retrieving and systematically organising legal information, they save time and ensure that judgments are well supported by legal authority.

3. The Council of Europe's extensive input

In terms of identifying and addressing the ethical (and related) risks that present when it comes to combining AI with ODR, no institution has been more to the fore than the Council of Europe, whose measures in this regard include the following. First, the European Ethical Charter on the Use of AI in Judicial Systems and Their Environment (2018) and the Framework Convention on AI and Human Rights (2024). (These are both considered in Chapter 17.) Second, the Guidelines on Artificial Intelligence and Data Protection (2019) and a Recommendation on Human Right Impacts of Algorithmic Systems (2020). (These are considered below.) Third, a Discussion Paper on a future legal instrument addressing criminal liability related to the use of AI (2024). (This is considered in Chapter 19.)

Figure 24: Challenges when implementing AI in ODR

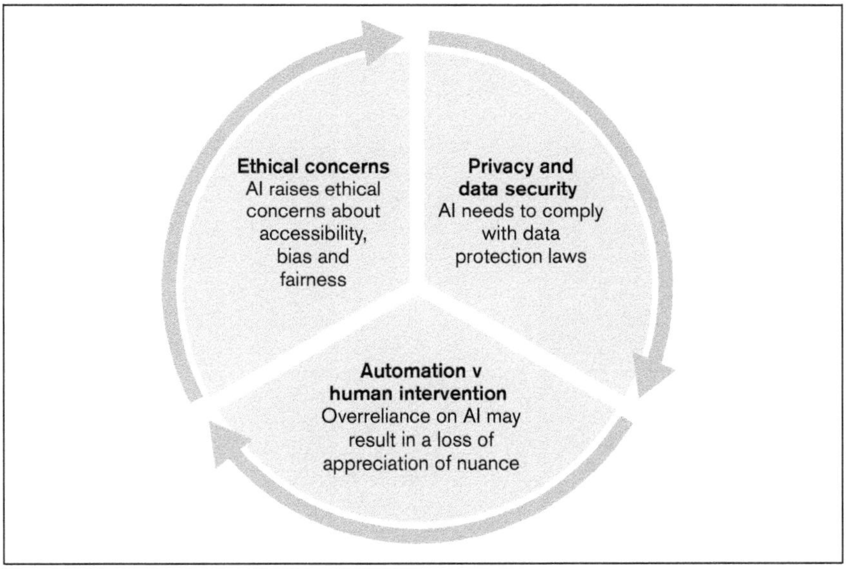

Figure 25: Designing an effective legal and regulatory framework for ODR[171]

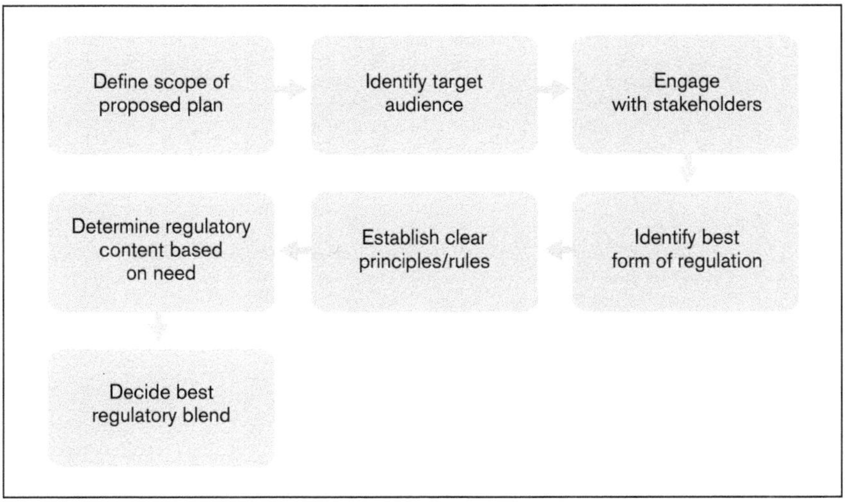

The Guidelines on Artificial Intelligence and Data Protection (2019) are divided into three parts which successively give general guidance; then guidance specific to developers, manufacturers and service providers; and finally, guidance for legislators and policymakers. The key provisions of the guidelines insofar as they relate to data protection are summarised in Figure 26.

Figure 26: Guidelines on AI and Data Protection (2019)

4. The OECD's input

The OECD in its Online Dispute Framework (2024) suggests that when it comes to the ethical and trustworthy use of data in the justice context, states might consider applying the following principles and precepts: deploying data so as to serve the public interest and give public value; managing data with integrity; ensuring that data is fit for purpose; incorporating data ethics into governance structures; striking a balance between social costs and the benefits of data collection and use; being clear and frank about the use of data; giving data subjects control over personal data; and maintaining accountability and proactiveness in risk management.

The OECD notes that there have been discussions as to whether AI involves such a radical transformation in the provision of justice services. Its sense is that existing values continue to be valid but require to be implemented in a manner that is complementary to the new context in which they now fall to be applied. That said, it suggests that as use of AI in justice systems becomes more prevalent, policymakers and leaders should commit to a set of core values in line with the OECD Recommendation on Artificial Intelligence (2019). This arguably seems less likely to occur following on from the anti-regulatory stance adopted by the United States at the AI Action Summit in Paris on 11 February 2025. That summit saw dozens of countries sign up to a declaration on the responsible use of AI, but not the United States (or the United Kingdom), with US Vice President JD Vance expressing open concern that, among other matters, "excessive regulation of the AI sector could kill a transformative industry".*

It is difficult to understand this last criticism when one has regard to the six "main priorities" identified in the declaration by its 64 signatories. First, prompting AI accessibility to reduce digital divides. Second, ensuring that AI is open, inclusive, transparent, ethical, safe, secure and trustworthy. Third, making innovation in AI thrive by enabling conditions for its development and avoiding market concentration (ie, competition law issues). Fourth, encouraging AI deployment that positively shapes the future of work and labour markets and delivers opportunity for sustainable growth. Fifth, making AI sustainable for people and the planet. And sixth, reinforcing international cooperation to promote coordination in international governance.

---

* Various reasons were suggested for the United Kingdom's stance, including that the wording on security in the declaration was (allegedly) not strong enough; the declaration did not represent the United Kingdom's general approach as a country; a United Kingdom outside the European Union had "little strategic room but to be downstream of the US"; and (indicative of the United Kingdom's challenges as a non-EU member state) US firms might simply decline to engage with British regulators if the United Kingdom were perceived to be taking too strict a regulatory approach (see Krupa).

5. Recommendation on the Human Rights Impacts of Algorithmic Systems (2020)

A key requirement of this recommendation is that member states of the Council of Europe should review their legislative frameworks and policies as well as their own practices with respect to the procurement, design, development and ongoing deployment of algorithmic systems to ensure that they are in line with the guidelines set out in the appendix to the recommendation. For the purposes of the recommendation, 'algorithmic systems' are understood as applications that – often using mathematical optimisation techniques – perform one or more tasks such as gathering, combining, cleaning, sorting, classifying and inferring data, as well as selecting, prioritising, making recommendations and making decisions.

The guidelines appended to the recommendation are very detailed. They identify an array of steps. As far as states are concerned, they establish principles of general application and principles concerning data management; analyses and modelling; transparency, accountability and remedies; the undertaking of precautionary measures; and research, innovation and public awareness. As far as private sector actors are concerned, a different array of principles are identified under the same headings. The key provisions of the guidelines are summarised in Figures 27 and 28.

6. AI, judgment writing and related research

AI can be used to streamline the judgment-writing process by automating routine tasks, providing some data analysis and ensuring text-wide consistency and accuracy. Justice Abdullah of the Supreme Court of Singapore has observed as follows when it comes to AI and judgment making and writing.[172] First, some form of machine or computer assessment will likely be introduced to assist human judges in avoiding or reducing errors and bias. Second, one area in which AI may be especially useful is when it comes to argument analysis. Third, while AI may not be aware of the reasons for a particular conclusion, it can assist in marshalling arguments in favour of such conclusion.

Effective use of AI begins with proper preparation. Thus, in any one circumstance, humans must decide whether it is wise and fair to use AI, conscious that AI will generally be best at augmenting, not supplanting, human judgement.[173] Effective use involves (at the least) the following steps. First, collecting data, understanding case details and setting up the necessary AI tools. The process of data collection (and of understanding the case at hand and previous cases) involves gathering relevant documents, evidence and legal texts, including pleadings, affidavit evidence, exhibits and previous judgments. Second, identifying key facts and issues. Here AI tools can be of assistance in extracting and summarising key facts and legal issues from the case documents. This process assists in focusing the judicial mind on the most relevant facts of the case before

Figure 27: Some obligations of states regarding algorithmic systems

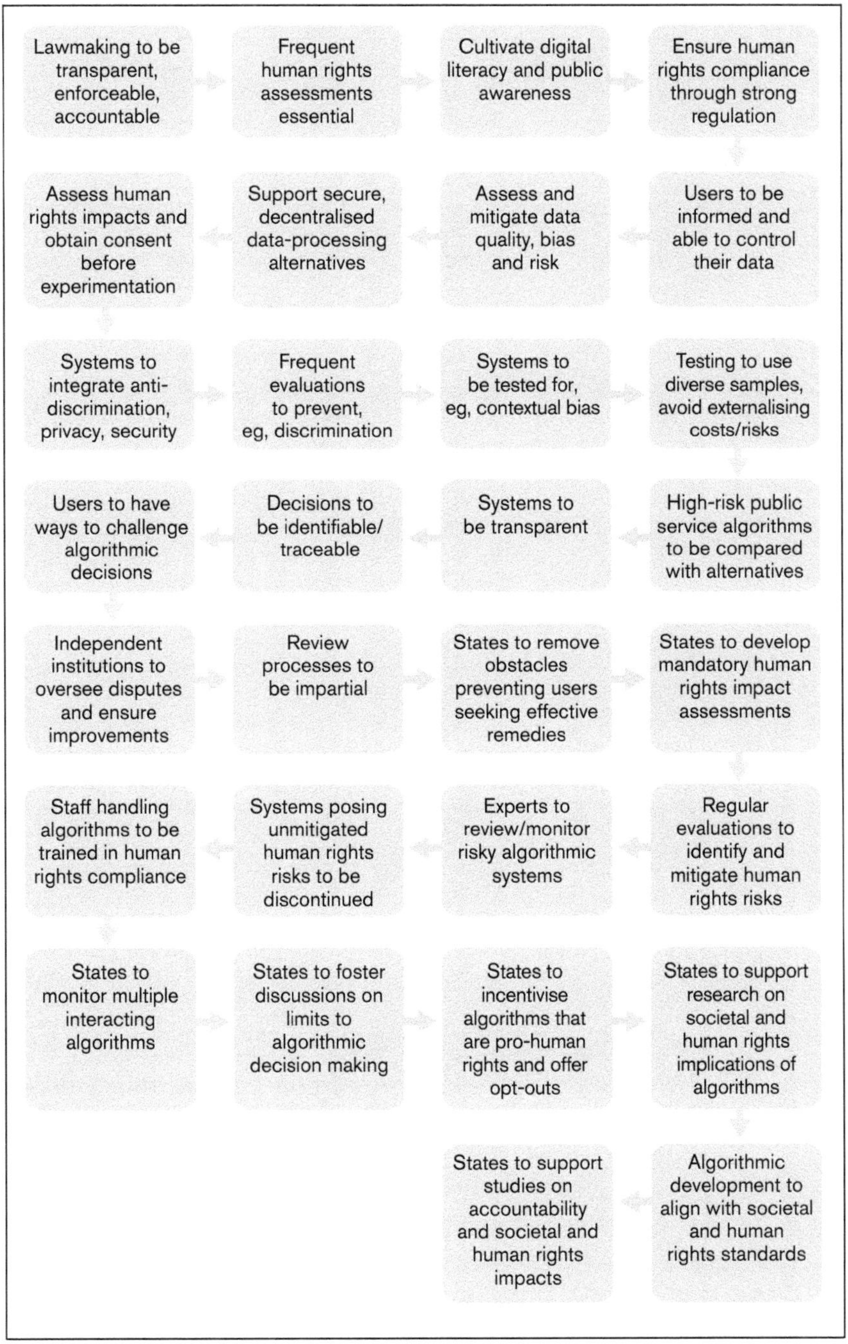

Figure 28: Some obligations of private sector actors regarding algorithmic systems

them. Third, analysing past judgments. ML tools can be used to review similar past judgments – a process which can assist in terms of better ensuring consistency and in the identification of relevant precedents.

In terms of setting up the required AI tools, the following steps can be identified: choosing the desired technology; training the AI; understanding the legal framework; and ensuring that any ensuing judgment complies with any guidelines as to form and substance. As to writing a judgment, this typically involves the steps identified in Figure 29. As is shown beneath that figure, AI (properly and cautiously used) can assist in each step, aiding in the swift production of a comprehensive, soundly reasoned and legally correct judgment.

Figure 29: Stages of the judgment-writing process

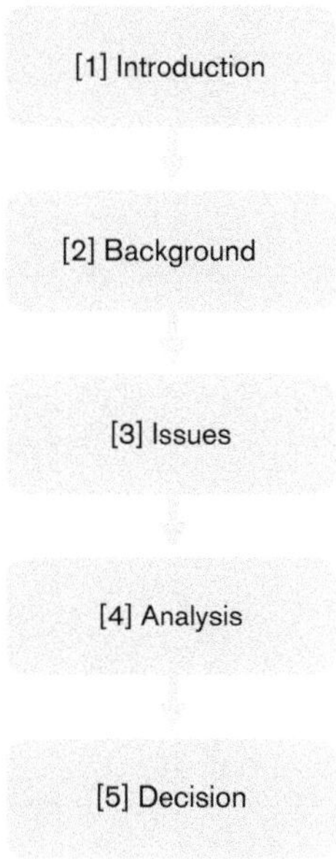

[1] **Introduction:** Sets the stage for the judgment and provides a summary of the case. At this stage, NLP tools can be used to summarise the background and offer a coherent overview. They can also be used to generate relatively standard introductory text.
[2] **Background:** Outlines relevant events and context. AI (document automation) can be used to compile facts and procedural history from the pleadings, evidence and legal information (eg, statute, case law and legal submissions) before the court.
[3] **Issues:** Identifies the questions that the court needs to answer. NLP tools can be used to identify the key legal issues and ensure that they are presented in an appropriate manner.
[4] **Analysis:** Provides legal rationale for decision. ML and legal research tools can be used to identify relevant statute law and case law.
[5] **Decision:** Concludes judgment with court's ruling. Although AI ought not to be deployed in terms of deciding the case (that is what judges are paid to do), it can assist in the drafting process (and in testing the logical soundness of a particular text) by offering arguments and counterarguments. AI can also assist the court official tasked with formulating the eventual order by identifying the proposed orders from the judgment as written.

While AI tools can enhance and improve the judgment-writing process, at this time, human oversight is necessary to ensure that any ensuing judgment meets the quality and consistency requirements expected by the public of any reputable court system. Thus, every AI-generated draft judgment should be reviewed carefully by a judge by reference to the key pleadings and any written legal submissions in order to ensure that the work product that has emerged from the just-described process is of optimal quality. Even in this regard, however, AI can be of some assistance in terms of identifying obvious inconsistencies or errors, even running a final spell-check.

As to research done with AI assistance, AI can rapidly analyse large volumes of legal documents, thus reducing the time required for legal research. By using AI, judges can minimise human error and ensure that their research is thorough and precise. AI tools can also uncover patterns and connections in legal data that might not be immediately apparent to human researchers. However, while AI offers numerous benefits for legal research, it presents with its own challenges and limitations. For starters, it relies greatly on the availability of good-quality data. Deficiencies in data sets can yield inaccurate results. Bias within AI algorithms can perpetuate biases in training data, yielding biased results. Some AI tools operate as so-called 'black boxes', yielding a lack of transparency in terms of how particular results have been arrived at. Compliance of AI tools with varying ethical guidelines in different jurisdictions may also present as an issue.

Figure 30: Some AI tools of note

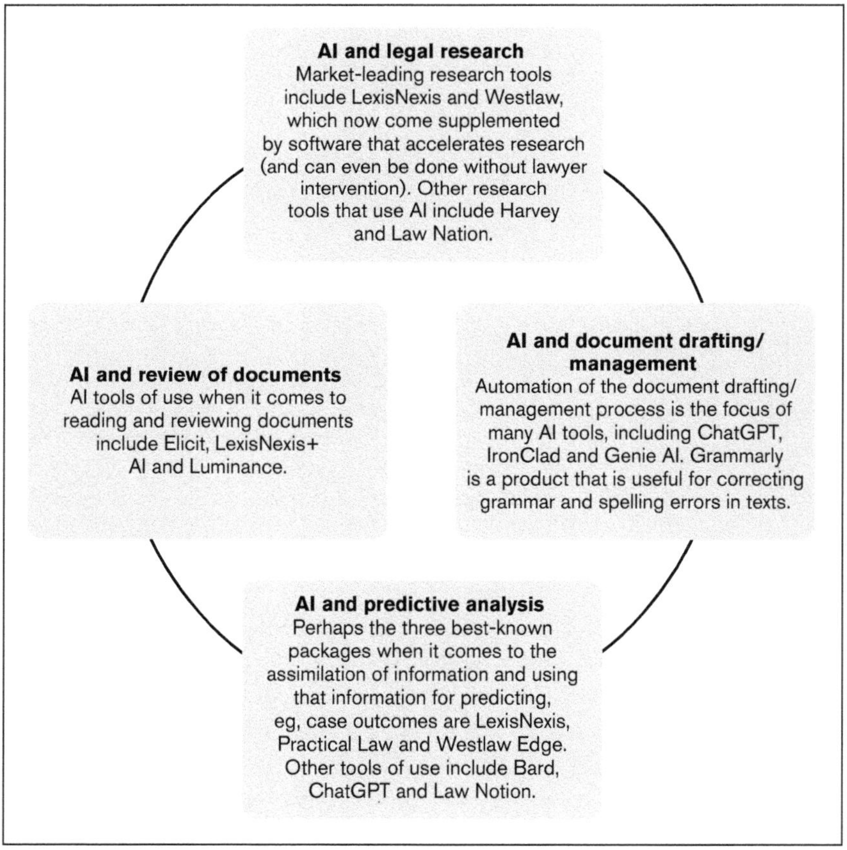

Four principal types of AI tool are useful in legal research: document analysis tools; predictive analysis tools; legal research databases; and citation tools. Document analysis tools use NLP to read and understand legal texts, extracting pertinent information. Predictive analytic tools use ML to predict legal outcomes based on historical data. Legal research databases provide access to an abundance of case law and periodical literature, with AI able, for example, to summarise what has been accessed and assist in identifying what might usefully be accessed. Citation tools generate and verify citations, ensuring that they are correct and comply with applicable citation guidelines.

To use AI effectively when undertaking legal research, judges, in tandem with their court administrators and IT advisers, need to select appropriate AI tools. This involves the tasks and steps identified below:

Task	**Step**
Assessing capabilities of AI tools	Identify specific research needs, evaluate AI tools based on their particular features and ease of use, and trial the tools in real-life scenarios before making a final decision as to what they need.
Integrating AI tools into workflow	As part of this process, a judge (or a court service) should ensure that proposed tools are compatible with existing office systems, ensure that adequate data protection measures are in place (in the European Union, these will need to be consistent with the GDPR) and undertake requisite training in the use of the AI tools.
Ensuring tools meet research needs	As part of this process, a judge (or a court service that is assisting the judiciary) should ensure that the selected AI tools are customised to focus, for example, on relevant cases and jurisdictions, and are subject to continuous improvement.

Once AI tools are set up, judges can begin using them to conduct legal research. There are perhaps three critical steps in this process. First, the formulation of research questions. (Key to the formulation of good research questions is clarity in terms of the question posed or the legal issue about which information is sought. Keywords and phrases are important in terms of producing more refined results.) Second, analysing legal texts with AI. (AI can be used to summarise long legal texts and to highlight key points in those texts. It can compare different cases and statutes, identifying patterns in them and discrepancies between them. And it can be used to identify supporting and opposing authorities.) Third, verification and validation. (Although there is an error rate even in AI results, one can reduce this error rate by having different AI tools cross-check results so as better to ensure the accuracy of the initial results. Even so, it remains imperative to have human oversight in order to ensure that the results returned are accurate and relevant.)

Key learnings

- *Have human oversight.* AI can streamline dispute resolution. However, maintaining human oversight ensures that the process caters to human nuance, though undue reliance on human oversight may unduly slow the AI-informed process.
- *Audit predictive models continuously.* Frequent auditing of AI models can help to ensure that they remain accurate and fair – though unduly frequent audits may disrupt proceedings and entail significant costs.
- *Carefully curate data.* A good ODR platform requires good and diverse datasets, though this can entail significant costs and time.
- *Be ethical but flexible in the usage of AI.* Applying ethics but retaining flexibility should facilitate an ethical approach to AI usage without unduly restricting innovation. That said, undue flexibility may compromise ethical standards.
- *AI usage should be explainable.* AI systems that explain their decision making should generate trust among users. If such an explanation is limited for confidentiality reasons or because aspects of the AI are proprietary in nature, the so-called 'explanation' may end up frustrating users.
- *Optimise human oversight to better ensure fairness.* Humans may appreciate nuances that AI does not. However, overcorrection of algorithmic bias by human intervention may engender human bias.
- *Proactively mitigate bias.* Countering bias in both algorithms and data is critical to user faith in an ODR system, though complete elimination of bias may not be achievable.
- *Conduct human rights assessments.* Check regularly whether AI usage conforms to human rights standards. Caution, however, would seem necessary: unduly frequent evaluations may be costly and disruptive.
- *Engage with stakeholders.* Engaging with stakeholders should better ensure that an ODR platform meets stakeholder needs. Of course, unduly extensive stakeholder consultation may impede swift ODR rollout.
- *Promote AI literacy.* Informed users can better utilise AI-informed ODR platforms – though financing extensive digital literacy programmes may be costly.

13. Blockchain

When the dispute in question involves fines or fees, the court may be responsible for enforcement and collection. An ODR solution can assist the adjudicator in understanding a defendant's ability to pay, set an appropriate payment schedule, provide automated payment reminders, and even be integrated with an online payment mechanism. More sophisticated ODR systems may incorporate Blockchain or similar technologies, providing automated enforcement.
Joint Technology Committee[174]

The advancement of information technology in the form of artificial intelligence ... big data, machine learning (ML) and blockchain can be increasingly embedded in legal processes ... One such example [is] ...in the realm of blockchain ... Smart contracts drafted in computer code can use technology to automate enforceability through transfer of rights and obligations.
NITI Aayog[175]

Improving ODR: 10 key lessons

- Blockchain ensures near-immutable transparency.
- Smart contracts automate and guarantee execution.
- Decentralised crowdsourced adjudication enhances fairness.
- Smart contract ambiguities are resolvable via blockchain.
- Blockchain enhances legal record-keeping.
- Blockchain dispute resolution reduces costs and expands access.
- Cryptographic protection should strengthen security.
- Blockchain enhances the integrity of evidence.
- Crowdsourced dispute resolution better ensures juror impartiality.
- Blockchain should be integrated within legal frameworks to maximise benefits.

1. Nature of blockchain

Blockchain is a particular type of database. Blockchains store data in blocks that are then 'chained together' by hashes (a mathematical method of sealing information in one direction only). As new data arrives, it is placed in a fresh block. Once a block is filled, it is chained onto the previous block. This is achieved by including the hash of the previous block in the data covered by the new block. Because of this interlocking hashing, the chain was thought to be effectively immutable. Latterly, however, it has proven to be hackable, upsetting its claim to provide absolute protection). Even so, one can exaggerate the significance of such hacks. Schmitz and Rule offer a balanced but carefully optimistic view in this regard, observing, among other things, as follows.[176] First, blockchain is more secure than general cloud-based systems, but can be hacked. Second, on a related note, hackers could create a copy of the blockchain which might allow the unscrupulous to steal information. Third, all that said, blockchain is now evolving in ways that make it less susceptible to attack. Fourth, the risks presenting have not slowed the increase in reliance on blockchain technology. Nor, it is submitted, should those risks impede the development of crowdsourced dispute resolution – not least (though not only) because of the evolution of blockchain in terms of becoming even more secure than it once was.

At root, blockchain is a form of distributed ledger technology (DLT) – a way of recording and sharing data across multiple data stores where each has the same data records, collectively controlled and maintained by a distributed network of computer servers called nodes. Because the chain is stored by all computers in a network, there is no central authority. Instead of a trusted validator, the system relies on a decentralised network of anonymous validators to maintain and update the ledger.

Blockchain's genesis can be traced back to a paper published in 2008 by the pseudonymous Satoshi Nakamoto. The author had noticed that e-commerce relied exclusively on financial institutions operating as trusted third parties in online transactions. However, these institutions were unable to offer completely non-reversible transactions for non-reversible services. Nakamoto saw in this situation a need for decentralised technology that no one person could control. And so, Bitcoin – which relies on blockchain technology – was born as a peer-to-peer version of electronic cash, allowing for online payments from Party A to B without need for the intermediation of any financial institution (or, indeed, any third party).*

* In fact, most people still have to trust some form of intermediary (eg, CoinBase) because the complexities of blockchain are not commonly understood.

2. Recommendation on Blockchain and Other Distributed Ledger Technologies (2022)

In 2022, the OECD Council adopted a Recommendation on Blockchain and Other Distributed Ledger Technologies.* The Recommendation offers a slightly tautologous definition of 'blockchain', describing it as "[referring to] all types of Blockchain technologies and distributed ledger technologies (DLT), including the protocol, network, and application layers". The definition continues:

- *Blockchain technologies and DLT are part of a broader ecosystem of technologies.*
- *DLT is a combination of technologies that together create a digital, shared and self-updating ledger of verified transactions or information among parties in a network based on innovative database technologies, including blockchain technologies.*
- *DLT uses various types of multi-party consensus mechanisms to validate and record transactions and has various governance systems, ranging from "centralised" models through to instances where there may be no control by a central authority(ies) (also known as "decentralised").*[177]

3. Blockchain and smart contracts

Before moving on to mention possible uses for blockchain in the ODR context, it is necessary to mention the concept of 'smart contracts'. A smart contract is self-executing software that automatically performs a function once prescribed conditions are met – for example, it will transfer crypto assets held in escrow from A to B immediately upon B satisfying the condition of winning in a blockchain dispute resolution process. Information on real-world occurrences is provided by so-called 'oracles' – that is, hardware (eg, scanners and sensors), software (eg, online downloads) or designated humans (eg, a certification officer). The certainty that Consequence Y will follow Event Y creates trust that a contract will be performed and creates a fairer 'playing field' – for example, for startups without a reputation or businesses in countries that have a less than reliable court or ADR system.

4. Blockchain dispute resolution platforms

Blockchain dispute resolution platforms offer services for disputes arising out of blockchain and smart contract transactions or for traditional disputes unrelated to blockchain transactions. In the process, they eliminate traditional decision-

---

* OECD/LEGAL/0470; adopted on 10 June 2022. The recommendation addresses six key issues relevant to all blockchain actors: compliance and coherence; governance, transparency, and accountability; interoperability; digital security and privacy; education and skills development; and environmental impact. The recommendation also contains specific policy recommendations for governments in five areas: to develop coordinated policy approaches concerning blockchain; to foster investment in blockchain research and development; to strive to build human capacity on blockchain; to support an enabling policy environment for blockchain; and to cooperate internationally on blockchain.

makers such as judges from the adjudicative process. What uses might blockchain serve in the context of ODR? A number of uses present, which are described below.

First, *dispute avoidance*. The use of smart contracts means that untampered evidence ought to be available. There is comfort for parties in this, though it would not pre-empt issues of interpretation arising.

Second, *ODR via smart contract*. ODR may itself be done via smart contract. An example of this is Kleros, a successful, decentralised decision protocol for use on smart contract platforms. It acts as a decentralised third party that can provide decisions upon applying a set of rules to various questions, whether simple or complex. This is achieved by having crowdsourced jurors analyse and rule correctly on cases. In this way, Kleros provides judgments in an inexpensive, reliable, swift and decentralised manner. A summary form of how the Kleros process works in practice is depicted in Figure 36. Another example of a blockchain dispute resolution platform is Aragon, the practical workings of which are shown in Figure 37. (These two figures appear at the end of this chapter.)

Third, *resolution of smart contract disputes*. The precise meaning of a smart contract may itself be the subject of a dispute that requires resolution. One commentator has described the use of smart contract and ODR procedures as the "digital symbiosis"[178] of contract and conflict resolution. Thus, there are already legal technology companies that offer software which sees a dispute about a smart contract sent directly to the ODR procedure so as to allow the dispute to be resolved as swiftly and efficiently as possible.[179]

Figure 31: Some challenges and risks presented by blockchain

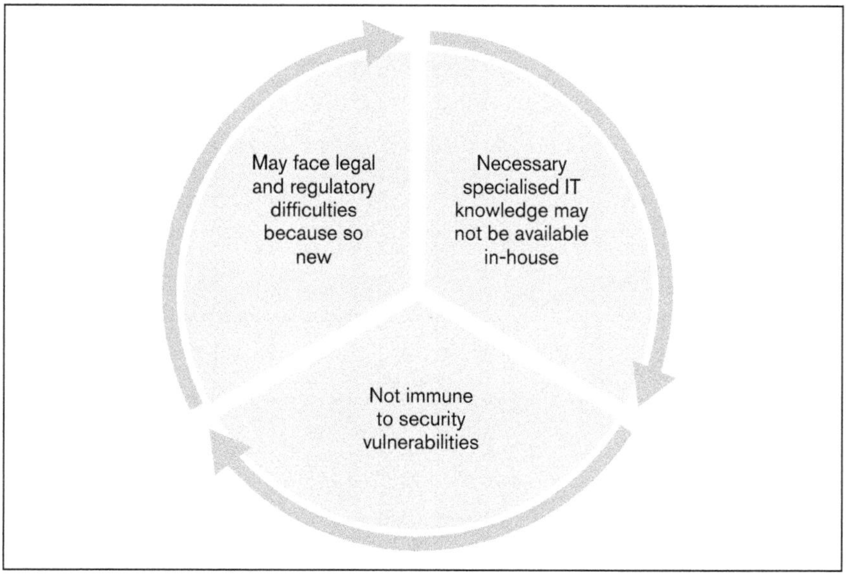

All that said, the world of smart contracts is not without challenges. A smart contract may be tainted by coding error (bugs). And it could reasonably be contended that, as a concept, smart contracts present more problems than they have resolved (as is perhaps to be expected of a new technology). Just to give a few examples of the issues presenting, it is not clear whether smart contracts invariably satisfy the requirements for a valid contract under the common law; whether, if a contract requires to be in writing, a smart contract satisfies this requirement; and what remedies are available if a party wants to prevent or reverse the operation of a smart contract.

Figure 32: Some types of dispute suitable for crowdsourced ODR[180]

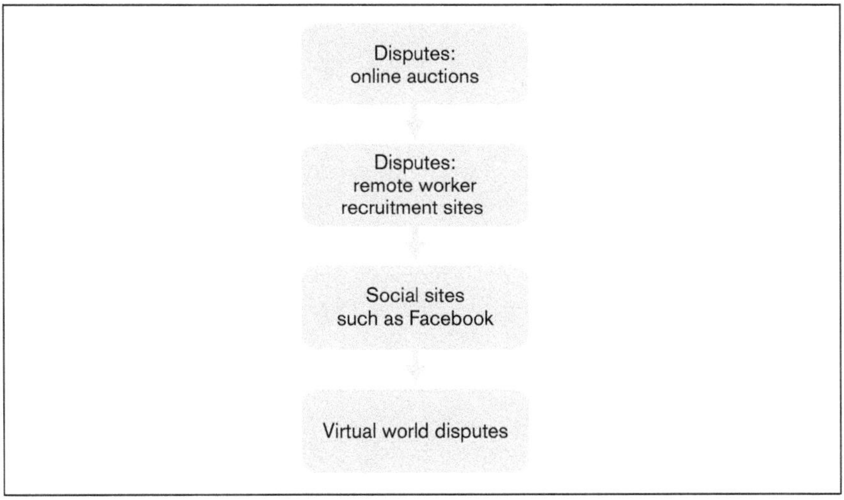

Figure 33: Some key attractions of blockchain dispute resolution[181]

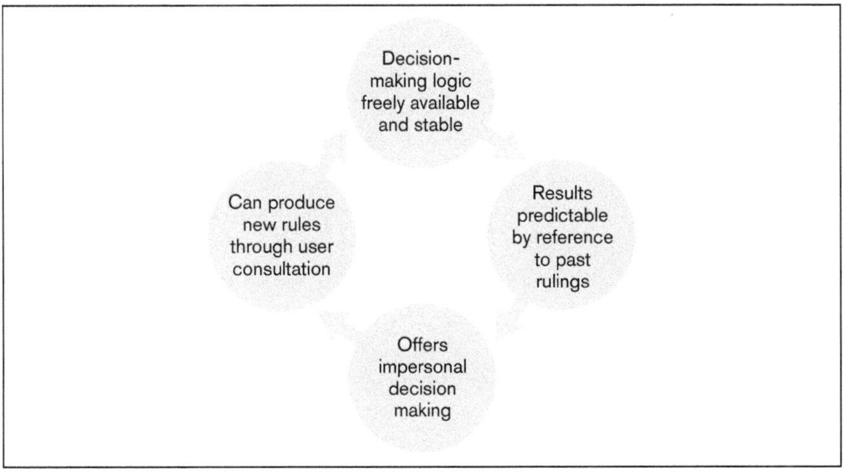

It has been suggested that blockchain may have a role to play in criminal courts in optimising the correctness and currency of court records, including court judgments, warrants and criminal histories.[182] The generally immutable nature of blockchain data also means that it can be relatively freely shared (subject to privacy constraints). In the non-blockchain context, virtual hearings (a more 'traditional form of ODR) may also have a role to play in reducing case backlogs. ODR blockchain dispute resolution has also been touted as a means of resolving personal injuries disputes, not least directing victims in the first instance down a non-litigation route.

5. Use of blockchain in China

As was touched upon in the account of ODR in China, blockchain also has significance when it comes to safeguarding online evidence. So, for example, in 2018, the Beijing Internet Court established a Balance Blockchain Project. This is a blockchain that connects hundreds of businesses in technical services, application services, intellectual property and financial exchanges. The project has proved valuable in copyright disputes. After copyright owners upload evidence of copyright ownership etc, that evidence is verified by accredited service providers and then encrypted as a 'block'. However, the process is not without challenges – for example, parties may have concerns about the security and stability of the e-evidence storage system and associated verification services. In a press release issued in November 2019 following its first blockchain case, the Beijing Internet Court indicated that the process involves the following steps:[183]

- In an online infringement case handled by the court, the plaintiff and defendant concluded a mediation agreement (a smart contract).
- They were told that the agreement would be executed automatically through blockchain smart contract technology.
- With a single click, the enforcement case was automatically filed to the Beijing Internet Court when the defendant failed to fully perform the obligations in the mediation (smart contract) agreement.

The press release issued by the Beijing Internet Court concerning the process continues as follows:[184]

> *This is the first automatic case filing powered by the blockchain smart contract technology in China. It means the judicial blockchain smart contract has been put into practical use, and the blockchain data has been highly integrated with the judicial off-chain information system ... The smart contract is a modular, auto-executing script that runs on blockchain, working for data processing, value transfer, and asset management. With the precision and unique specificity of computer language code, the application of smart contracts in the integration of trials with blockchain can avoid misunderstandings caused by language loopholes.*

In addition, it reduces manual intervention and promotes a smarter and more open and transparent process of judicial enforcement.

Figure 34: Types of blockchain dispute resolution processes[185]

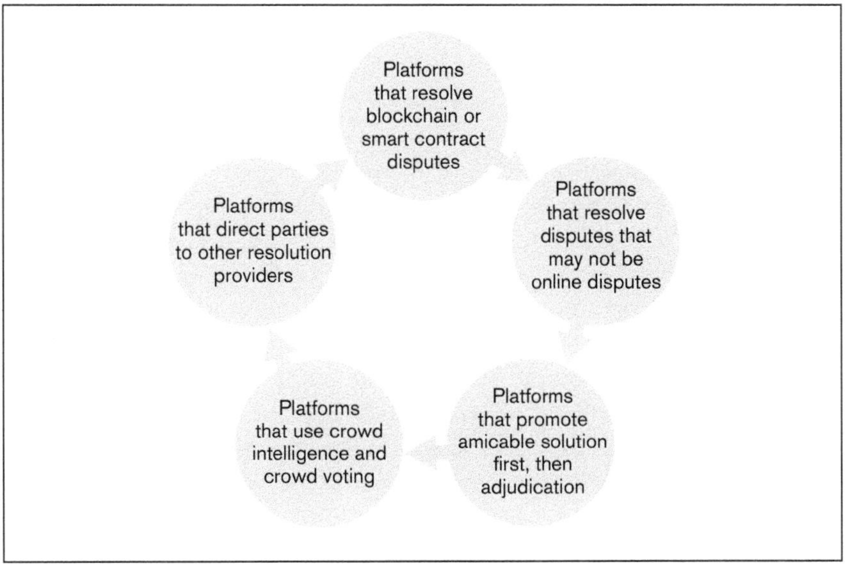

6. Advantages and weaknesses of blockchain dispute resolution

One learned commentator has distinguished between five general categories of blockchain platform according to their functions and structures, while noting that any one platform may slot into a number of categories.[186] Her fivefold categorisation is summarised in Figure 34.

The use of blockchain in the context of ODR is arguably more suitable than traditional adjudication for a world in which distrust of third parties is commonplace and traditional adjudication is not reflective of a growing counterculture that sees people distancing themselves from central authority.

The key advantages of blockchain dispute resolution include the following. First, individual users cannot be identified. Second, it should lead to the amicable resolution of disputes. Third, it offers assurance that the data in issue is real and reliable. Fourth, the verdict can be executed by smart contract – for example, by placing crypto-assets in escrow and distributing when a decision is made. Fifth, if viewed as arbitration, it may have *res judicata* effect. Sixth, it relies on collective wisdom (assuming this to be a good thing – and it may not be). Seventh, it reduces costs and may increase efficiency. Eighth, the diversity of jurors should facilitate fairness. Ninth, it eliminates the need to invoke cross-border enforcement. Tenth, typically simplified procedures facilitate accessibility. Eleventh, there is an informality of approach. Twelfth, in some systems, users can choose whether to accept the outcome. Thirteenth, there is independence from decisionmakers. Fourteenth, the services are typically available on a 24/7 basis.

The key challenges of blockchain dispute resolution include the following. First, it is hard to trust and cooperate with unknown persons. Second, technology can be a barrier for the digitally challenged. Third, platform operators enjoy no power to coerce. Fourth, it relies on crowd wisdom. Fifth, it relies on an aggregate of decisions, not collective decisions. Sixth, aggregate decision making may lead to 'herding'. Seventh, jurors may have very different understandings of justice. Eighth, it is potentially open to the risk of an individual having multiple juror accounts. Ninth, consensus is no guarantee of correctness. Tenth, it may tend towards the application of some group concept of fairness rather than law. Eleventh, jurors may be more narrowly specialised than offline judges with wide experience. Twelfth, there may be language (and hence communication) difficulties. Thirteenth, simplified procedures may mean that crowdsourcing is unsuitable for complicated disputes. Fourteenth, simplified procedures may yield procedural unfairness. Fifteenth, blockchain is hackable. Sixteenth, it is as yet unclear whether blockchain dispute resolution would be so cost effective that it could be used for the swathe of digital small claims in need of an effective resolution mechanism. Seventeenth, it is unclear whether courts will recognise blockchain rulings.

Blockchain offers decentralised platforms on which disputes can be resolved efficiently and cost effectively. Blockchain dispute resolution platforms such as Kleros and Aragon have pioneered mechanisms that replace traditional adjudicators with crowdsourced jurors who analyse cases based on predefined rules. These jurors deliver verdicts that can be enforced via smart contracts, ensuring the immediate execution of decisions, such as the transfer of digital assets. It has even been suggested that only ODR systems which include an in-built enforcement mechanism can ensure that the twin goals of speed and effectiveness are attained.[187]

Applications or potential applications of blockchain in the ODR context include dispute avoidance, smart contracts disputes, criminal justice and the preservation and storage of digital evidence. Van Den Herik and Dimov divide crowdsourced ODR into three principal types: online opinion polls, online trials and procedures that render decisions that are enforceable.[188] The mechanisms considered in this chapter are a mix of all three (though the enforceability comes via the crowdsourced platform; enforceability via traditional enforcement mechanisms may remain a challenge).

The advantages and weaknesses of blockchain dispute resolution have been considered above. While blockchain dispute resolution cannot entirely replace traditional legal systems, it offers a viable complement where conventional methods prove inaccessible or inefficient. Dimov has suggested that there are 14 criteria by reference to which a crowdsourced ODR platform can be gauged.[189] These are summarised in Figure 35 and, in effect, offer a litmus test by which to gauge the adequacy or degree of adequacy of a blockchain dispute resolution process. Blockchain-based dispute resolution is not a panacea but represents a potentially significant step forwards as regards establishing a more accessible, transparent and efficient justice system. As legal frameworks evolve to accommodate this new paradigm, blockchain will play an increasing role.

Figure 35: Dimov's 14 criteria (a summary)

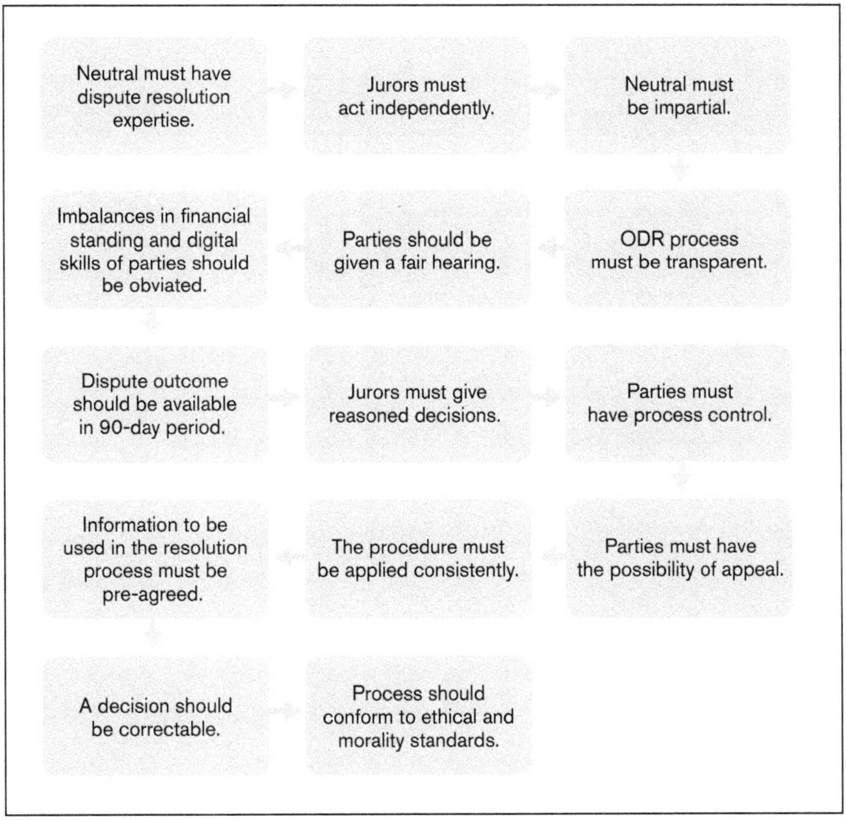

Figure 36: Summary version of the Kleros process[190]

[a] The more tokens James stakes, the more likely that he will be selected as a juror. Staking avoids selection of an inactive jury. Selection is done by random number generator.
[b] To incentivise honest rulings, jurors lose some stake for rulings that are out of line with those of other jurors. A special court can separately rule on alleged juror violations of court policies.
[c] Appeals courts are less specialised, prompting more effort to arrive at a correct solution.

Figure 37: Summary version of the Aragon process[191]

System design means that judges are incentivised to dismiss request and take bond money. However, they also know that if they are reversed on appeal, they will be penalised. Supreme Court judges will lose standing as top nine network judges if they do not vote in the same way as the aggregate.

Key learnings

- *Blockchain ensures near-immutable transparency.* Blockchain provides almost tamper-proof record-keeping, better ensuring that all dispute resolution actions remain transparent and immutable. Unfortunately, blockchain has proven to be hackable. So, while blockchain ensures transparency, concerns about data privacy and the risk of exposing sensitive information remain live.
- *Smart contracts automate and guarantee execution.* Smart contracts ensure that rulings and settlements are enforced instantly and automatically. That said, errors in smart contract code can lead to enforcement issues. So, there is need for some mechanism to correct unintended execution of smart contracts.
- *Decentralised crowdsourced adjudication enhances fairness.* Blockchain-based ODR platforms provide swift, cost-effective and impartial rulings. However, lack of judicial oversight could lead to inconsistencies in rulings.
- *Smart contract ambiguities can be resolved via blockchain.* Blockchain-powered ODR can ensure that smart contract disputes are resolved, but traditional legal systems may not yet recognise smart contracts as legally binding, raising concerns about their enforceability via traditional court mechanisms.
- *Blockchain enhances legal record-keeping.* Blockchain enhances legal record-keeping, though again it has proven to be hackable.
- *Blockchain dispute resolution reduces costs and expands access.* Blockchain eliminates intermediaries, significantly reducing dispute resolution costs while making justice systems more accessible. That said, the digital divide could limit participation for some in blockchain ODR systems.
- *Cryptographic protection should strengthen security.* Blockchain's cryptographic security better ensures that ODR data remains protected from tampering and cyberattacks. However, while blockchain is highly secure, it is susceptible to hacking.
- *Blockchain enhances the integrity of evidence.* Blockchain provides time-stamped evidence that better ensures disputes are resolved based on verifiable facts. Challenges arise in verifying the authenticity of off-chain data, ensuring its admissibility in legal proceedings and avoiding hacking.
- *Crowdsourced dispute resolution better ensures juror impartiality and anonymity.* Blockchain-based juror selection better ensures fair decision making, reducing the potential for external influences and bias. That said, while anonymity enhances neutrality, it can also reduce accountability and render it difficult to challenge incorrect rulings.

- *Blockchain dispute resolution should be integrated within legal frameworks:* Blockchain ODR should be integrated within legal frameworks to better ensure its benefits while preserving due process and fairness. However, excessive integration and regulation may hinder blockchain innovation.

14. Cybersecurity and chatbots

Courts will need to thoughtfully define who owns ODR system data, how it will be protected, how it can be used, and how and where audit trails are maintained ... Courts are responsible for final agreements, judgments, and any officially filed documents as part of the court record. Negotiation and private communication between parties are not part of the court record, and therefore not retained and not discoverable.

Joint Technology Committee[192]

The endeavour towards mainstreaming ODR needs to address the issue of trust at every level. Like other emerging technologies, ODR is bound to be met with scepticism from potential users, especially regarding its effectiveness given the lack of in-person interactions, as well as regarding data security and confidentiality.

NITI Aayog[193]

Improving ODR: 10 key lessons

- Prioritise cybersecurity as a core ODR requirement.
- Ensure legal and regulatory compliance from outset.
- Use AI-powered chatbots to improve ODR accessibility.
- Build and maintain trust in ODR systems.
- Have clear data ownership and security policies (and related auditing policies).
- Use strong encryption and access controls.
- Establish a strong cybersecurity incident response plan.
- Continuously update AI chatbots for accuracy and compliance.
- Integrate human oversight into AI-reliant ODR.
- Provide cybersecurity training.

1. The need for security

It is perhaps a statement of the obvious, though still a statement worth making, that security is a key concern when it comes to any computer system, including an ODR system.[194] The use of digital platforms introduces vulnerabilities to dispute resolution processes that fraudsters might exploit. Some of the more prominent cybercrimes of relevance include malware attacks (using harmful software to gain unauthorised access to or harm computer systems), phishing (the fraudulent use of emails or websites to obtain personal information) and distributed denial of service (DDoS) attacks (using several computers to overwhelm a network or server with traffic.)* A DDoS attack might be used to disrupt ODR sessions or restrict access to an online case management system. One learned commentator has even suggested that in India, ODR will only prove a success when, among other things, there is improved cybersecurity.[195]

2. The Cybercrime Convention

This chapter focuses on cybersecurity in the ODR context. At the European level, cybercrime has latterly been the subject of the Council of Europe's Cybercrime Convention (2001). Within the European Union, a number of measures of note have also been or are in the course of being adopted in the realm of cybersecurity generally. They have fairly limited relevance when it comes to ODR. However, they form part of the legal backdrop in which, for example, blockchain dispute resolution (as well as ODR generally) is now designed and operated. These wider measures include the following:

- *Second Network and Information Systems Directive:*[196] This amends the rules on the security of network and information systems, the aim being to further improve the resilience of public and private entities against cybersecurity threats.
- *Critical Entities Resilience Directive:*[197] This aims to strengthen the security of critical infrastructural entities across the European Union.
- *Cybersecurity Act:*[198] This enhances the mandate of the EU Agency for Cybersecurity and establishes a cybersecurity certification framework for products and services.
- *Digital Operation Resilience Act (DORA):*[199] DORA responds to the need for harmonised rules on the digital operational resilience of individual financial entities and the financial system as a whole, including a new framework for the oversight of third-party providers that are critical to the European financial system.
- *Cyber Resilience Act:*[200] This seeks to ensure the production of more secure

---

* Some of these attacks are from unexpected sources. For example, in the international context, one learned commentator has observed how consumer information has been accessed by North Korea (Oh, 319).

hardware and software products – for example, by setting rules for the placing on the market of products with digital elements.

- *Proposed Cyber Solidarity Act:*[201] This aims to improve the response to cyber threats across the European Union. It will involve the creation of a European Cybersecurity Alert System, a Cybersecurity Emergency Mechanism and a European Cybersecurity Incident Review Mechanism.

It is worth discussing the Cybersecurity Act in a little more detail. Much of it is concerned with the establishment of a European cybersecurity certification framework. This framework provides for a mechanism to establish European cybersecurity certification schemes, which seek to meet the various security objectives mentioned in Figure 38. A European cybersecurity certification scheme may specify one or more of the assurance levels in Figure 38 for ICT products, services and processes.

Figure 38: Security objectives of European cybersecurity certification schemes

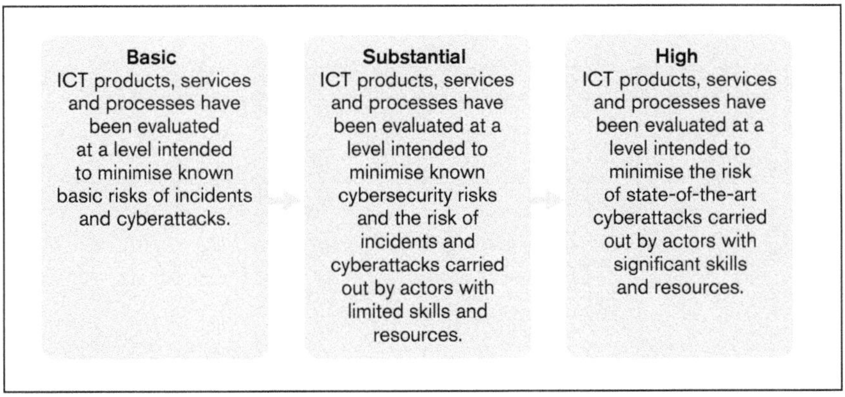

ICT products, services and processes certified under a European cybersecurity certification scheme are presumed to comply with the requirements of that scheme. Cybersecurity certification is voluntary, unless otherwise specified by law.

3. Guidelines on ODR Mechanisms in Civil and Administrative Court Proceedings (2021)

The Council of Europe's Guidelines on Online Dispute Resolution Mechanisms in Civil and Administrative Court Proceedings (2021) touch briefly on the issue of cybersecurity, stating, among other things, that an appropriate level of cybersecurity should be ensured to satisfy Articles 6 and 13 of the European Convention on Human Rights (ECHR) (the right to a fair trial and the right to an effective remedy), and to ensure the necessary trust and confidence in ODR. The associated explanatory memorandum elaborates on these guidelines a little. A cybersecurity checklist for Council of Europe member states is also appended to the explanatory memorandum. It provides that states should implement the following in designing ODR: protect stored, transmitted or otherwise processed data; manage user access through secure identification and authentication; identify and document known dependencies and vulnerabilities; log data access, use and processing; allow consultation of log files to enable auditing; test for vulnerability; provide back-up facilities and technical support; proceed by way of security by design and by default; and use up-to-date hardware and software.

The guidelines do not impose binding legal obligations on Council of Europe member states. Instead, they serve as a practical and reputable framework within which to ensure that ODR mechanisms uphold the principles enshrined in the ECHR. The guidelines are considered in Chapter 15. However, it is appropriate to consider, at this juncture, the provisions of those guidelines and to make some comment on them. Six key principles are identified in the guidelines when it comes to cybersecurity:

- An appropriate level of cybersecurity should be ensured in order to meet the requirements of Articles 6 and 13 of the ECHR and ensure the necessary trust and confidence in ODR mechanisms.
- The level of cybersecurity should be considered appropriate when there are safeguards against unauthorised access to confidential data; unwanted alteration or deletion of data; improper access to the system and the data contained therein; uncertainty over the identity of the judge and other professionals involved; and identity fraud. (Confidentiality safeguards should also consider the risks of state or corporate surveillance.)
- The use of ODR mechanisms should not infringe data protection rights, including, where applicable, the right to information, the right to access data, the right to object to processing data and the right to erasure. (For data protection rights to be upheld, enforcement mechanisms for breaches must also be robust.)
- Technical and organisational measures should be implemented to ensure that rules on personal data protection are respected, both when determining the means of processing and during data processing.
- ODR mechanisms should be designed and developed by applying the principles of personal data protection by default and by design. (While privacy by design is important, in reality, cost and technical constraints may limit its application.)
- Outsourcing of the technology used in ODR should not lead to the processing of personal data for commercial purposes. (Commercial exploitation risks require strict oversight.)

4. The Cybersecurity Protocol for International Arbitration (2020)

A Cybersecurity Protocol for International Arbitration was adopted in 2020 by the International Council for Commercial Arbitration, the New York City Bar Association and the International Institute for Conflict Prevention (CPR). The protocol is the most comprehensive measure of its type. Among the objectives it seeks to achieve are to provide a framework to determine reasonable information security measures for individual arbitration matters; to provide practical and procedural guidance in the assessment of security risks and the identification of related measures that might be implemented; and to increase awareness about information security in international arbitration.

Figure 39: Security objectives of certification schemes

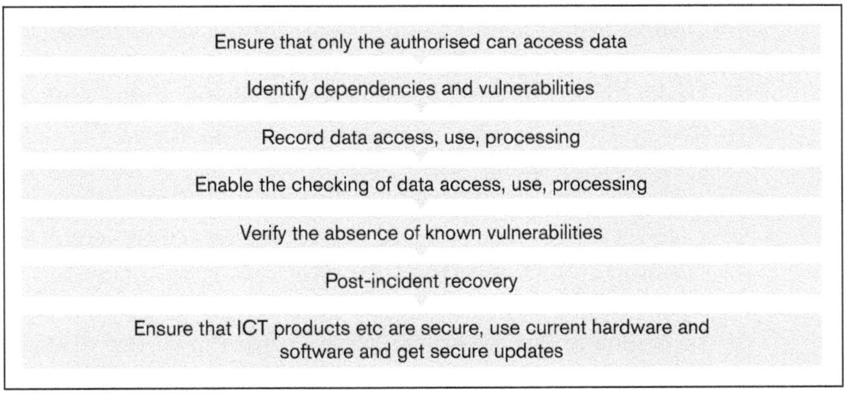

From a cybersecurity perspective, the following requirements of the protocol are perhaps of greatest interest:

- *Keep abreast of security threats and solutions.* (A problem presenting in this regard is that cyberthreats evolve so rapidly that keeping abreast of them may prove remarkably challenging.)
- *Consider industry standards and governmental regulations.* (Such standards and regulations can be dense and complex, making compliance with them a challenging process, even with legal advice.)
- *Know one's assets and infrastructure.* (This requires the maintenance of a comprehensive and current asset inventory.)
- *Identify sensitive data and take steps to minimise and protect it.* (Errors in classification increase the risk of accidental release of sensitive data.)
- *Avoid having unnecessary multiple copies of documents.* (To proceed otherwise is to increase the risk of accidental release of data.)
- *Establish document retention and destruction practices.* (If such practices are not rigorously observed, an increased risk of the accidental release of data will present.)

- *Enable remote location tracking and data wiping functions.* (Such functions are subject to abuse by hackers if not properly secured.)
- *Minimise access to sensitive data while travelling.* (The problem with such access is that it increases the risk of malicious interception.)
- *Back up data.* (Back-up failures increase the risk of data loss if a cyberattack occurs.)
- *Consider access control policies.* (Inadequate or inadequately observed control policies enable unauthorised people to access data.)
- *Establish strong passwords or biometric controls.*
- *Encrypt data that is in transit.* (Unencrypted data is more susceptible to unauthorised access.)
- *Be cautious as regards opening attachments and using links.* (A lack of caution yields a heightened exposure to phishing and other cyberattacks.)
- *Use share filing services instead of email.* (A failure to do so may lead to sensitive files being exposed to interception.)
- *Control physical access to information resources.* (Unauthorised physical access may lead to device tampering and data theft.)
- *Use professional/commercial products and tools.* (Use of inferior products may yield unnecessary IT susceptibilities.)
- *Avoid sharing accounts/devices.* (Sharing increases the risk of unauthorised access or unintended data disclosure.)
- *Guard digital perimeters.* (The problem with this precaution is that it will not prevent internal attacks or guard against unknown weaknesses.)
- *Promptly install software patches/updates.* (Delayed patching yields a security risk.)
- *Monitor for security weaknesses.* (If such monitoring is inadequate or merely reactive, any weaknesses may continue or may not be caught in a timely manner.)
- *Have specific plans and procedures for dealing with cybersecurity breaches.* (Absent such plans and procedures, an ODR operator may find it difficult to meet any cyberattacks.)
- *Put cybersecurity risk insurance in place.* (The usefulness of such insurance may be diminished by policy terms and exemptions.)

Some obligations on states under the Cybercrime Convention (2001)

The convention provides for international cooperation in the area of cybercrime; the criminalisation of various online behaviours; and procedural tools to investigate cybercrime and secure related electronic evidence. The main conduct that the convention anticipates as suitable for criminalisation is described below:

- *Illegal access:* Intentional access to the whole or any part of a computer system without right (Article 2).

- *Illegal interception:* Intentional interception without the right of non-public transmissions of computer data to, from or within a computer system (Article 3).
- *Data interference:* Intentional damage, deletion, deterioration, alteration or suppression of computer data without right (Article 4).
- *System interference:* Intentional serious hindering without the right of the functioning of a computer system (Article 5).
- *Misuse of devices:* The production, sale or procurement of a device aimed at committing Article 2–5 offences or a password allowing access to computer system with view to committing Article 2–5 offences (Article 6).
- *Computer-related forgery:* Issue of inauthentic data with the intent that it be considered or acted upon for legal purposes as if it were authentic (Article 7).
- *Computer-related fraud:* Intentional causing of a loss of property to another person by input of data or interference with a computer system, with fraudulent or dishonest intent (Article 8).
- *Child pornography:* Various child pornography-related behaviours (Article 9).
- *Copyright breaches:* Infringement of copyright where such acts are committed wilfully, on a commercial scale and by means of a computer system (Article 10).
- *Aiding and abetting:* Intentional aiding or abetting of commission of any Article 2–10 offences.

5. Chatbots

Chatbots are computer programs designed to interact with humans through natural language, typically over the Internet. At their most basic, chatbots operate using a rules-based approach, responding to user inputs with pre-programmed replies from a predetermined database. Two quotes from learned commentators suffice to give a sense of the present reach and limitations of chatbots:

> *[L]arge language model (LLM) chatbots ... can seemingly "do everything that a human being [can] do except drink and swear and go on strike." Of course, LLM chatbots are not truly intelligent: they ... derive statistical patterns from enormous amounts of training data ... [They] do not so much provide information as produce "information-shaped" sentences ... [W]hat Marshall McLuhan wrote of the television might be the most accurate and damning description of ... [chatbots]: the chatbot "speaks, and yet says nothing".*[202]

> *Is a bot worse than the human mind? When I first had a chat with ChatGPT, it offered the following disclaimer: "... May occasionally generate incorrect informa-*

> *tion ... May occasionally produce harmful instructions or biased content ... Limited knowledge of world and events after 2021." Do these limitations make ChatGPT unique? I have seen many legal briefs and awards that suffer from these shortcomings: the law or the facts are incorrect, the judgment or award is biased, or the drafter has ignored crucial evidence.*[203]

The cybersecurity risks posed by AI chatbots include the following.[204] First, the generation of harmful content. Second, the promotion of bias and discrimination. Third, the generation of misinformation. Fourth, the potential for disclosures of private information. And fifth, the potential for copyright infringement.

When it comes to ODR, chatbots are invaluable in terms of automated assistance, streamlined processes and user accessibility. They can guide users through the dispute resolution process, classify cases or offer general (and general legal) information. Automating these functions lightens the human workload, renders the resolution process more expeditious and ensures the 24/7 availability of information and assistance.

A chatbot's effectiveness depends on its design. Chatbots must be user-friendly, transparent and capable of delivering accurate and clear information. Additionally, their design should incorporate robust security and privacy measures, ensuring compliance with applicable laws, including data protection laws.

Viewed negatively, chatbots can struggle with complex legal language or nuanced disputes. Additionally, they lack the empathetic, interpersonal qualities that can be critical in resolving emotionally charged disputes. It follows that chatbots should be integrated with human oversight. This should ensure accuracy and efficiency while maintaining the accessibility advantages of automated systems. A key function of chatbots in ODR is their triaging of claims. Sometimes, a simple questionnaire with multiple-choice options may suffice for accurate claim classification. However, in more sophisticated cases, a chatbot with AI capabilities may be required – which comes at a cost.

An emerging development in ODR chatbot technology is the integration of external NLP application programming interfaces (APIs), such as ChatGPT, into ODR systems. With these APIs, institutions can enhance existing platforms, enabling chatbots to assist users more effectively. This innovation entails significant potential when it comes to consumer protection platforms (when one will be dealing with an audience that may well be unfamiliar with legal processes and language), fostering trust in dispute resolution systems and ensuring greater accessibility to justice.

Despite the advantages, reliance on AI-driven chatbots also introduces potential risks. For example, they may not be trained up as regards jurisdiction-specific laws, leading to dissemination of inaccurate legal information – a sure recipe for a lawsuit. (This risk underscores the importance of ensuring that chatbot knowledge bases are continuously updated to reflect applicable laws and regulations. For providers, it is also possible to limit liability through the use of suitable disclaimers.)

Figure 40: Potential uses of chatbots in ODR

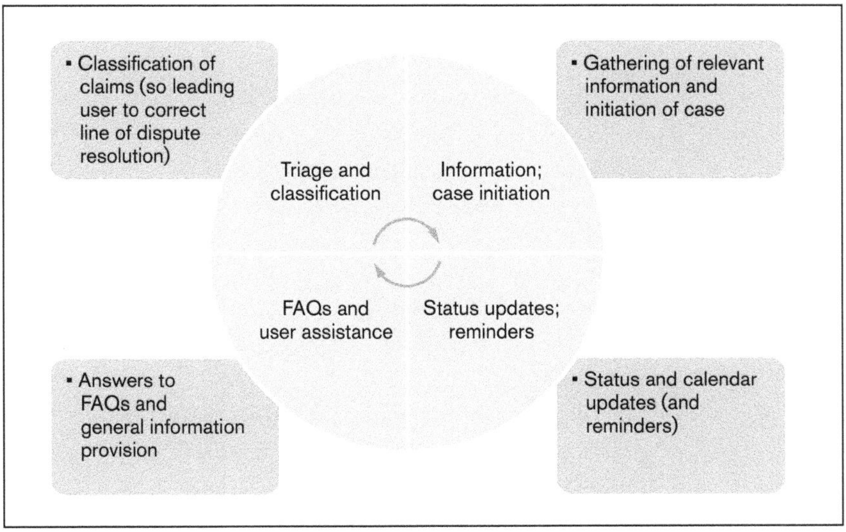

Key learnings

- *Prioritise cybersecurity as a core ODR requirement.* Strong cybersecurity measures are critical for ODR platforms. Implementing high-level protections can be costly. Striking a balance between good security measures and platform usability may be challenging.
- *Ensure legal and regulatory compliance from outset.* Ethically run ODR platforms should comply with cybersecurity law and regulation. Such compliance frameworks can be burdensome, not least in terms of legal cost.
- *Use AI-powered chatbots to improve ODR accessibility.* Chatbots enhance user experience, ensuring that users can navigate ODR platforms with ease. That said, chatbots are less useful when it comes to legal or emotionally charged issues. Over-reliance on chatbots without human oversight could yield errors that weaken general public confidence in ODR.
- *Build and maintain trust in ODR systems.* ODR platforms generate user trust by being perceived to be fair, reliable, secure and transparent. Cultivating user trust may be challenging, especially among the less digitally literate.

- *Have clear data and auditing policies.* ODR platforms should have clear policies on data access, ownership, retention and related auditing. The establishment of suitably rigorous policies needs to be balanced against the need for transparency.
- *Use strong encryption and access controls.* There should be strong encryption protocols to secure data – albeit that implementation may lead to usability challenges.
- *Establish a strong cybersecurity incident response plan.* ODR platform providers should develop and update incident response protocols. (Addressing every possible outcome is resource-intensive and might not be feasible for smaller ODR platform providers.)
- *Continuously update AI chatbots.* Chatbots should frequently be updated with accurate information. Absent such maintenance, chatbots risk giving misleading or wrong information.
- *Integrate human oversight into AI-reliant ODR.* AI systems should complement, not replace, human decision-makers. That said, striking the right balance between automation and human involvement may be challenging.
- *Provide cybersecurity training.* ODR platform providers should offer cybersecurity training to staff. It is important that such training be comprehensive but not overwhelming.

15. Guidelines on ODR mechanisms

ODR can expand access by helping eliminate a wide variety of obstacles that prevent individuals from understanding and exercising their rights.
Joint Technology Committee[205]

ODR can play an important role in promoting legal health by making people aware about the law, their rights and duties, and the remedies available with them … [T]ools can be developed where parties can feed in questions and get answers on the rights and protections. Thus overall, ODR can help in moving towards a more 'rule of law' based society.
NITI Aayog[206]

Improving ODR: 10 key lessons

- Prioritise human rights compliance.
- Eliminate algorithmic bias.
- Enhance explainability and transparency.
- Preserve confidentiality and data privacy.
- Ensure user control.
- Cultivate trust through frequent audits.
- Balance innovation with regulation.
- Develop a vigorous appeals mechanism.
- Ensure that AI is accurate and reliable.
- Promote digital literacy.

Ensuring that ODR aligns with fundamental human rights protections has been a pressing concern. The ECHR guarantees the right to a fair trial (Article 6) and the right to an effective remedy (Article 13). However, as of 2021, there was a conspicuous absence of ODR-related human rights standards at the international, European or national level. To address this gap, the Council of Europe's Committee of Ministers adopted guidelines aimed at safeguarding human rights in civil and administrative ODR mechanisms.[207] These guidelines do not impose binding legal obligations on member states but serve as a practical framework to ensure that ODR mechanisms uphold the principles enshrined in the ECHR. The guidelines are founded on four overarching principles. First, member states should seek to ensure trust and confidence in ODR. Second, ODR should not create substantial barriers to access to justice. Third, procedural rules which apply to court proceedings in general should apply to court proceedings involving ODR. Fourth, parties to proceedings involving the use of ODR should be identified using secure mechanisms.

Moving on, the Council of Europe outlines 43 more specific guidelines which are detailed below, along with some related observations.

1. Access to justice

Six key points are identified in the guidelines when it comes to access to justice. First, ODR should be easily understood, affordable and user friendly so that it can be used comfortably by as many people as possible. (These are subjective criteria; more concrete usability benchmarks would seem desirable.) Second, parties should be informed about how ODR operates, how to file an application, how to monitor progress of the proceedings and how to access decisions. (Of course, information alone does not ensure comprehension and there may need to be further user support.) Third, use of ODR should not be disadvantageous to the parties or give unfair advantage to one of the parties. (Ensuring absolute neutrality is as challenging in ODR as in real life.) Fourth, ODR should be designed and implemented in accordance with internationally recognised technical standards, in order to allow its use by as many people as possible with as much autonomy as possible. (While technical usability is key, digital literacy gaps may still exclude some users.) Fifth, the cost of court proceedings involving ODR should not be higher than that of proceedings not involving an ODR element. (Implementation costs may create hidden expenses.) Sixth, parties should be notified when it is intended that their case will be processed with the involvement of an AI mechanism. (While AI use ought to be disclosed, users also need avenues to challenge automated outcomes.)

2. Equality of arms

The term 'equality of arms' describes the notion that there ought to be a generally fair balance between disputants in terms of the opportunities extended to them to put forward their case in litigation. Three key points are identified in the guidelines when it comes to equality of arms between parties. First, participation in ODR proceedings should not prejudice an individual's right to participate effectively in the proceedings or their right to an effective remedy. (It might be more beneficial to set measurable criteria in this regard.) Second, ODR proceedings should ensure an independent and impartial adjudicative process. Third, parties to proceedings involving ODR should have knowledge of the materials in the case file, including those submitted by the other parties. (While full access to materials is necessary, real-time updates and easy retrieval could also usefully be ensured.)

3. Evidence and legal certainty

Three key points are identified in the guidelines when it comes to evidence and legal certainty. First, fairness requires that parties to proceedings involving ODR should be permitted to present evidence in a manner that does not place them at a disadvantage *vis-à-vis* other parties. (That said, digital access disparities could undermine the capacity to present evidence and that offline alternatives are thus needed.) Second, parties should have the opportunity to present their case and to contest evidence submitted by other parties. Third, ODR should respect the principles of legal certainty and protection of the legitimate expectations of the parties.

4. Effective proceedings

Three key points are identified in the guidelines when it comes to the effectiveness of proceedings. First, the implementation of ODR should aim to improve the effectiveness of the proceedings by allowing parties to participate without being physically present in court and by streamlining the whole process as far as possible. (Of course, efficiency should not come at the cost of procedural fairness or thorough adjudication.) Second, technical difficulties in the functioning of ODR should not prevent the courts, even for short periods, from examining cases and performing appropriate procedural steps. (While backup solutions must be robust, ensuring availability at all times may be impracticable.) Third, where national law provides that ADR constitutes a prerequisite for instituting court proceedings, including those involving ODR, this should not protract the dispute resolution process unnecessarily or result in a substantial increase in costs for the parties.

5. Decision delivery and enforcement

Four key points are identified in the guidelines when it comes to decision delivery and enforcement. First, the outcomes of the proceedings involving ODR should be transparent. (Of course, transparency falls to be balanced with privacy, especially in sensitive cases such as family law or immigration disputes.) Second, any final decision reached using ODR should be made public in accordance with the jurisprudence of the European Court of Human Rights. (Public accessibility is of course important, but anonymisation measures require also to be considered.) Third, sufficient reasons should be given for decisions reached using ODR or with the assistance of ODR – in particular, decisions reached with the involvement of AI mechanisms. (As with offline judgments,

AI-informed judgments need to explain not just outcomes but also the process by which the decision was reached.) Fourth, the mere fact that the decision is a result of an ODR mechanism should not prevent it from being enforceable.

6. Transparency

Eight key points are identified in the guidelines when it comes to judicial review and transparency. First, where national law allows for purely automated decisions, such decisions should be open to review before a judge. (That said, judicial backlogs in producing work outside of court may make full review impractical.) Second, the design and operation of ODR mechanisms should be made transparent and explained in an intelligible manner using clear and plain language. (However, too many or too detailed explanations may confuse self-represented disputants.) Third, the use of ODR mechanisms should guarantee appropriate ways to ensure public scrutiny of proceedings. (The confidentiality of sensitive disputes also needs to be respected.) Fourth, the use of ODR in courts should not in itself deprive parties of a right to request an oral hearing before at least one court. Fifth, parties to proceedings involving ODR should be informed about any potential conflicts of interest related to the operation of an ODR mechanism. Sixth, ODR should be designed in such a way that all documents generated, including the final judgment and other decisions or notifications, are written in clear and plain language. (Clear language is essential, but legal nuances must still be conveyed accurately.) Seventh, procedural rules applicable to ODR should be transparent. Eighth, parties to proceedings involving ODR should be aware of and have the ability to access information concerning the procedural rules applicable to ODR. (Arguably, interactive guidance may be more effective.)

7. Cybersecurity

Six key points are identified in the guidelines when it comes to cybersecurity. These have already been considered in Chapter 14.

8. Human rights protection

The guidelines require that Council of Europe member states assess the impact of ODR use throughout its entire lifecycle. They should also identify the specific requirements for both ethical and fair use of ODR and respect for human rights as part of the development and operation of any ODR mechanism. (It is submitted that ethical oversight is needed, but that defining measurable human rights impacts may well be difficult.)

9. Testing, monitoring, upgrading and research and development

Nine key points are identified in the guidelines when it comes to testing, monitoring, upgrading and research and development. First, Council of Europe member states are encouraged to allocate appropriate public funding for the development of ODR mechanisms to be used in court proceedings, including relevant research. (Public funding is valuable but public-private collaboration may assist from a cost perspective.) Second, the ease of use of ODR mechanisms should be sufficiently tested before implementing them, albeit that real-world adaptation may still reveal unanticipated flaws. Third, the judiciary, lawyers and other relevant stakeholders should be actively involved in designing ODR mechanisms. (Conversely, too much reliance on the traditions that such stakeholders might bring may stifle innovation.) Fourth, continuous monitoring and timely upgrading of ODR mechanisms, ensuring safety, fairness, efficiency and other quality standards, should be included in the lifecycle of all such systems. (Balancing continuous monitoring with efficiency may be challenging.) Fifth, Council of Europe member states should encourage individuals and legal entities to use ODR mechanisms – in particular, by informing them about the existence of such an option, its reliability and its compatibility with the requirements of the ECHR. (Such public awareness campaigns might also usefully address any public scepticism as regards digital justice.) Sixth, judges, legal practitioners and all those involved in court proceedings should be made aware of the benefits and value of ODR mechanisms and their compliance with the ECHR, as well as with other relevant laws. (It is submitted that judicial training should be practical, as over-reliance on technical staff may impede judicial autonomy.) Seventh, judges and legal practitioners as well as court staff should have access to appropriate training on ODR, delivered by legal and IT professionals. The training should be as practical as possible and tailored to the needs of specific target groups. (Of course, legal education that includes ODR should not replace foundational legal training. In other words, lawyers should be able to reason separately from AI.) Eighth, just as ODR mechanisms should not compromise parties' procedural rights, judges should be able to identify risks that might arise and eliminate them. (Developing 'tech literacy' in a national judiciary may be a slow process.) Ninth, legal education should include modules on the use of IT tools in courts. (The ethical implications of technology-driven ODR could also usefully be a core focus.)*

---

* Training is also the subject of some consideration in the EBRD's document, *Are You Ready for Online Courts?* (2023). There, it is addressed in the context of capacity training – that is, ensuring that stakeholders (eg, judges, court staff, legal professionals) are empowered to use e-justice systems effectively. To develop an effective capacity-building programme, the EBRD suggests, for example, that states should consider the following: assessing the training needs and skill gaps among judges and other stakeholders, identifying key areas of judicial knowledge and/or skills that require additional training, educational development programmes, etc; designing a bespoke, comprehensive training framework for stakeholder groups; offering online/offline training, education, etc; setting up peer-learning and mentoring programmes; ensuring that training is regularly evaluated/updated to allow for changing needs and technology; and developing a store of resources for continued learning and support. Among the benefits of taking such measures, the EBRD suggests, are greater knowledge/skills among stakeholders regarding e-justice systems; better court performance and resolution rates; more consistent application of e-justice laws; and stakeholders that are empowered to leverage the benefits of e-justice.

Key learnings

- *Build trust through fairness and transparency.* ODR systems must uphold fair trial principles. Transparency in decision making, particularly with AI involvement, is crucial to fostering public trust. That said, excessive transparency may expose sensitive data and create security vulnerabilities.
- *Make ODR accessible to all.* ODR should enhance access to justice rather than create new barriers. Caution is required in this regard. Efforts to make ODR universally accessible could diminish its efficiency and increase costs.
- *Ensure that digital disputes meet court standards.* ODR should align with conventional court procedures. However, unduly strict adherence to conventional court procedures may reduce the very flexibility that makes ODR attractive.
- *Prevent identity fraud with secure verification.* Strong authentication mechanisms, such as digital certificates, are essential to prevent fraud and maintain the integrity of ODR proceedings. That said, unduly stringent identity verification requirements may create new barriers to access.
- *Disclose and justify automated decisions.* AI and automated decision making in ODR must be disclosed and users should have a way to challenge outcomes. Of course, full disclosure of automated decision-making processes may not always be feasible due, for example, to proprietary algorithms. Additionally, excessive human oversight could undermine the efficiency benefits of automation.
- *Protect user data with strong cybersecurity.* ODR platforms must implement privacy by design principles, comply with data protection laws and prevent unauthorised access. Stronger cybersecurity measures may, however, increase costs and complexity, potentially making ODR systems less user-friendly.
- *Ensure that ODR decisions are legally enforceable.* ODR rulings should be legally binding.
- *Provide human oversight and the right to a hearing.* Purely automated decisions should always be reviewed by a human judge. Additionally, parties should retain the right to an oral hearing at some stage of the adjudicative process. By way of counterpoint, mandating human oversight and oral hearings in every case could conceivably erode the efficiency gains of ODR.
- *Continuously improve ODR with expert input.* ODR platforms must undergo rigorous usability testing and continuous monitoring for efficiency and fairness. Involving legal professionals and IT experts

should ensure ongoing improvements. Care is required in this regard: overreliance on legal and technology experts for system improvements may yield a framework that overlooks everyday user needs.

- *Educate the public and train legal professionals.* Public awareness campaigns should inform users about their rights and options when it comes to ODR. Additionally, legal education should cover digital lawyering skills to prepare professionals for the world of ODR.

16. Two European charters

Courts must weigh a variety of legal, technical, practical, and ethical considerations as they evaluate the potential for ODR in their jurisdictions. Those considerations range from technology essentials (customisable off-the-shelf or in-house cloud-based products that meet the court's requirements for integration and security) to implications to the court's mandate to provide access to justice and procedural fairness.

Joint Technology Committee[208]

Platforms should be designed to be transparent and accountable to all ... They should be transparent in their use of artificial intelligence and provide the manner of its use in a non-technical language. They should clearly disclose their funding structure, affiliations, privacy and security measures that have been adopted while designing the platforms.

NITI Aayog[209]

Improving ODR: 10 key lessons

- Prioritise fundamental rights.
- Ensure transparency and fairness in AI decision making.
- Design AI to avoid bias and discrimination.
- Maintain user autonomy and access to courts.
- Develop a multidisciplinary approach.
- Implement strong security and data protection measures.
- Expand ODR beyond low-value disputes with caution.
- Allow legal professionals to override AI decisions.
- Foster digital literacy and public engagement.
- Assess AI's role in ODR on a case-by-case basis.

The integration of AI into ODR raises fundamental questions about accountability, fairness and transparency in automated decision making. The European Ethical Charter on the Use of AI (2018) and the Framework Convention on AI and Human Rights (2024) provide guidance on these questions, offering ethical and legal frameworks that help to ensure that AI-driven ODR systems respect fundamental rights.

1. European Ethical Charter on Use of AI in Judicial Systems and Their Environment (2018)

In 2018, the European Commission for the Efficiency of Justice (CEPEJ), acting under the auspices of the Council of Europe, adopted the European Ethical Charter on the Use of AI in Judicial Systems and Their Environment.[210] The growing intersection of AI and ODR warrants a look at the charter's guiding principles. These principles, along with observations from an accompanying study on AI and ODR, offer valuable insights into the ethical deployment of AI in the legal context. The charter rests on five key principles:

- *Respect for fundamental rights:* The design and implementation of AI tools and services must be compatible with fundamental rights.
- *Non-discrimination:* The development or intensification of any discrimination between individuals or groups of individuals must be prevented.
- *Quality and security:* With regard to the processing of judicial decisions and data, certified sources and intangible data with models conceived in a multi-disciplinary manner (and in a secure technological environment) must be used.
- *Transparency, impartiality and fairness:* Data processing methods must be made accessible and understandable, and external audits authorised.
- *'Under user control':* A prescriptive approach must be avoided and it must be ensured that users are informed actors in control of their choices.

Each of these principles is supplemented by more detailed provisions which are considered below.

1. Respect for fundamental rights

The design and implementation of AI tools and services are compatible with fundamental rights.

A number of supplementary provisions are made in this regard.

First, the processing of judicial decisions and data must serve clear purposes, in full compliance with the fundamental rights guaranteed by, for example, the ECHR. (Of course, by insisting on predefined purposes, the potential for useful exploratory research might be unduly constrained.)

Second, when AI tools are used to resolve a dispute or as a tool to assist in judicial decision making or to give guidance to the public, they must not undermine the guarantees of the right of access to the judge and the right to a fair trial.

Third, AI tools should be used with due respect for the principles of the rule of law and judicial independence. (This is perhaps one of the key concerns that arises as regards AI – namely, that judicial independence and impartiality could be compromised by algorithmic bias or opaque decision making.)

Fourth, preference should be given to ethical-by-design or human rights-by-design approaches. This means that right from the design and learning phases, rules prohibiting direct or indirect violations of fundamental rights are fully integrated. (A question perhaps arises as to whether such a design approach may unduly impede innovation.)

2. Non-discrimination

The development or intensification of any discrimination between individuals or groups of individuals must be prevented.

A number of supplementary provisions are made in this regard.

First, stakeholders must ensure that processing methods do not reproduce or aggravate such discrimination. (All due caution should of course be observed; however, a question perhaps arises as to whether undue caution could impede innovation. A tricky balance must be struck in this regard.)

Second, particular care must be taken in both the development and deployment phases, especially when the processing involves sensitive data. (Again, a challenging balance act arises in this regard if data privacy is to be preserved but lawful and effective use of data is not unduly to be impeded.)

Third, when such discrimination has been identified, consideration must be given to corrective measures to limit or, if possible, neutralise these risks, as well as to raise awareness among stakeholders. (To be guarded against is the potential for overcorrection and hence the substitution of human error for algorithmic error.)

Fourth, the use of ML and multidisciplinary scientific analyses to combat discrimination should be encouraged. (Attention should also be given to the deeper social and structural roots of discrimination, rather than merely deploying technical fixes in this regard.)

3. Quality and security

With regard to the processing of judicial decisions and data, certified sources and models conceived in a multi-disciplinary manner (and in a secure technological environment) must be used.

A number of supplementary provisions are made in this regard.

First, designers of ML models should be able to draw widely on the expertise of the relevant legal profession and the social sciences. (Such an interdisciplinary approach should enrich model design; however, it might conceivably also complicate the design process unduly.)

Second, ethical safeguards should be constantly shared by project teams and enhanced by reference to feedback. (Adopting such a continuous approach could be resource intensive and potentially even confusing.)

Third, data based on judicial decisions should come from certified sources and not be changed in any way until used by the learning mechanism. (A question perhaps arises as to whether reliance solely on certified sources might unduly limit the diversity of inputted data.)

Fourth, the whole process should be traceable to ensure that no modification has occurred to alter the content or meaning of the processed decision.

Fifth, the models and algorithms created must also be able to be stored and executed in secure environments. (Though an ostensibly sensible measure, the cost of operating rigorously secure environments may impose an exclusionary cost on smaller market participants.)

4. Transparency, impartiality and fairness

Data processing methods must be made accessible and understandable, and external audits authorised.

A number of supplementary provisions are made in this regard. Key among them is that a balance must be struck between the intellectual property of certain processing methods and the need for transparency when tools are used that may have legal consequences or may significantly affect people's lives. (One option is complete technical transparency – for example, open-source code and documentation.* However, this may be restricted by the protection of trade secrets. An alternative possible approach is to explain in clear and familiar language, for example, the nature of the services offered and the risks of error.)

---

* The European Ethical Charter on the Use of Artificial Intelligence in Judicial Systems and Their Environment (2018), which is considered at some length in Chapter 16, contains a glossary which defines 'open source software' as "[s]oftware for which the source code is available to everyone. The software can therefore be freely used, modified and redistributed".

The authors of the charter suggest that independent persons could be tasked with certifying and auditing processing methods or providing advice, and that public authorities could grant temporary certification. (A question perhaps arises as to whether a process of private – that is, non-state – certification, if that is what is contemplated in this regard, could lead to an inconsistency of standards.)

5. *'Under user control'*

A prescriptive approach must be avoided and users must be informed and in control of their choices.

A number of supplementary provisions are made in this regard.

First, user autonomy should be increased through use of AI tools and services.

Second, professionals in the justice system should, at any moment, be able to review decisions and the data used to produce them and should not necessarily be bound by them. (A question perhaps arises as to whether such an approach could rob ODR of the very efficiencies that make it attractive to begin with.)

Third, the user should be informed in clear and understandable language of whether the solutions offered by the AI tools are binding, the different options available to them and their right to legal advice and to access a court.

Fourth, the user must also be clearly informed of any prior processing of a case by AI before or during a judicial process and have the right to object, so that their case can be heard directly by a court. (This appears to exclude the potential for mandatory ODR, which has been touted as one of the reasons for the success of Utah's ODR scheme.)

Fifth, generally, when any AI-based information system is implemented, there should be computer literacy programmes for users. (Offering comprehensive computer literacy programmes to all may prove an unsustainable cost for some jurisdictions.)

A study appended to the charter provides deeper insights into AI's impact on judicial systems. These include the following. First, bias and reasoning limitations in AI models could negatively impact judicial reasoning and the rule of law. (That said, AI also has the potential to reduce the human bias that can present in human judicial decision making.) Second, AI may undermine judicial discretion, replacing individualised rulings with standardised, statistical calculations. (On the other hand, standardisation should enhance predictability and fairness and reduce the risk of inconsistent rulings.) Third, AI's impact on fundamental legal rights must be carefully managed – particularly in criminal law, where AI risks undermining the principle of individualised sentencing. (A careful balance falls to be struck in this regard: AI can assist in ensuring proportionality and consistency by analysing and applying past rulings.) Fourth, AI should enhance, rather than replace, human judicial decision making. (That said, as the example of China shows, AI can validly lead to reduced reliance on human decision making in instances where it may introduce unnecessary delay or error.) Fifth, broad public engagement is necessary to fully assess AI's role in justice systems and develop appropriate ethical frameworks. (Again, there is perhaps a balance to be struck in this regard. While consultation is important, timely implementation is also important if legal systems are not to fall behind as regards the rollout of technological advancements.)

2. The Framework Convention on AI and Human Rights (2024)

The Framework Convention on AI and Human Rights (2024) aims to ensure that activities within the lifecycle of AI systems are fully consistent with human rights, democracy and the rule of law. The European Union, the United States and the United Kingdom are among the signatories to the convention. (It is questionable how keen an adherent the United States now is, given the observations of Vice President JD Vance at the Paris AI Summit in February 2025 to the effect that "excessive regulation of the AI sector could kill a transformative industry just as it's taking off, and we'll make every effort to encourage pro-growth AI policies").[211]

Among the obligations imposed on parties to the convention are the following. Parties must:

- ensure that activities within the lifecycle of AI systems are consistent with their obligations to protect human rights;
- seek to ensure that AI systems do not undermine the integrity, independence and effectiveness of democratic institutions and processes;
- adopt or maintain measures to respect human dignity and individual autonomy in relation to activities within the lifecycle of AI systems;
- ensure that adequate transparency and oversight requirements tailored to the specific contexts and risks are in place in respect of activities within the lifecycle of AI systems;
- ensure that there is accountability and responsibility for adverse impacts on human rights, democracy and the rule of law resulting from activities within the lifecycle of AI systems;
- ensure that activities within the lifecycle of AI systems respect equality;
- ensure that, with regard to activities within the lifecycle of AI systems, the privacy rights of individuals and their personal data are protected;
- promote the reliability of AI systems and trust in their outputs;
- enable, as appropriate, the establishment of controlled environments for developing, experimenting with and testing AI systems under the supervision of competent authorities;

- ensure the availability of accessible and effective remedies for violations of human rights resulting from the activities within the lifecycle of AI systems;
- adopt or maintain measures for the identification, assessment, prevention and mitigation of risks posed by AI systems by considering actual and potential impacts to human rights, democracy and the rule of law;
- implement the convention without discrimination on any ground;
- take due account of any specific needs and vulnerabilities in relation to respect for the rights of persons with disabilities and of children;
- ensure that important questions concerning AI systems are duly considered through public discussion and multistakeholder consultation in light of social, economic, legal, ethical, environmental and other relevant implications; and
- encourage and promote adequate digital literacy and digital skills for all segments of the population.

To some extent, the requirements of the Framework Convention are very much of the 'motherhood and apple pie' variety – that is, no one could sensibly object to them. But the practical implementation of the convention's requirements seems likely to present with challenges:

- *Protection of human rights:* Ensuring that AI-driven dispute resolution remains accessible to all is a challenge, because people with limited digital literacy or internet access may struggle to engage properly.
- *Ensuring the integrity of democratic processes and respect for the rule of law:* The evolving nature of AI technology creates an ongoing regulatory challenge. (This is because legal frameworks may struggle to keep pace with technological developments.)
- *Human dignity and individual autonomy:* Ensuring that AI-driven ODR respects human dignity may prove challenging if users lack visibility as to how AI reaches decisions. (Reliance on AI may lead unavoidably to a more impersonal approach to dispute resolution.)
- *Transparency and oversight:* The opacity of AI decision making can create obstacles to transparency. (Even when transparency mechanisms are in place, explaining AI-driven outcomes in a comprehensible manner may remain challenging.)
- *Accountability and responsibility:* Assigning accountability for AI-driven decisions may be challenging. (This will become more challenging if private AI developers resist assuming liability for possible harms.)
- *Equality and non-discrimination:* Preventing bias in AI-driven ODR is challenging, as bias can emerge in the training data. (Ensuring the accessibility of ODR to the digitally challenged may also be difficult.)

- *Privacy and personal data protection:* Protecting personal data may present significant security challenges. (Ensuring compliance with different privacy laws across different jurisdictions is also likely to be challenging.)
- *Reliability:* Ensuring the reliability of AI-driven ODR systems may require addressing the potential for inaccuracies or inconsistencies in algorithmic predictions. (Implementing testing and validation processes measures at scale could be resource intensive.)
- *Safe innovation:* Promoting safe innovation in AI-reliant ODR may be challenging, not least as regulatory approval processes may be frustratingly slow, to the point of delaying the deployment of new technology.
- *Remedies:* Designing appeal avenues that do not undermine an ODR platform's efficiency could be complex, not least in terms of balancing swiftness of process with procedural fairness.
- *Risk and impact management framework:* Anticipating the wider legal and societal impacts of AI-driven dispute resolution could prove difficult. This is because unintended consequences may only emerge after widespread rollout.
- *Non-discrimination:* Ensuring that ODR platforms function properly across different cultural and linguistic scenarios may be challenging. (Even with safeguards in place, automated decision making can still produce unintended disparities of treatment.)
- *Public consultation:* Arranging for meaningful public consultation on AI-informed ODR may present challenges. (This is because the complexity of AI governance may make it difficult for the public to understand and engage with the detail.)
- *Digital literacy and skills:* Promoting digital literacy may prove challenging, given society-wide disparities in education levels and access to technology.

Charter checklist

This checklist reduces the above-considered obligations of the Ethical Charter and the Framework Convention to a series of questions to which the answers of a compliant party should be 'yes'. A question arises as to whether the level of governance captured by this checklist is entirely appropriate for a still-nascent AI industry.

European Ethical Charter on the Use of AI in Judicial Systems

Fundamental rights

- Is design and implementation of AI tools and services compatible with fundamental rights?
- Does processing serve clear purposes, in full compliance with fundamental rights?
- Do AI tools used to resolve disputes, to assist judicial decision making or to give public guidance avoid undermining the right of access to a judge and the right to a fair trial?
- Are AI tools used with due respect for the principles of the rule of law and judicial independence?
- Has preference been given to ethical-by-design or human rights-by-design approaches?

Non-discrimination

- Has the development or intensification of any discrimination been prevented?
- Have stakeholders ensured that processing does not reproduce or aggravate discrimination?
- Has care been taken in the development and deployment phases, especially when processing sensitive data?
- If discrimination has been identified, has consideration been given to corrective measures?
- Has use of ML and multidisciplinary scientific analyses to combat discrimination been encouraged?

Quality and security

- When it comes to processing judicial decisions and data, have certified sources and intangible data with models conceived in a multi-disciplinary manner (and in a secure technological environment) been used?
- Can ML model designers draw widely on the expertise of relevant justice system and social science professionals?

- Are ethical safeguards constantly shared by project teams and enhanced by reference to feedback?
- Does data based on judicial decisions come from certified sources and remain unmodified until used by the learning mechanism?
- Is the process traceable to ensure that no modification occurs to alter the content or meaning of the processed decision?
- Can models and algorithms be stored and executed in secure environments?

Fairness, impartiality and transparency

- Are data processing methods accessible and understandable, and are external audits authorised?
- Is a balance struck between the intellectual property of certain processing methods and the need for transparency when tools are used that may have legal consequences or significantly affect people's lives?

'Under user control'

- Has a prescriptive approach been avoided and are users informed and in control of their choices?
- Is user autonomy increased through the use of AI tools and services?
- Can professionals in the justice system review judicial decisions and the data used to produce them at any moment, and are they not necessarily bound by such decisions?
- Is the user informed in clear, understandable language as to whether solutions offered by AI tools are binding, the different options available to them and their right to legal advice and to access a court?
- Is the user clearly informed of any prior processing of a case by AI so that they have the right to object and have their case heard directly by a court?
- Are there computer literacy programmes available to all?

Framework Convention on AI and Human Rights (2024)

Is it ensured that ...

- ... activities within the lifecycle of AI systems are consistent with their obligations to protect human rights?
- ... AI systems do not undermine the integrity, independence and effectiveness of democratic institutions and processes?
- ... the adoption or maintenance of measures to respect human dignity and individual autonomy in relation to activities will take place within the lifecycle of AI systems?
- ... adequate transparency and oversight requirements tailored to the

specific contexts and risks are in place in respect of activities within the lifecycle of AI systems?

- ... there is accountability and responsibility for adverse impacts on human rights, democracy and the rule of law resulting from activities within the lifecycle of AI systems?
- ... activities within the lifecycle of AI systems respect equality?
- ... with regard to activities within the lifecycle of AI systems, the privacy rights of individuals and their personal data are protected?
- ... the reliability of AI systems and trust in their outputs are promoted?
- ... the establishment of controlled environments for developing, experimenting with and testing AI systems under the supervision of competent authorities is possible?
- ... accessible and effective remedies are available for violations of human rights within the lifecycle of AI systems?
- ... measures are adopted or maintained for the identification, assessment, prevention and mitigation of risks posed by AI systems by considering actual and potential impacts on human rights, democracy and the rule of law?
- ... the Framework Convention is implemented without discrimination on any ground?
- ... due account is taken of any specific needs and vulnerabilities in relation to respect for the rights of persons with disabilities and of children?
- ... important questions concerning AI systems are duly considered through public discussion and multistakeholder consultation in light of social, economic, legal, ethical, environmental and other relevant implications?
- ... adequate digital literacy and digital skills for all segments of the population are encouraged and promoted?

Key learnings

- *Prioritise human rights compliance.* ODR platforms must be designed to protect fundamental rights. Ethical-by-design and human rights-by-design approaches should be integrated from the start.
- *Eliminate algorithmic bias.* ODR designers should seek to ensure that AI-informed decisions do not disproportionately impact specific groups. A careful balance needs to be struck in this regard to guard against overcorrection.
- *Enhance explainability and transparency.* An ODR platform should be transparent, with clear explanations of how decisions are made. That said, unless dealing with an open-source AI model, proprietary concerns may impede the fullest transparency.

- *Preserve confidentiality and data privacy.* AI models should rely on certified sources, operate in secure environments and be traceable. (Care should also be taken to ensure that datasets continue to be sufficiently diverse.)
- *Ensure user control.* ODR users must retain control, be fully informed and have access to legal advice. Excessive user control could diminish the efficiency of an ODR platform.
- *Cultivate trust through frequent audits.* ODR platforms should be regularly audited by independent entities for legal and ethics compliance. That said, if audits are done by independent entities, this could lead to inconsistent standards being applied.
- *Balance innovation with regulation.* AI-informed ODR should seek to protect human rights while allowing for technological innovation. A careful balance must be struck in this regard, with the greater weight falling to human rights protection.
- *Develop a vigorous appeals mechanism.* ODR platforms must offer a clear, effective means of appeal. That said, an unduly extensive appeals system has the potential to undermine ODR efficiency.
- *Ensure AI is accurate and reliable.* AI models should be continuously tested. That said, such testing comes at a cost that may not be sustainable in some jurisdictions.
- *Promote digital literacy and access.* ODR platforms and providers should seek to cultivate digital literacy. Again, such programmes come at a cost that may not be sustainable in some jurisdictions.

17. ODR and people in need

ODR eliminates many of the obvious physical barriers and can also mitigate many of the financial barriers that limit individuals from accessing court processes. The "level playing field" of ODR can improve fairness. Together, these benefits improve disputant satisfaction with the process.

Joint Technology Committee[212]

The potential benefits of ODR do not have to be limited to the economically advantaged individuals from urban areas, with easy access to technology, but also [need to be accessible] to the marginalised and less privileged. It is also necessary that ODR platforms account for the cultural diversity of its users ... [T]he technology should not be allowed to become a barrier for one or both the parties to present their case.

NITI Aayog[213]

Improving ODR: 10 key lessons

- Design for mobile accessibility.
- Address scepticism by prioritising fairness.
- Empower self-represented litigants.
- Prioritise fair outcomes over speed.
- Respect the importance of low-value claims.
- Make complex cases work online.
- Balance transparency and privacy.
- Remove barriers to accessibility.
- Guide users without restricting choice
- Refine ODR through responsible data usage.

1. ODR and low-income people

Judges and other lawyers are well educated and nowadays often technology-savvy individuals, to whom a more virtual world may present a lesser challenge than for others.[214] Low-income individuals often will not have the same advantages.* A Buzzfeed article, published in 2020, highlighted the difficulties that lower-income people encountered as a result of court closures during the COVID-19 pandemic (see Figure 41), in effect pointing to the challenges that they face if and as courts move online.[215] Challenges notwithstanding, in Florida's Miami-Dade County, for example, during the COVID-19 pandemic, callers were encouraged to sign up for e-filing, were sent hearing reminders by email as well as regular mail and eventually were sent reminders by text message.

At the Los Angeles Superior Court, efforts were made to make its website more user-friendly, a self-help phone line was available on weekdays and a series of online programmes were offered that sought to assist self-represented disputants in knowing what to do.** Both Michigan and Ohio established internet platforms for dealing with minor litigation, such as traffic citations. In Michigan, "forward-thinking court leaders"[216] have been credited for the state's pioneering position when it comes to ODR – pointing to the fact that court support for ODR considerably assists in ODR rollout.

2. The NLADA report on *Ensuring Equity in Efficiency*

In the United States, the National Legal Aid & Defender Association (NLADA) is the nation's oldest and largest non-profit association focused on excellence in the delivery of legal services to those who cannot afford legal advice. More particularly, NLADA acts as an advocate for equal justice practitioners, providing them with guidance, information, training and technical assistance. In 2021, NLADA produced a report entitled *Ensuring Equity in Efficiency: The Civil Legal Aid Community's Views of Online Dispute Resolution.*[217] The report drew on the insights of legal aid practitioners, legal aid clients and legal technologists. The report is focused on the United States. However, it is of more general interest because it offers a view of ODR through the prism of persons who are, or who work to assist, underprivileged individuals.

NLADA found that in almost every interview it conducted, the initial response

---

* How best (or better) to serve lower-income people in the courts system is a challenging issue. As one learned commentator had observed, policymakers have largely focused on supplying unrepresented parties with lawyers; and little attention has been paid to demand-side reform to or to changing the rules that structure litigation processes and govern the resolution of disputes involving the unrepresented poor (Steinberg, 806).

** The need to process cases remotely during the COVID-19 pandemic was a prompt for small claims ODR in Los Angeles (and for its expanded use post-2020 expanding the use of Moria, a proprietary ODR platform, in child custody and visitation issues). In the small claims programme, parties can use electronic devices – for example, smartphones – to share documents and liaise at convenient times. Parties are also guided through questions about their cases. If litigants settle, the ODR system provides the forms needed to 'close' the deal and file the agreement with the court (*id*, 59).

Figure 41: Some problems encountered by courts moving online

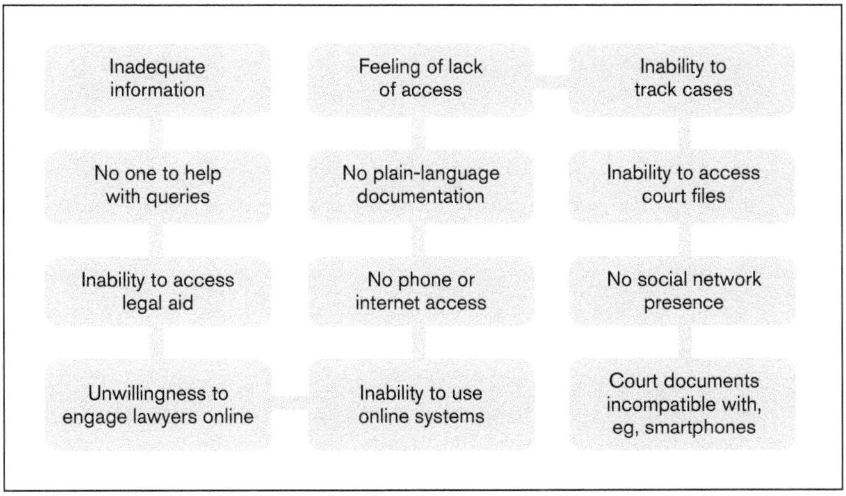

to ODR was one of great mistrust. One client considered that offering any form of assistance through the Internet was bound to be problematic. Legal aid providers expressed concerns as to equity versus efficiency, a worsening of existing power imbalances and doubts as to the true motivating factors for ODR. However, some of this mistrust may not be entirely ODR specific but more reflective of a society-wide mistrust[218] in the United States of legal institutions and a sense that when it comes to state actors addressing systemic social issues, there is a level of doubt about whether government actions will produce desired outcomes.[219]

A number of NLADA's interviewees were dubious as to who ODR was intended primarily to benefit. In this regard, the true motivations of government, technology vendors and even the courts were questioned. When it came to government, one commentator observed that she did not think that a shortage of judges would be cured by enabling disputants to litigate through the night.[220] However, at first glance, empowering disputants to litigate online at a time that best suits them seems to be a user-friendly development.

NLADA found that ODR seemed to cause particular disquiet among advocates for equal justice. To them, ODR was being touted as a benefit to their clients in ways they found dubious. So, for example, advocates did not consider that clients would find an especial convenience in not attending a physical court building. Notably, however, the California Access to Justice Commission has stated in a study on enhancing rural access to justice, published in 2020, that "legal technology can play an especially significant role in increasing access to justice. This is because legal tech can alleviate the need to travel to an attorney's office or even to the courthouse".[221] In other words, it very clearly sees the elimination of the necessity to attend in-person hearings as a key attraction of ODR.

Among the people polled, NLADA found a sense that the greatest beneficiaries of ODR were the courts themselves, and that the discussion of ODR was not sufficiently candid in this regard.[222] In truth, the benefits seem (to use a colloquialism) to cut both ways. As Lord Dyson, a senior English judge, notes in his foreword to the Susskind Report: "At a time of major pressure on public spending and high legal costs, ODR offers a major opportunity to help many people for whom public funding to resolve disputes is not available, or for whom legal costs are prohibitive." So, yes, ODR enables the courts to help more people, though in a manner consistent with the need for limits on government expenditure.[223] In fact, NLADA found that when existing problems in the courts system were highlighted with interviewees, they tended to become less negative about ODR.

Third, there was a sense that the point of ODR was "to ... devote fewer resources to already vulnerable and underserved clients".[224] This is a concern that merits the most serious consideration. It perhaps finds an answer in the observation in the Susskind Report (written in the UK context, but it is hard to see that this does not hold true more generally) that:

> *ODR holds enormous potential to bring two great benefits to our justice system: a lower cost court system and an increase in access to justice. In appropriate cases, we are therefore saying that ODR can deliver more affordable and accessible dispute resolution.*[225]

Returning to the NLADA data, many advocates – even those who acknowledged the capacity of ODR to offer convenience and efficiency – were dubious as to whether it could deliver equitable outcomes and whether there was enough focus on equitable outcomes. There was even some concern that ODR could make existing inequities worse – for example, that for a self-represented disputant to deal with an attorney for an opposing party (if the opposing party had an attorney – and one aim of ODR is to reduce reliance on attorneys) could be an even worse experience online than in real life, especially if the attorney was more familiar with navigating the ODR system.

While the legal aid advocates who were interviewed by NLADA were not opposed to the idea of ODR focusing on high-volume, low-value cases, there was some concern that lower-value claims would be perceived not to matter as much as higher-value claims. However, as Lord (then Lord Justice) Briggs has observed, writing in the English context:

> *It is ... because claims are of such importance to ordinary disputants, and currently cannot be litigated at proportionate cost using lawyers, or satisfactorily without representation, that the large effort and investment to create an Online Court [in England and Wales was] ... being made.*[226]

The same point can be made of ODR generally.

One area of concern that came up in almost every conversation conducted by NLADA was that of data privacy. As has been seen in previous chapters, this is a concern that is addressed (in the United States) by the NCTDR in its Online Dispute Resolution Standards and (in Europe) by the Council of Europe's Guidelines of the Committee of Ministers of the Council of Europe on Online Dispute Resolution Mechanisms in Civil and Administrative Court Proceedings. So, it is a concern of which law and policymakers are well aware.

NLADA raised a variety of questions concerning accessibility, assistance and autonomy, including the following:

- Who has the technology to access ODR (and who does not)?
- How serious a problem is the digital divide?
- Having accessed an ODR platform, how accessible does it thereafter continue to be?
- Does ODR work with whatever existing technology a person may have to hand?
- Is ODR accessible to people with disabilities?

In addressing these issues, the following points cropped up in the conversations between NLADA and its interviewees.

Consistent with publicly available data and estimates, NLADA's interviewees flagged concerns about access to technology among Black, Hispanic, limited-education, low-education, Native American and rural households. But even urban legal aid advocates pointed to the absence of high-speed Internet in some urban areas. On balance, NLADA's view was that while concerns about technology ought not to be dismissed, requiring people to attend in court can also pose significant barriers for some individuals.

Many of those whom NLADA interviewed expressed concerns about how ODR would function as regards people with cognitive impairments, disabilities, literacy issues and a non-native command of English. One interviewee even suggested that an ODR system should be designed to screen out those for whom it was unsuitable. However, there were competing views: one legal advocate was opposed to what she styled "legal paternalism"; and one client with a disability said: "Let me try and fail, you know? Don't tell me up front and not even let me try. Because I'm not my disability."[227] This last view seems to have been the dominant one. NLADA observes in this regard that although legal aid advocates had some concerns about how ODR might not suit some clients, those clients with whom it spoke expressed a "universal desire"[228] to make their own choices and not be automatically screened out.

Advocates accepted that ODR offered the potential for increased access, reduced defaults through inability to attend at court and overall afforded a more convenient and less traumatic experience. Notably, a significant number of child and family law issues were posited as being appropriate for ODR, such as child custody, child support (maintenance), child visitation and divorce mediation. Small claims, traffic tickets and bench warrants were also mentioned. As with the final Briggs Report, housing law was generally perceived as ill-suited for ODR, though at least one advocate departed from the consensus, suggesting that, for example, deposit-related disputes would be suitable for ODR. On a related note, another advocate noted that most landlord-tenant cases ended up being settled via mediation or negotiation, suggesting that there might be a role for ODR at the initial stage of such disputes (with the potential for a dispute to be referred to court if and when appropriate). Various advocates considered that ODR could generally be useful at the 'pre-filing' stage – that is, before litigation was commenced, with a view to arriving at a settlement (and the potential for a reference to court in the event that efforts at settlement failed). Ultimately, NLADA noted that while interviewees identified various concerns with ODR, they were receptive to the notion that ODR could reshape the civil legal system in ways that could benefit low-income disputants.

3. NLADA on ODR platform design

When it came to designing ODR platforms that would be accessible and inclusive and increase the prospects of equitable outcomes for low-income clients, NLADA suggested that the following guiding principles should apply:

- *"Be Transparent."*[229] NLADA recommended that there be transparency in terms of allowing public access, ensuring technological transparency (eg, through the use of open source software),* communicating openly to consumers what an ODR platform could and could not do, using plain language and making the choice as to whether to use the system a matter for user election (ie, no automatic screening out).[230] (By way of counterpoint, undue transparency could yield security difficulties.)
- *"[Be] Client-Centered."*[231] What NLADA means in this regard is that ODR developers should be able to identify the clients who would use the platform, with an eye towards prospective vulnerable users, and ensure that it works for all. In this regard, NLADA notes, the need for mobile phone access was emphasised to it "[o]ver and over again".[232]
- *"Create Multiple and Easy to Use Off Ramps."*[233] NLADA suggested that it should be easy for people to opt out of ODR; and that when a user does choose to opt out, there should be no penalty and no costs, and their personal data should be removed within clearly defined periods. (By way

* The term 'open-source software' is defined in the European Ethical Charter on the Use of AI In Judicial Systems and Their Environment (CEPEJ, 2018), 74, as "[s]oftware for which the source code is available to everyone ... [and thus which can be] freely used, modified, and redistributed".

of counterpoint, allowing users to opt out too easily could conceivably lead to abuses of the ODR system.)

- *"Get Good Data, But Not Too Much."*[234] NLADA highlighted the need for data privacy and then suggested various mechanisms that are possibly specific to the United States and not of equal concern in, for example, the European Union, which benefits from quite stringent data protection legislation in the form of the GDPR. (Excessive privacy standards, if there are such things, could impede platform rollout.)

Key learnings

- *Design for mobile accessibility.* ODR must be designed to accommodate users without high-speed internet or computers – though it may be that reliance on mobile devices could restrict functionality.
- *Address scepticism by prioritising fairness.* In a bid to convince sceptics, ODR systems should emphasise equity, procedural safeguards and user education.
- *Empower self-represented litigants.* ODR can empower users with guided workflows, AI-driven assistance and mediation options. That said, self-representation seems unlikely to replace lawyer expertise, potentially leaving users vulnerable if they face represented parties.
- *Prioritise fair outcomes over speed.* Efficiency should not come at the cost of fairness.
- *Respect the importance of low-value claims.* ODR should make justice more accessible by providing a cost-effective dispute resolution platform. However, it does potentially sideline those who prefer in-person justice.
- *Make complex cases work online.* Simple cases are ideal for ODR but complex disputes can also be handled with the right design. Over-complex features may make an ODR system challenging to use, thus diminishing accessibility.
- *Balance transparency and privacy.* Excessive disclosure may overwhelm ODR users. Conversely, reducing transparency too much could diminish user trust in ODR.
- *Remove barriers to accessibility.* ODR should integrate, for example, chat tools, translation tools, text-to-speech tools and AI-supported guidance. That said, this may require investment of a level that some states cannot afford.
- *Guide users without restricting choice.* ODR should offer users a guided pathway to help them choose the resolution method best suited to them.

- *Refine ODR through responsible data usage.* Data collection is essential for refining ODR platforms, so limiting data collection unduly could conceivably impede innovation.

18. Domain name dispute resolution

Improving ODR: 10 key lessons

- Aim for accessibility and speed.
- Aim for jurisdictional neutrality.
- Streamline decision making.
- Balance efficiency and fairness when choosing panels.
- Protect legal rights but avoid overreach.
- Use registrars as gatekeepers.
- Apply rigorous timelines but avoid undermining due process.
- Reduce legal barriers but be watchful for the self-represented.
- Maintain transparency through publicity.
- Audit, adapt and improve.

1. The Uniform Dispute Resolution Policy: an ODR success story

The UDRP is one of the great ODR success stories. So, for example, it has been observed that:[235]

> *The UDRP has evolved as a unique means of resolving disputes in a relatively unique context. It has shown itself to be efficient, relatively inexpensive (both in terms of filing fees and in terms of its simplicity), competently administered by its providers and panellists and enforceable as a model for dispute resolution in twenty-first century electronic commerce, there may be nothing closer in form and substance than the UDRP.**

2. The role and operation of the UDRP

The UDRP is operated by ICANN, a non-governmental, non-profit organisation generally accepted as the key player when it comes to designing internet governance policies. (ICANN was formed under the auspices of the US government, which later surrendered its controlling role, only to question in recent years whether it should assume control again given, for example, perceived 'mission creep' on the part of ICANN, as well as perceived ICANN budgetary issues.)[236]

* Not all would agree. Hornle (at 289) suggests that the UDRP has sacrificed due process in the interests of convenience, efficiency and speed.

The key function of ICANN is to coordinate Internet Assigned Numbers Authority functions. Simply put, to reach another person on the Internet, one must enter an address (name or number) into a computer. That address must be unique so that computers know where to find each other. ICANN coordinates these unique identifiers across the world. Absent that coordination, there would not be a single global Internet. A secondary but still important function has been the establishment and operation of the UDRP – a policy which has been used to resolve thousands of disputes over the rights to domain names. The UDRP was initially adopted in 1999; the most recently amended version dates from 2024.

The primary reason that the UDRP was established was to address the problem of cybersquatting – that is, registration of a domain name in a bid to block a trademark owner from accessing the Internet via a website under its own name.[237] Ill-intentioned individuals could readily obtain such domain names because registrars assigned addresses for a flat fee on a first come, first served basis. A variety of (some simple, some sophisticated) cybersquatting abuses were practised, including registration of another person's mark or personal name (either correctly spelled or misspelled) as a domain name (or part of a domain name); and registration of another person's mark other than with a '.com' suffix.[238] In truth, however, trademark owners faced a cybersquatting landscape that one learned commentator has compared to the game of 'Whac-A-Mole', with a new problem arising once a previous one had been solved.[239] The problem was so bad, the same commentator observed, that countering it exceeded the enforcement budgets of many brand owners.

3. *Panavision* and other cybersquatting disputes

Panavision International, LP v Toeppen (1998)[240] offers a good example of the type of cybersquatting issues that prominent businesses faced in the late 1990s. Panavision held registered trademarks to the names 'Panavision' and 'Panaflex' in connection with motion picture camera equipment. Panavision promoted its trademarks through motion picture and television credits and other media advertising. In December 1995, Panavision attempted to register a website on the Internet with the domain name 'panavision.com'. It could not do that, however, because Mr Toeppen had already registered the Panavision domain name. In December 1995, Panavision's counsel sent a letter to Mr Toeppen informing him that Panavision held a trademark in the name 'Panavision' and telling him to halt what Panavision considered to be his objectionable behaviour. Mr Toeppen then offered to settle the dispute if Panavision paid him $13,000 in exchange for the domain name. After Panavision refused Mr Toeppen's demand, he registered Panavision's other trademark with Network Solutions Inc (NSI) as the domain name 'panaflex.com'. Separately, Mr Toeppen had registered domain names for various other companies – including Delta

Airlines, Neiman Marcus and Lufthansa – and over 100 other marks. Panavision alleged claims for dilution of its trademark under the Federal Trademark Dilution Act of 1995. The district court determined that it had personal jurisdiction over Mr Toeppen and granted summary judgment in favour of Panavision on both its federal and state dilution claims. The US Court of Appeals affirmed this decision, holding that Mr Toeppen had engaged in a scheme to register Panavision's trademarks as his domain names on the Internet and then to extort money from Panavision by trading on the value of those names; that he had made commercial use of Panavision's trademarks; and that his conduct diluted those marks.

Panavision and other cybersquatting disputes revealed a number of problems that made national litigation a notably challenging process. These include the following.* First, multi-jurisdictional complexity: different national courts could each assert jurisdiction over the same dispute. Second, parallel legal actions: parties had to initiate multiple lawsuits in different jurisdictions. Third, urgency of resolution: due to the ease and speed of domain name registration, disputes often required swift resolution. Fourth, disproportionate costs: the low cost of registering a domain name contrasted sharply with the potential economic harm caused by wrongful registrations. Fifth, registrar involvement: domain name registration authorities were frequently drawn into legal proceedings due to their role in managing domain registrations. Given these challenges, there was a strong push for an ADR mechanism that would be fast, inexpensive and globally enforceable. And so the UDRP was born.

4. The UDRP process

The UDRP introduced a streamlined administrative procedure for domain name disputes.** The system meets the ends identified in Figure 42. The ODR model adopted by ICANN is particularly appropriate for domain name disputes, for

---

* See generally WIPO, *The Management of Internet Names and Addresses: Intellectual Property Issues* (Final Report of the WIPO Domain Name Process) (WIPO (2)). Among other matters, that report identified (at para 22) domain name registration disputes to present with a number of special characteristics, including the following: "(i) Because a domain name gives rise to a global presence, the dispute may be multijurisdictional in several senses ... (ii) Because of the number of [top level domain names] ... essentially the same dispute may manifest itself in many TLDs ... [requiring] multiple court actions throughout the world. (iii) In view of the ease and speed with which a domain name registration may be obtained ... and the global access to the Internet that is possible, the need to resolve a domain name dispute may ... be urgent ... (iv) A considerable disjunction exists between...the cost of obtaining a domain name registration ... and the cost [of] ... remedying the situation through litigation ... (v) The registration authority has often been joined in domain name disputes because of its role in the technical management of the domain name." As can be seen, it is the need to pursue multiple lawsuits in multiple jurisdictions that, to use a colloquialism, repeatedly 'raised its head' as perhaps the most pressing need for change.

** Before ICANN was established, the leading domain name registrar in the United States was NSI. It had a policy whereby trademark owners could ask it to place a domain name 'on hold' in certain circumstances. Once the domain name was placed on hold, the relevant parties had to settle their dispute through negotiation, arbitration or litigation. One of the flaws of this approach was that disputes continued over a protracted period before a matter was resolved (McMurry, 381). The adoption of the UDRP sought to improve on the NSI policy (*id*).

several reasons. First, geographical distance is eliminated as an issue. Second, it offers a swiftness of resolution that is simply unavailable in the domestic context. Third, it means that many domain name disputes can be resolved based on written submissions alone, eliminating the need for witness testimony or in-person hearings. Fourth, for individuals and businesses that are unfamiliar with legal proceedings, the UDRP reduces complexity and improves accessibility. That said, it is not a perfect system: no injunctive relief is available and no damages are available. So, if one hopes for injunctive relief or damages, "UDRP cases are no substitute for a civil action for trademark infringement, dilution, or cybersquatting [for example]".[241]

Figure 42: Objectives of the UDRP

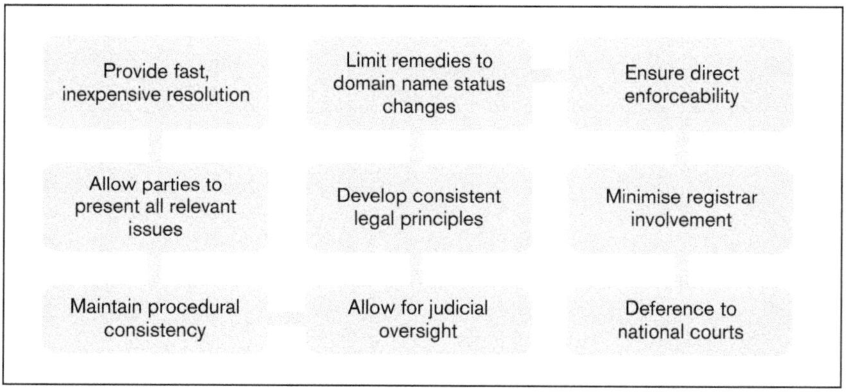

The UDRP is considered in some detail later below. However, to understand the UDRP, it is first necessary to understand the role of registrants and registrars. A domain name registrant is an individual or entity that registers a domain name. Upon registration of a domain name, a registrant enters into a contract with a registrar. The contract describes the terms under which the registrar agrees to register and maintain the requested name. After registration, registrants manage their domain name settings through their registrar. A registrant has various rights, including the right to defend itself if its domain name registration is disputed or challenged under the UDRP or the Uniform Rapid Suspension (URS) system (on which, more below). These procedures seek to provide trademark holders with a dispute resolution process for cybersquatting and other types of trademark-related abusive domain name registrations. There are five key points that every domain name registrant should know:

- The UDRP and URS systems are administrative proceedings that a trademark holder may initiate against a domain name registrant when seeking either to recover or cancel an allegedly cyber-squatted domain name or to have an allegedly cybersquatted domain name suspended.

- The burden of proof in the complaint process is on the filing party. There are three criteria that it must establish to succeed: its trademark rights and use of the trademark; that the domain name subject to the UDRP or URS is identical or confusingly similar to the trademark; and that the domain name was registered and has been used in bad faith and the registrant has no rights to or legitimate interests in the domain name.
- The dispute resolution process is very swift: a registrant will be notified of the commencement of the proceedings and the timing for a response; there is limited time to respond (20 days for the UDRP and 14 days for the URS, subject to an extension in some circumstances); there is no in-person hearing, absent exceptional circumstances; and the proceedings proceed to judgment even if a disputant does not manage to get its side of matters on record.
- Legal input is not needed to respond to a UDRP or URS complaint, but it may be advisable to engage a suitably qualified lawyer.
- If the complainant prevails, the UDRP panel will order the offending domain name to be cancelled or transferred to the complainant. (In a URS filing, the panel will order the domain name to be suspended for the remainder of its registration period.)

Briefly put, the UDRP process unfolds as follows. First, the registrant submits to mandatory administrative proceedings if the third party makes a valid complaint. Second, the complainant selects an ICANN-approved provider to administer proceedings. Third, the circumstances in Figure 43 are among those that may indicate bad-faith registration. Fourth, the circumstances in Figure 44 are among those that may indicate good-faith registration. Fifth, the cost of the resolution process depends ultimately on two factors: the number of domains at issue in the dispute and the number of panellists (arbitrators), be it one or three. In the case of a single-member panel, the full fee is due from the complainant. If a three-member panel is requested by the complainant, the full fee is again due from the complainant. In the case of a three-member panel requested by the respondent, the fee is split equally between the complainant and the respondent. Sixth, ICANN does not participate and disclaims liability for the process. Seventh, remedies are limited to cancellation or transfer to a complainant of a domain name. (Damages or injunctive relief cannot be ordered.) Eighth, save in exceptional circumstances, decisions are published on the Internet. Ninth, the disputants may proceed to judicial proceedings before the administrative process commences or after it completes. (In fact, matters tend not to proceed to court.)

Figure 43: Some indicators of bad faith by registrant

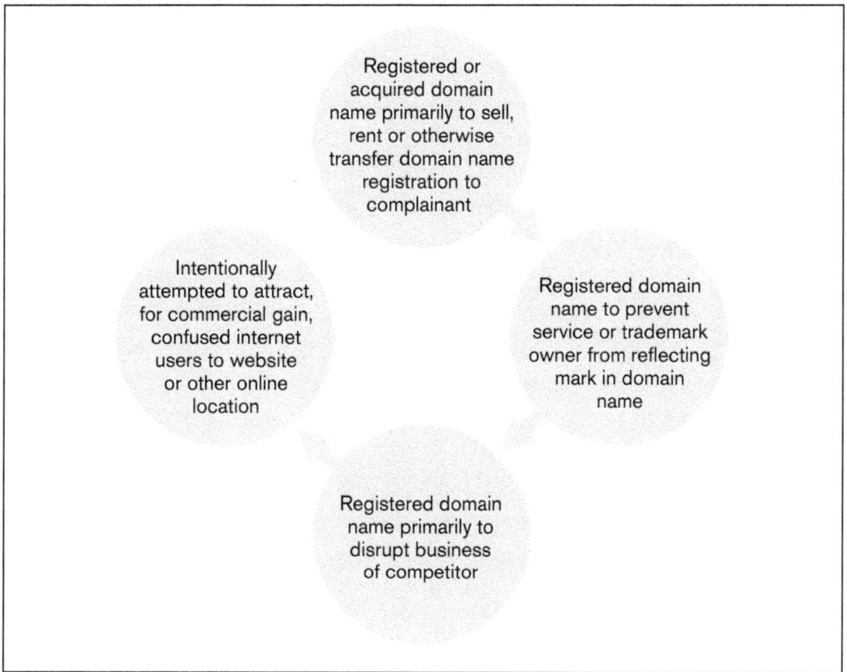

5. The URS process

Briefly put, the URS process unfolds as follows. First, the registrant must make a valid complaint. Second, the complainant must pay the requisite fees. Third, an administrative review is undertaken to check for compliance with the filing rules. Fourth, if the filing is compliant with the filing rules, the domain name is locked and the registrant is then notified. The registrant has 14 days to file a response. (The circumstances in Figure 45 show some defences to allegations of bad-faith usage.) Fifth, after 14 days, the complaint proceeds, with an examiner being selected by the provider to preside over the URS proceeding. The standards that an examiner applies are shown in Figure 46. Sixth, if the determination favours the complainant, the domain name is suspended for the balance of the registration period. Seventh, there is a right of appeal (by way of *de novo* determination). Eighth, a URS determination does not preclude a UDRP or court determination.

6. Conclusion

The UDRP is one of the most successful and widely used ODR mechanisms in the world. By providing fast, cost-effective and enforceable resolutions, it has become a model for modern digital dispute resolution frameworks. It demonstrates the effectiveness of ODR processes – particularly in contexts where speed,

Figure 44: Some indicators of good faith by registrant

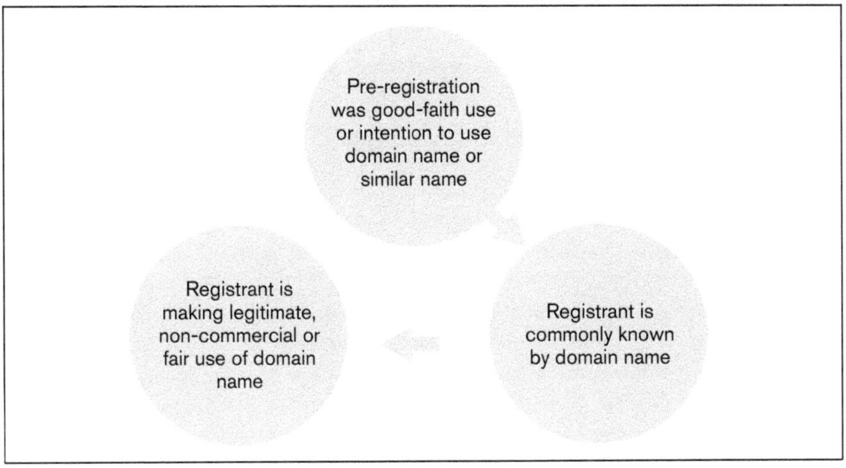

Figure 45: Some defences to bad-faith use

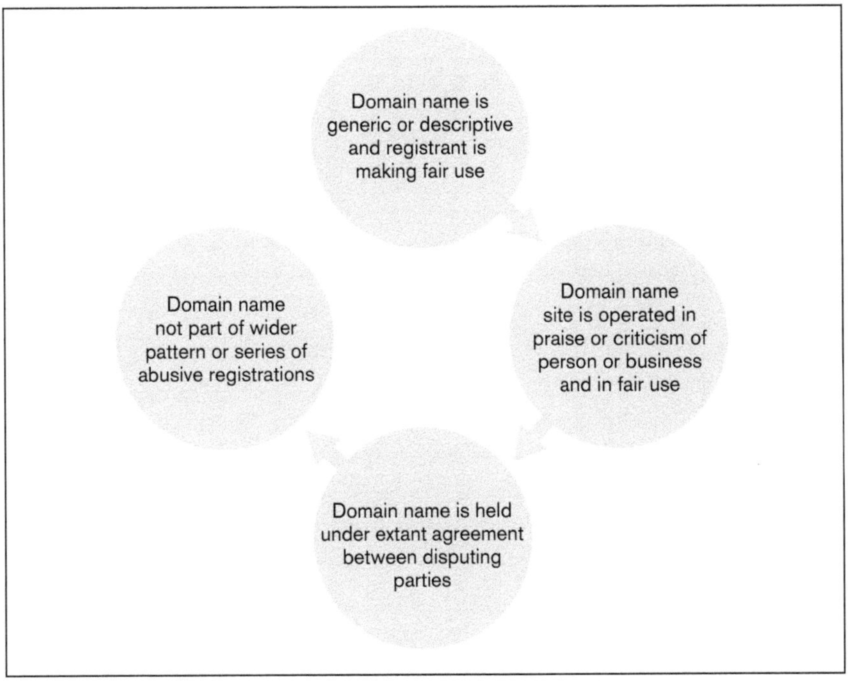

jurisdictional neutrality and enforcement efficiency are paramount. As digital transactions continue to expand, the lessons from the UDRP's success almost certainly will serve as a blueprint for future international ODR initiatives. That said, as with any human-designed process, the ICANN process is doubtless capable of improvement. Among the suggestions made in this regard are that[242] the process of registration be tightened up and proceed on the basis of validity of application, not on mere priority in time; that there be a supervisory body to ensure that decisions are fair; and that there be an appeals process.

Figure 46: Standards examiners apply

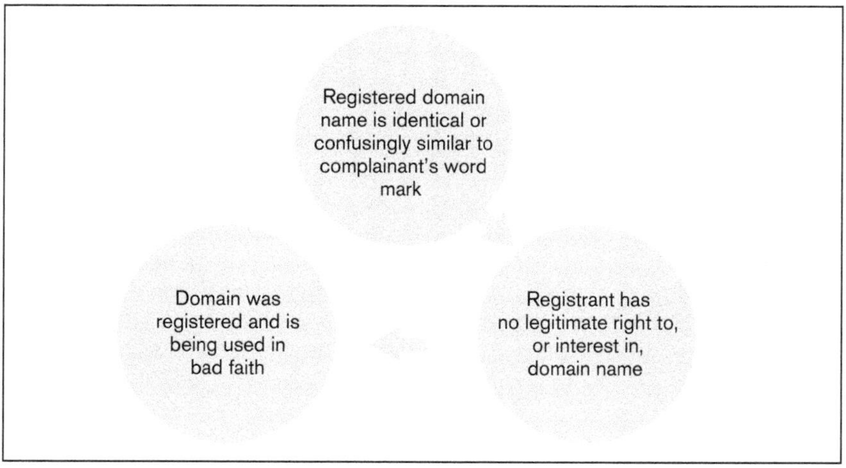

Examples of UDRP case law

Case D99-0001
Registered domain name:
'worldwrestlingfederation.com'

This was the first decision under the UDRP. The complainant was World Wrestling Federation Entertainment, Inc. It was authorised to use and had used its service mark in connection with entertainment services and all manner of related merchandise. The respondent individual registered the above domain name. Three days after doing so, he contacted the complainant, notified it of the registration and stated that his primary purpose in registering the domain name was to sell, rent or otherwise transfer it to the complainant for valuable consideration in excess of his out-of-pocket expenses. The complainant contended that the respondent had registered as a domain name a mark which was identical to the complainant's; that the respondent had no rights or legitimate interests with respect to the domain name at issue; and that the respondent had registered and was using the domain name at issue in bad faith. The respondent did not contest the complainant's allegations. The deciding panel held that the domain name registered by the respondent was identical or confusingly similar to the complainant's mark; that he had no rights or legitimate interests in respect of the domain name; and that his domain name had been registered and was being used in bad faith. Accordingly, the panel required that the registration of the domain name 'worldwrestlingfederation.com' be transferred to the complainant.

Case CPR 0231
Registered domain name:
'southwesttexasstateuniversity.com'

Here, the complainant had used the name 'Southwest Texas State University' (since renamed 'Texas State University') for its educational services since 1968 and had registered the name with the State of Texas in 1983. With the exception of the '.com' top-level domain, the domain name was identical to the complainant's mark. Additionally, the complainant cited a number of cases of actual confusion by users of the domain name. The arbitrator considered that the respondent's domain name was identical or confusingly similar to a trademark or service mark in which the complainant had rights; that the respondent had no rights or legitimate interests in respect of the domain name; and that the respondent's domain name had been registered and was being used in bad faith. The arbitrator further noted that the fact that the domain name was the obvious name of a university should have put the respondent on notice that he was not acquiring from the original owner any legitimate rights in the domain name. By purchasing the domain name (the arbitrator concluded), the respondent became party to a pattern of registration in order to prevent the complainant from reflecting the mark in a corresponding domain name. Given the finding as to bad faith, the complainant prevailed.

Key learnings

- *Aim for accessibility and speed.* The UDRP is a success because it is swift, inexpensive and enforceable. However, it cannot provide injunctive relief or monetary damages, making it unsuitable for certain disputes.
- *Aim for jurisdictional neutrality.* This is really a point for ODR schemes with a cross-border dimension. By its international nature, the UDRP is widely applicable. Even so, it is constrained by the fact that its only power of compulsion relates to domain name transfers.
- *Streamline decision making.* Most UDRP complaints are resolved without the need for hearings. Such an approach may disadvantage people with limited writing skills, who are unfamiliar with the applicable procedures or who may, for example, have especially complex defences.

- *Balance efficiency and fairness when choosing panel forms.* A one-person panel may be more efficient. However, a preponderance of one-person panel decisions may increase the risk of inconsistency.
- *Protect legal rights but avoid overreach.* The UDRP combats cybersquatting. However, it may enable wealthy corporations to claim domains even when poorer opponents have valid interests at stake.
- *Use registrars as gatekeepers.* Registrars play an important role when it comes to enforcing UDRP decisions – for example, by transferring disputed domains; but because enforcement depends on different registrars, inconsistencies may arise.
- *Apply rigorous timelines but avoid undermining due process.* A key appeal of the UDRP is the swift pace of dispute resolution. That said, it is important that swiftness not undermine due process.
- *Reduce legal barriers but be watchful for the self-represented.* Under the UDRP, legal representation is not required. Even so, decision makers may need to be watchful for the unrepresented insofar as neutrality and impartiality allow.
- *Maintain transparency through publicity.* By publishing decisions, consistency and trust are cultivated. However, it is important not to expose parties to undue reputational harm.
- *Audit, adapt and improve:* It is important to seek continuously to improve an ODR platform's offering. A careful balancing exercise is required in this regard if self-review and improvement are not to compromise the very efficiencies that make the UDRP and ODR so attractive.

19. ODR and specific sectors

Franklin County, Ohio is using ODR to resolve a variety of small claims case types, including City of Columbus tax cases … British Columbia's Residential Tenancy Branch uses ODR for landlord-tenant disputes … The Ohio Board of Tax Appeals … has been using ODR since late 2014 … Ottawa County, Michigan's Family Court Compliance ODR provides automated notifications, reminders, a secure communication mechanism for case managers and parents, and tools for managing "show cause" hearings. The system has reduced in-person hearings … and arrest warrants.

Joint Technology Committee[243]

Improving ODR: 10 key lessons

- Use ODR for high-volume, low-complexity cases.
- To begin with, ODR should be optional, not mandatory.
- Video hearings should be used strategically.
- ODR aids in reducing power imbalances between parties.
- ODR should be user friendly for consumers.
- ODR requires to be used cautiously in the criminal arena.
- Balance transparency and privacy.
- AI should be used as a support tool, not as a judge.
- The digital divide must be addressed.
- ODR should be continuously evaluated and adapted accordingly.

1. Asylum and immigration law

Since the early 1990s, video teleconferencing technology has been used by US agencies in administrative hearings and other adjudicatory proceedings.[244] Advances in technology coupled with reduced personnel and increased travel costs have made the use of such technology more attractive to government at all levels. However, government is not the only party present at asylum and immigration hearings. Thus, as one learned commentator has observed:

> *Given that video technology has been used in immigration courts since the 1990s to serve the interests of ICE and EOIR by not physically bringing detained immigrants to the courthouse, it is high time to explore ways to use video to also facilitate access to representation for immigrants.*[245]

('ICE' stands for 'US Immigration and Customs Enforcement', a federal law enforcement agency. 'EOIR' stands for the 'Executive Office for Immigration Review', a sub-agency of the US Department of Justice.)

The use of video technology for administrative hearings is not without controversy. Some applaud the use of video technology by administrative agencies because it yields efficiency benefits, such as reducing the need for travel and associated costs, reducing case backlogs, increasing scheduling flexibility for agencies and attorneys, and increasing access for parties.[246] However, critics have suggested that hearings and other adjudicatory proceedings conducted by video can hamper communication between parties and decision-makers, and between parties and their attorneys; and can hamper a decision-maker's ability to make credibility determinations.[247] (In truth, these are but claims and complaints made regarding ODR generally and have already been addressed extensively in previous chapters.)

In the United States, a succession of cases has cast doubt on whether videoconferencing is adequate to satisfy the so-called 'right of presence' at a hearing. Specifically in the immigration context, the US Court of Appeals observed in *Rusu v INS* (2002)[248] that:

- *[R]egardless of how rapidly technological improvements, such as video conferencing, may advance, the Government remains obliged to ensure that asylum petitioners are accorded a meaningful opportunity to be heard before their cases are determined ...*
- *The utilization of video conferencing, although enhancing the efficient conduct of the judicial and administrative process, also has the potential of creating certain problems in adjudicative proceedings.*
- *As Chief Judge Wilkinson has appropriately observed, "virtual reality is rarely a substitute for actual presence and ... even in an age of advancing technology, watching an event on the screen remains less than the complete equivalent of actually attending it".*[249]

One has to wonder, respectfully, whether Chief Judge Wilkinson's observation is still correct. As discussed in Chapter 2, videoconferencing as a technology seems about to be replaced by holography (the use of light transmission to broadcast a three-dimensional image of a person into a place where they are not physically present).[250] This will enable someone to have an almost traditional, in-person, face-to-face form of communication with a person who is in a remote venue, making virtual reality a true substitute for actual presence.

In any event, regardless of the observations of the US Court of Appeals, the trend to videoconferencing in administrative hearings has continued unabated. In 2011, the US Administrative Conference issued a recommendation regarding the use of videoconferencing in federal agencies with high-volume caseloads. (The Administrative Conference is an independent federal agency with a statutory mission to identify ways to improve the procedures by which federal agencies protect the public interest and determine the rights, privileges and obligations of private persons.)

The recommendation suggests that federal agencies (for which one might substitute those tasked with operating ODR platforms) should, when determining whether to use video technology in adjudicatory proceedings, consider whether the use of video technology is legally permissible; whether the nature and type of the hearings/proceedings are conducive to the use of video technology; whether video technology can be used without affecting the outcome of cases heard; whether the available budget would allow for investment in appropriate and secure technology given the costs of video technology; whether the use of video technology would create cost savings; whether the use of video technology would reduce the waiting time for a hearing; whether users of video technology would find the use of such technology beneficial; whether the use of video technology would adversely affect the representation of a party; and whether communication between the various individuals present at a hearing or proceeding would be adversely affected.

The recommendation is also of interest because it identifies certain best practices insofar as remote hearings are concerned. These include the following. Video technology should be used on a voluntary basis, with a party free to have an in-person hearing or proceeding if they so choose. Its use should periodically be evaluated to ensure that it is outcome neutral and meets user needs. Feedback and comments should be solicited from regular users. Its use should commence with a pilot programme, which should then be evaluated before moving to wider use. Training should be done at the outset and technical support provided. And prospective users should consult other agencies that have used video technology to solicit best practices, guidance and advice.

One of the more exciting developments in recent years when it comes to the interaction between ODR and asylum and immigration law is the creation in Greece of a smartphone app that seeks to prevent the escalation of disputes involving refugees (eg, with other refugees, with nearby locals or with camp administrators), and to facilitate the resolution of those disputes online.[251] One of the prompts for the creation of the app was the realisation that almost all refugees coming to Greece had smartphones (because they are easy to carry and enable contact with family members left behind or accommodated elsewhere).[252] Among the app's features are personalised texts, multiple languages, language selection, a disputes menu, a facility to appoint a mediator and (thanks to the smartphone) audio, text and video communication.[253]

Another app (this one is used in the United States) triages immigrants through their various possible options by having them complete an online interview designed to take 10 to 30 minutes to complete. At the end, the user receives a personalised result that explains their immigration options and potential risks.[254] Though not an ODR mechanism, the triaging is akin to the type that is a part of ODR platforms and brings immigrants to the right silo in which to progress their case with the immigration authorities. Technology is also being brought to bear in preparing the sometimes-complex analysis that is required in so-called 'crimmigration' law – that is, the challenging area of the law in which criminal law, asylum law and immigration law all overlap.[255]

One as-yet unmet challenge is the creation of an app that would assist immigrants and asylum seekers through the related court process. One learned commentator has observed that the complex nature of immigration law and the fact that detained people tend not to have access to their own information or technology further complicate the creation of such an app.[256]

In terms of improving the existing asylum and immigration court process in the United States through the use of technology, the following suggestions (which have more general resonance) have been made: using online case resolution to ease the pressures on all sides that in-court attendance imposes; making such usage voluntary only, so that those applicants who wish to attend in court can still do so; providing online facilities in Spanish and other common languages; allowing attorneys to appear online – all the evidence points to cases being adjudicated more fairly if attorneys are present, so facilitating their presence is a boon to judges and applicants alike; and using technology to match prospective clients with *pro bono* attorneys – for such a process to work effectively, it has been suggested that the court should be involved in designing and promoting the relevant programme.[257]

2. Child and family law

In the United States, ODR platforms of note in the child and family law context include CREK, which offers a complete ODR process; Mondrian, a popular ODR platform; and Our Family Wizard, through which one can arrange all the practical details of joint custody.

In the divorce context (though the point holds true in the child and family law context more generally), it has been suggested that ODR offers a notably therapeutic method of going about arranging a divorce, and in some circumstances can be a more appropriate method than traditional means.[258] Among the advantages attributed to ODR in the child and family law context are the following.[259] It provides a remoteness that reduces tension. It offers an environment in which it is very difficult to intimidate. It follows from the first two points that it helps to redress power imbalances. It offers the benefit of asynchronous (and hence more considered) communications. It enables efficient and less costly online engagement with third-party practitioners. It facilitates the negotiation (and operation) of post-separation/divorce parenting plans. And it means that most, if not all communication between disputants is in writing, reducing the potential for 'he said/she said' conflicts in evidence.

One of the many good examples of ODR being used as a crutch in the family law context is offered by the Pinal County Superior Court in Arizona. It facilitates online mediated discussion between parties in the divorce law context. Discussions that might be held online include considerations of financial matters, development of a parenting plan and discussion as to decision making regarding children of the marriage. Parties with a history of domestic violence are allowed to participate but the mediator may terminate a session if they are concerned for the safety of either party or of children. If agreement is reached, a document outlining the agreement is sent to the parties for signature and the mediator then liaises with the trial judge for the issuance of a court order; if no agreement is reached, the matter then proceeds through an in-person court process.

In the United Kingdom, it is also possible for divorces to be sought and granted via an online process. It operates a highly simplified seven-step process which is summarised in Figure 47. Notably, there is at least one case internationally of ODR making divorce so easy that lawmakers considered it appropriate to slow the pace at which online divorces were available. Thus, in 2018, Denmark changed its existing online divorce process (which enabled a divorce to be obtained in less than a week at a cost of about €60).[260] Instead, it substituted a process which required a three-month 'reflection period' before a divorce took effect. (Free elective counselling was available during this three-month period; there is also a mandatory online course on the challenges of divorce.) The previous arrangements were continued for childless couples and also for marriages where abuse presented.

Ottawa County, Michigan, uses ODR as a means of reducing the number of parents in breach of a maintenance order who are sent to prison. Obviously, being sent to prison is not likely to improve the affected parent's ability to pay maintenance, so non-paying parents are instead routed through a process which sees them invited to discuss with county officers their ability to pay. If there is no reply or no progress, a further SMS message is sent advising the parent that a hearing is pending at which an order for committal may be made. There is also the opportunity for an online meeting with county officers. Through these relatively simple steps, Ottawa County has greatly reduced the number of parents who are committed to prison. The related reduction in the number of committal hearings frees up judges and court staff to do other work.

Innovation in the family law field in the United States is not limited to state-sponsored initiatives. For example, one Californian attorney who noticed that there was an increasing number of self-represented litigants seeking to navigate the divorce law system created a highly user-friendly online service, Hello Divorce (www.hellodivorce.com), which seeks to help divorcing couples through the divorce process. Available services include a personalised divorce plan, a free and highly informative worksheet on creating a co-parenting plan, useful free DIY videos, instructional templates, mediation and (if wanted) access to an attorney at an affordable rate. Another commercial platform which seeks to assist those going through the divorce process, including those who wish to progress matters as self-represented litigants, is www.divorce.com.

Figure 47: Seven-step online divorce process in the United Kingdom[261]

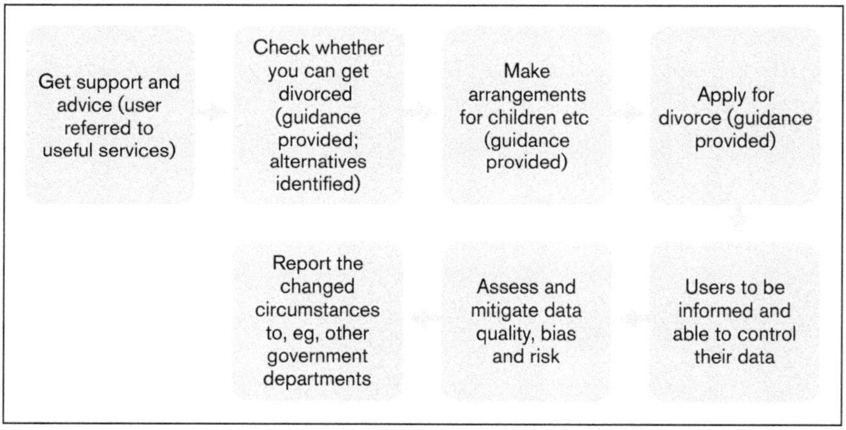

ODR in the family law context has benefited from AI development. In family law, AI (as well as assisting with functions such as scheduling and document generation) is helping to defuse tensions by, for example, assisting with financial assessments and highlighting issues for resolution. In doing so, it frees up disputants to focus on resolving the substantive issues between them, with far less emotional strife. AI can also assist with such varied matters as domestic violence screening, obviating any power imbalance (it is difficult to dominate physically in a remote hearing) and generating case-specific parenting solutions.

* There is also a process known as 'med-arb' ('mediation-arbitration'). This involves the parties seeking an agreed solution to their dispute with the aid of a mediator. If the mediation fails, the mediator then 'changes hat' and thereafter functions at an arbitrator, arriving at a binding arbitration decision. Sometimes the mediator and arbitrator may be different persons (to ensure that the arbitrator has no pre-formed ideas concerning the dispute). The key attraction of adding in arbitration means that the process ultimately will end in some form of (agreed or imposed) solution. The desire to avoid an imposed solution may also provide an incentive to arrive at an agreed solution.

3. Consumer disputes

The usefulness of ODR in consumer disputes has already repeatedly been touched upon. However, a few additional points might usefully be made. ODR (particularly online mediation) has shown itself to be valuable in terms of consumer disputes regarding an online transaction that involves a vendor or service provider based in another jurisdiction.* Consumers are notably vulnerable when it comes to such disputes: they cannot inspect before they buy; the transactions are generally low-value ones that would not justify the cost of litigation; and there is the ever-present risk of online fraud. Against this background, ODR is seen as an attractive alternative to international litigation and even mandatory arbitration in the context of cross-border consumer transactions.[262] The challenge presenting when it comes to ODR uptake among consumers in the cross-border context is a certain level of mistrust, with consumers uncertain as to whether ODR can provide useful results and how these results may be recognised and enforced.[263]

There are a number of advantages to ODR in the business-to-consumer (B2C) context. These are, in truth, the same advantages as apply to ODR generally. Thus, the process is typically convenient and simple. ODR providers are usually available on a 24/7 basis. Parties can engage in asynchronous communications. There is no need for parties to be physically present in the same place. It is less confrontational. Experts can be involved remotely. Relative anonymity levels the playing field. And the written nature of the process encourages directness and succinctness and creates a written record.

There are also a number of disadvantages when it comes to applying ODR in the consumer law context. These include the following. People may not be at their best in written communications. Typically, consumers are self-represented and may not be very good at representing themselves. If neutrality is to be preserved, the mediator can do little to assist a self-represented consumer who is not very good at self-representation. If there is no guarantee of an end agreement, why would a consumer invest their time in the process? There is no binding judgment at the end of the process. There may be no meaningful incentive for a merchant to participate. Recognition and enforcement of an end agreement may be challenging. And there is a lingering concern about the maintenance of confidentiality in the online context.

A good example of courts using ODR to resolve consumer debts is offered by the system in operation in Alabama's Montgomery, Morgan and Tuscaloosa Counties since 2022, for claims up to a value of $6,500. The process employed is as follows (and is relatively familiar when one has regard to other ODR systems considered thus far):[264]

- Plaintiff e-files small claims case.
- Summons and copy of complaint served on defendant.
- Plaintiff notified that case assigned to ODR and options explained.

- Defendant receives information sheet about ODR.
- If defendant decides to opt in, they can; otherwise, case proceeds offline.
- Once defendant has registered, they are directed to answer the complaint.
- Defendant can enter proposal of some kind.
- Defendant may upload documents or pictures to support arguments.
- System generates email to plaintiff with defendant's proposal.
- Plaintiff may respond with another proposal or accept offer.
- Parties respond in open text format.
- Exchange continues until settlement agreed or one party requests that matter go to trial. (There does not appear to be any facilitation or mediation. The parties enter negotiation. Absent settlement, they go to trial. So, the process can be seen as a pre-litigation measure to see whether solution via negotiation is possible.)
- If the parties agree to a settlement, the system generates an agreement, which the parties can sign electronically and then send to a judge for review. The settlement becomes part of the judge's order. Communications between the parties do not. The court does not have access to communications at any point.

In 2023, the US National Consumer Law Center published an issue brief addressing various topics of interest for courts that were considering whether to use ODR in the online context. The box below outlines some general considerations that the centre highlighted in this regard.

US National Consumer Law Center

General Considerations for ODR System Design (2023)[265]

Court legitimacy
Problem: Court-sponsored ODR has not had time to build trust and establish legitimacy.
Solution: Courts adopting ODR should make it optional. Consumers should be able to try ODR without penalty and be allowed to transfer back to a traditional court at any time. There should be no negative consequences for a consumer who does not opt in to ODR.
Comment: A question surely arises as to whether making ODR optional could limit its adoption and impede its ability to win popular acceptance.

Access to online resources
Problem: Participants may encounter a variety of barriers to accessing or using ODR platforms, such as disabilities, limited internet access and low literacy.

Solutions: Courts should offer options such as telephone participation.
Comment: Specifically as regards telephone assistance, it is not a complete solution: some people may still find dispute resolution to be unduly complex and require assistance.

Language
Problem: Limited English proficiency can be a barrier to accessing the courts.
Solution: Early in the process, users should be screened for translation and interpretation needs.
Comment: It is submitted that plain language materials and ongoing support may also be required.

Readability
Problem: Some participants may struggle to understand complicated or technical materials.
Solution: Prioritise readability.
Comment: Legal matters cannot always be completely simplified and ongoing assistance may be required by some users.

Accessing court
Problem: Users may have difficulty accessing courts – for example, because they are unable to take time off work, lack childcare or face transportation issues.
Solution: Remote access ODR should be of assistance in this regard.
Comment: For people without internet access or private space, remote access may not assist.

Top-down design
Problem: ODR design may involve little user feedback.
Solution: Involve stakeholders and their advocates.
Comment: Regular testing would also be useful.

Data confidentiality and privacy
Problem: ODR platform will involve processing of personal data.
Solution: Clear data security protocols required.
Comment: Clear communication about process and procedure is also required to cultivate trust.

Also of interest is the National Consumer Law Center's consideration of the types of in-process issues that can arise when using an ODR platform to resolve consumer debt lawsuits. These include the following.

First, *abusive practices*. Unsupervised chatroom spaces in ODR platforms present opportunities for abuse. All chatroom spaces, the centre suggests, should be monitored by neutrals who are empowered to act in response to abusive practices. (That said, such monitoring may raise privacy concerns. A better approach might be to use AI-informed moderation that detects abusive behaviour while also maintaining confidentiality.)

Second, *asynchronous communication*. The asynchronous nature of ODR raises questions about how mass filers (typically creditors) will manage large portfolios of lawsuits simultaneously. (It is a little difficult to understand this concern. ODR, even asynchronous ODR, can streamline case management for all.)

Third, *casualness*. ODR would allow debt collection lawsuits to be resolved from a consumer's living room. In this regard, the centre observes:

- *[D]ue to the informal environment, some consumers may fall into a trap of not appreciating the seriousness of the matter. They may not recognize that the agreement that they are entering into on their phone in their pajamas is a legal agreement that can impact their lives for years or even decades.*
- *Courts that adopt ODR should require waiting periods during which the consumer has the ability to cancel any settlement agreement without penalty and the opportunity to consult with an attorney, family, or friends.*
- *ODR platforms should state clearly at all times that the platform is being used to resolve a lawsuit.*[266]

(Two comments might be made as regards the centre's above-quoted observations. Ease of access need not equate to reduced seriousness. And having waiting periods could conceivably unduly slow matters; offering an option to seek legal advice may be a preferable approach.)

Fourth, *financial literacy*. Many consumers have limited financial literacy. Courts that adopt ODR, the centre suggests, should build 'reality checks'[267] into the ODR system – for example, showing how much a potential settlement will cost over time. (In order not to impede settlements unduly, the use of such tools should be elective.)

Fifth, *information about the relevant debt*. Consumers may lack basic information about an alleged creditor (which may not have been the original lender) and hence be confused as to what debt is in issue. This is obviously unsatisfactory if and when it occurs.

Sixth, *lack of information about legal rights, etc*. ODR platforms, the centre suggests, should be designed to provide relevant legal information using an interactive interface. To avoid users becoming overwhelmed, the information should be provided on a tiered basis, with more detail available if a user elects to proceed through successive hyperlinks.

Seventh, *legal representation*. This is among the more interesting of the points addressed by the centre. Most consumers in the United States, the centre observes, are not represented by attorneys in collection lawsuits. By contrast, most creditors appear regularly in court and are almost always represented by attorneys. ODR platforms could, the centre notes, screen for legal aid eligibility, include links to request referral to an attorney and provide information about representation options. (All of these are useful steps. However, in the event that a person is ineligible for free legal aid and cannot otherwise afford legal representation, ODR platforms should continue to be designed to provide relevant legal information using an interactive interface.)

Eighth, *notice*. The notice that a consumer receives when a debt collection lawsuit is filed is often difficult to understand and does not give the consumer enough information on how to defend their case. The National Consumer Law Center suggests that the adoption of ODR represents an opportunity to improve on existing notice forms to ensure understanding. (This is clearly a sensible step. However, sight should not be lost of the fact that ODR can improve the efficiency of the notification process through, for example, digital tracking and read receipts.)

Ninth, *imbalance of power*. There is a power imbalance between the unrepresented consumer on one side and the collection attorney on the other. Some courts have attempted to mitigate the power imbalance by using mediators or other neutrals to facilitate conversations between parties in court-sponsored ODR. (Even without such neutrals, ODR can in any event mitigate power imbalances through reliance on automated negotiation tools, standard templates and structured responses.)

Tenth, *resolution post-ODR*. Courts that adopt ODR need to decide what to do with collection lawsuits that are not resolved via ODR. Consumers should have the same rights to appeal whether the judge/magistrate resolves the case online or in a traditional court. (As a standard, ODR should integrate seamlessly with offline court processes, so that online cases proceed offline without any disadvantage to disputants.)

Eleventh, *service of documents*. The centre suggests that the adoption of ODR likewise offers courts an opportunity to consider whether they need to reform service requirements. (It is submitted that if digital service methods are to be adopted, safeguards need to be included.)

As can be seen, while ODR presents clear advantages in consumer disputes, it is not without its challenges. Issues such as those highlighted by the National Consumer Center require careful consideration in system design. However, the concerns that it highlights should not overshadow the broader benefits of ODR in terms of providing a practical, cost-effective means of effecting consumer litigation.

4. Criminal proceedings

In many countries, the criminal legal system is overstretched and underfunded. In the United Kingdom, concerns have been expressed by senior judges that constant cuts to the justice system will lead to a collapse in the rule of law.[268] In the United States, the court system has been described as "largely broken".[269] Yet for all these difficulties, when the world was struck by the COVID-19 pandemic, the criminal justice system proved remarkably resilient in the face of unexpected adversity, with an online system of criminal proceedings springing rapidly into being, replacing centuries-old offline processes.[270] Instead of attending in court, lawyers began attending online bail, motion, sentencing and other hearings from the comfort of their homes.

COVID-19-related changes, when they came, took place with little planning, less debate and no meaningful input from impacted parties.[271] And they were not uncontroversial. It was even suggested that defendant rights stood the potential to become COVID-19 victims.[272] In a review of the issues that the move to online proceedings during the COVID-19 pandemic presented in the United States, the US National Association of Criminal Defense Lawyers (NACDL) made various remarks from which the following observations may be drawn.[273] (These seem likely to have resonance for other liberal democracies also.)

First, criminal proceedings demand a robust lawyer-client relationship, which requires ample opportunities for the two to confer. Second, any modifications necessitated as a result of an online hearing/trial must not abridge the rights of a defendant and should be expressly agreed to by that defendant. Third, modifications should not exacerbate any traditional weaknesses of the criminal justice system. Fourth, the view of the NACDL was that online mechanisms cannot be reconciled with US law and practice as to the right of confrontation, the right to due process and the right to the effective assistance of counsel. Fifth, virtual mechanisms run the risk of fundamentally altering the psychology of jurors. Sixth, jurors participating virtually may be deprived of the complete panoply of non-verbal cues used to assess witness credibility. Seventh, jurors may pay less attention to testimony when observing via Zoom or other online platforms. Eighth, when it comes to virtual or remote hearings, courts must avoid placing a defendant in the position of having to elect between one set of rights to the detriment of others. Ninth, care should be taken to ensure that a move online does not benefit well-funded institutional actors to the detriment of others.

These are all legitimate concerns. But perhaps the following counter-observations might be made. First, as to lawyer-client meetings, virtual platforms can provide generally secure breakout rooms. Second, as to defendant rights, online modifications can be made subject to express consent. Third, it may be that in the wider global perspective, different countries will take a different view from the NACDL as to the feasibility of assuring defendant rights online. Fourth, as to juror behaviour, virtual environments can be constructed to mitigate any potential difficulties presenting; judges alive to the risks can seek to manage them; and suitable video shots can empower jurors to take account of visual cues. Fifth, virtual proceedings can be structured to ensure that accessibility, fairness and transparency are all adequately protected.

Even with the fastest internet speed, glitches in communication are inevitable. One possible solution is that cost savings to government from online justice should be used to finance better internet access for all. Other solutions to internet glitches include the following. First, requiring jurors to tell the judge if their internet connection fails at any time (presumably immediately after it has been restored.) Second, checking with jurors after each witness whether any of them suffered an access failure during that witness's testimony – in which case, for example, the relevant evidence could be replayed to the jury from the point at which it failed for one of the jurors. Or the witness in question could be re-examined. The point is not so much that these are the correct solutions as that there are potential solutions.

There appears to be a widespread sense among lawyers that evidence can better be evaluated when a witness is viewed in person. Meeting such concerns does not seem an impossible task. For example, it has been suggested that by placing a webcam at a certain distance, the entirety of a person's body can be viewed (so allowing that person's body language to be seen).[274] As to difficulties with observing demeanour, it has been suggested that these can be overcome by giving clear, high-quality instructions as to how a person should compose themselves.[275] The privacy (and safety) concerns that witnesses sometimes have in criminal trials can be allayed through the use of virtual technology as it places a physical distance between the witness and the trial (and opens up the possibility of using technology to obscure a witness's appearance or voice).[276] Also, as mentioned previously, videoconferencing as a technology appears to be on the verge of being replaced by holography – that is, the use of light transmission to broadcast a three-dimensional image of a person into a place where they are not physically present.[277] This will have the result that one can have an almost traditional, in-person, face-to-face form of communication with a person who is in a remote venue, thus obviating some or all of the just-mentioned concerns.

There are also, it should be noted, attractions for criminal defendants in a virtual criminal justice system.[278] Technology enables easier contact between clients and their lawyers. It may also improve the array and choice of lawyers available, with clients freer to choose lawyers from beyond their local high streets. It could allow free legal aid (public defender) budgets to go further, provided that those budgets are not cut in anticipation of the reduced cost that online justice can reasonably be expected to yield.[279] There are also attractions for criminal lawyers in terms of allowing them to work more efficiently.[280]

Defendants in criminal proceedings present with particular needs when it comes to privacy. Principal among these concerns is the presumption of innocence. So, in the course of online broadcasts, spectators will at some point see persons who will eventually be acquitted. To some extent, this is possible already, given that the public may attend trials and the media often covers such trials. However, the potential for a swathe of people to follow such proceedings is likely enhanced by their being online. The knee-jerk reaction would be to keep such proceedings private. However, a preferable way of resolving such concerns – and one more consistent with the notion that justice should be done in public – would be to limit courts to a livestream, archive court hearings for only a short period and forbid third-party recordings.[281]

As to the use of AI in the criminal justice context, AI potentially can assist when it comes to risk assessment, sentencing recommendations and offender profiling.* (Whether it should is another matter.) AI models such as Correctional Offender Management Profiling for Alternative Sanctions (COMPAS), which is used in the United States to assess recidivism risks, have faced scrutiny for racial and socio-economic biases and regarding the transparency of a system which rests ultimately on privately developed, proprietary software. The authors of the expert report appended to the European Ethical Charter on the Use of Artificial Intelligence in Judicial Systems and Their Environment (2018) were notably critical about the use of AI in the context of criminal proceedings, stating the following, among other things:

- *[I]nclusion of algorithmic variables such as criminal history and family background means … the past behaviour of a certain group may decide the[ir] fate …*
- *[H]uman decisions can be based on values and considerations … that would not be retained by the machine …*
- *[I]nstead of correcting … problematic policies, technology may end up legitimising them …*
- *[L]ack of transparency … by proprietary companies and their accountability to the public is a cause for concern …*
- *[W]hen algorithms are used in the context of a criminal trial it seems essential to fully guarantee respect for the principle of equality of arms and presumption of innocence …*
- *The party concerned should have access to and be able to challenge … an algorithm …*
- *[A] judge who decides against the prediction of an algorithm is likely to take risks as [the judge is thereby assuming] … greater [personal] responsibility.*

If one had to give a short response to each of these seven points, perhaps the following observations might be made:

- Algorithms can be refined to mitigate bias, and it is worth remembering that human decision making can itself be influenced by unconscious prejudice.

* The European Ethical Charter on the Use of Artificial Intelligence in Judicial Systems and Their Environment (2018), which is considered in Chapter 16, contains a glossary which defines 'profiling' as: "An automated data processing technique that consists of applying a 'profile' to a natural person, in particular in order to make decisions about him or her or to analyze or predict personal preferences, behaviours and attitudes."

- While human judges might have regard to broader social factors, this ability could lead to inconsistencies and subjective bias.
- Technology can be used to make decision-making processes more transparent and measurable.
- Proprietary algorithms undoubtedly present transparency challenges but these can be addressed by requiring the use of open-source or government-audited models.
- Algorithmic tools, correctly used, can enhance fairness by reducing human biases.
- A balance falls inevitably to be struck between the right to privacy and the need for IP rights to be respected if innovation in legal technology is to be fostered.
- Any frailty among judges can surely be addressed by courts establishing appropriate judicial guidelines which encourage informed usage.

In passing, it should be noted that US courts have not proceeded blind to concerns about the use of AI in the criminal law context. A good example of this awareness is offered by the decision of the Wisconsin Supreme Court in *Wisconsin v Loomis* (2016).[282] Insofar are they are relevant to this book, the details of that case are as follows. The state of Wisconsin had contended that Mr Loomis was the driver in a drive-by shooting. Loomis denied involvement in the shooting but entered a guilty plea to two lesser charges. After accepting Loomis's plea, the trial court ordered a pre-sentence investigation (PSI) that included a COMPAS risk assessment. In her opinion for the Wisconsin Supreme Court, affirming the lower court's judgment, Bradley J later described the COMPAS risk assessment in the following terms:

- *COMPAS is a risk-need assessment tool designed … to provide decisional support for the Department of Corrections when making placement decisions, managing offenders, and planning treatment.*
- *The COMPAS risk assessment is based upon information gathered from the defendant's criminal file and an interview with the defendant.*
- *A COMPAS report consists of a risk assessment designed to predict recidivism and a separate needs assessment …*
- *The risk assessment portion of COMPAS generates risk scores … intended to predict the general likelihood that those with a similar history … are … less likely or more likely to commit another crime following release …*
- *[T]he … risk assessment does not predict the specific likelihood that an individual offender will reoffend …*
- *The PSI … cautions that a COMPAS risk assessment should not be used to determine … severity of … sentence or whether an offender is incarcerated.*[283]

At sentencing, the state of Wisconsin argued that the sentencing court should use the COMPAS report when determining an appropriate sentence. Ultimately, the sentencing court referred to the COMPAS risk score along with other sentencing factors in ruling out probation.[284]

Loomis subsequently filed a motion for post-conviction relief requesting a new sentencing hearing. He argued, among other matters, that the sentencing court's consideration of the COMPAS risk assessment at sentencing violated his due process rights. On appeal, he offered the testimony of an expert witness regarding the use at sentencing of a COMPAS risk assessment. That expert witness opined that a COMPAS risk assessment should not be used for decisions regarding incarceration because a COMPAS risk assessment was not designed for such use and yielded a tremendous risk of overestimating an individual's propensity to reoffend. The expert witness further testified that sentencing courts have very little information about how a COMPAS assessment analyses the risk.[285] Denying the post-conviction motion, the sentencing court explained that it had used the COMPAS risk assessment to corroborate its findings, and that it would have imposed the same sentence regardless of whether it considered the COMPAS risk scores. Loomis appealed. In her opinion for the Supreme Court on appeal, Bradley J described the background to the use of risk assessment tools (and struck a cautionary note as to their use) in the following terms:

- *Initially risk assessment tools were used only by probation and parole departments to help determine the best supervision and treatment strategies for offenders. With nationwide focus on the need to reduce recidivism and the importance of evidence-based practices, the use of such tools has now expanded to sentencing. Yet, the use of these tools at sentencing is more complex because the sentencing decision has multiple purposes, only some of which are related to recidivism reduction.*
- *When analyzing the use of evidence-based risk assessment tools at sentencing, it is important to consider that tools such as COMPAS continue to change and evolve. The concerns we address today may very well be alleviated in the future. It is incumbent upon the criminal justice system to recognize that in the coming months and years, additional research data will become available. Different and better tools may be developed. As data changes, our use of evidence-based tools will have to change as well. The justice system must keep up with the research and continuously assess the use of these tools.*[286]

Closer to home, when it comes to the use of AI in the criminal arena, the Council of Europe's Committee on Crime Problems published a discussion paper on this topic in 2024.[287] That discussion paper touches on a number of points of interest when it comes to ODR. As regards the *bona fide* use of AI that results in harm (eg, a chatbot defames someone), the paper makes a number of points of interest as regards the foreseeable unforeseen – for example, it is foreseeable that a chatbot could slander someone but it is not predictable when it will do so. The question is: who should be liable if and when it does do so? The operator of the search engine? Its designers? This creates what the discussion paper refers to as the 'negligence dilemma'. The dilemma is this: one could argue that none of the human actors can be held liable because AI systems act on their own; or one might maintain that the deployer/designer should foresee any and all potential harm caused and thus face strict liability. The authors of the discussion paper were not convinced by either argument. As to the inherent unpredictability of AI systems offering a basis for exempting human actors from liability, the authors consider that it is this very unpredictability that offers a basis for liability. However, they also consider that imposing strict criminal liability on anyone involved in the lifecycle of AI systems would be disproportionate, as individuals and society benefit from AI.

The authors suggest that Council of Europe member states might wish to consider limiting criminal liability to situations where actions in the lifecycle of an AI system do not adhere to state-of-the-art standards or lack reasonable measures to control associated risks. The immediate question that arises is: at what point would the state of the art fall to be gauged? The discussion paper also notes that AI systems are typically produced by corporations, not by individuals, and hence the question of corporate criminal liability arises. Specifically, regarding ODR, the discussion paper observes as follows:

- *It is a fundamental question in the era of vastly and rapidly developing AI systems whether only humans should judge humans. Or if it is conceivable to have a criminal trial in which a software architecture autonomously applies the law ...*
- *Today, we still view human judges as guarantors of the separation of powers and the democratic legitimacy of jurisprudence, and we are reluctant to risk undetectable errors in judgment that may arise from using AI systems that are prone to hallucination. [At the present time, generated text may contain possibly contradictory or harmful text that is colloquially known as 'hallucinatory text'.]*[288]
- *However, in the near or distant future, procedural safeguards such as the right to a fair hearing and the opportunity for meaningful dialogue could be adapted for use with AI systems.*[289]

If this book has shown nothing else, it has hopefully shown how far some countries have already gone when it comes to the practical rollout of ODR, in the process having to address (and having addressed) issues that may seem novel in the European purview but are not so novel when one has regard to the wider international experience of ODR.

Key learnings

- *Use ODR for high-volume, low-complexity cases.* ODR has proven efficient in handling minor criminal cases, as well as family, landlord and tenant, small claims and tax cases. That said, complex cases may suffer from the lack of human interaction that ODR typically involves.
- *Initially, ODR should be optional.* Voluntary participation should build public trust. Conversely, if ODR remains permanently optional, its impact may be diminished.
- *Video hearings should be used strategically.* Remote hearings increase accessibility and efficiency. However, they also present technical and other challenges which may yield unfairness.
- *ODR aids in reducing power imbalances.* ODR can assist in reducing power imbalances through providing a neutral platform where parties can negotiate without, for example, fear of intimidation.
- *ODR should be user-friendly for consumers.* ODR is an attractive dispute resolution process for cross-border B2C disputes. Even so, consumers may find self-representation challenging and business may simply decline to engage.
- *ODR requires to be used cautiously in the criminal arena.* Remote criminal hearings occurred during the COVID-19 pandemic. However, online or offline, such proceedings require strong procedural safeguards to protect defendant rights.
- *Balance transparency and privacy.* Maintaining confidentiality is key to the proper operation of ODR platforms. That said, courts need to strike a balance between maintaining privacy and conducting proceedings transparently.
- *AI should only be used as a support tool.* AI can assist with ODR. However, as yet, it is not good when it comes to empathy or nuance.
- *The digital divide must be addressed.* ODR can increase legal accessibility, but care needs to be taken to ensure that it does not decrease accessibility for those on the wrong side of the digital divide.
- *Continuously evaluate ODR and adapt accordingly.* ODR should be continuously evaluated and flaws remediated. However, continuous evaluation may present a financial and practical challenge in practice.

20. Conclusion

[I]f the first twenty years of ODR's growth has been impressive, the next twenty years are poised to be truly revolutionary.
Wing and Ors (2021)[290]

The future of ODR is assured. Unsurprisingly, perhaps, given that it is the birthplace of the Computer Age, the United States is at the fore of the world's liberal democracies in terms of incorporating ODR into (or grafting ODR onto) its existing court structures. Among smaller jurisdictions, Canada and the United Kingdom have also achieved notable successes. What lessons might usefully be gleaned by experienced and less experienced jurisdictions from the international rollout of ODR to date? Perhaps the following.

1. **Access**

ODR requires general access to digital technology and a degree of digital literacy among users. In some jurisdictions, the digital divide is such that it may prevent significant segments of the public from utilising ODR. To maximise accessibility, ODR platforms need to be designed with inclusivity in mind. That said, designing inclusive platforms is a complex task because user needs vary so widely. A 'one-size-fits-all' approach to platform design seems doomed to failure in terms of addressing certain disabilities or language barriers. Targeted campaigns may be necessary to encourage the use of technology – though ingrained habits or mistrust of technology may persist among some. It is submitted that private sector innovations which support marginalised persons or groups should be encouraged by states. Finally, a reasonable level of regulatory oversight would appear crucial to ensure that ODR's benefits and efficiencies do not come at the expense of fundamental rights and freedoms.

2. **Competence**

Competent, trained professionals are essential for a well-developed ODR scheme. In some jurisdictions, state intervention may be required to establish adequate training standards. Remote training for ODR professionals may be feasible. Moreover, such training need not await a person's qualification as a lawyer and could begin in law school – though law school curricula tend already to be heavily loaded. Judges and court staff should be trained to ensure familiarity with ODR processes. However, judicial training is slow to implement, and resistance from traditionalist judges and staff may hinder its rollout. Governments do not have to build ODR capacity by themselves; they can leverage off the private sector. This might involve establishing legal tech hubs to foster innovation, encouraging the adoption of new technology and developing customised ODR solutions for different disputes.

3. Trust

ODR can be applied to a broad array of disputes, including commercial law, contract law, employment law* and family law disputes. If minor criminal offences and asylum cases are included, ODR actually covers a large portion of a typical court calendar. That said, not all cases are suited to digital resolution. Popularising ODR requires building trust in ODR processes. This can only be achieved through the combined efforts of stakeholders. Even with such efforts, building trust in ODR can take time. Launching new technologies can prompt public scepticism. One possible way to address such scepticism is to increase awareness of ODR. Even so, public awareness campaigns alone may not be sufficient to shift attitudes towards ODR: engagement with key stakeholders is essential if any negative public perceptions are to be changed. Targeted incentives could also be introduced to build trust in ODR. For example, ODR centres could draft suggested ODR clauses for businesses to use; lawyers could be facilitated in developing the skillset necessary to act as ODR operatives; and courts could be encouraged to refer cases to ODR so as to legitimise the process and build trust in ODR within the legal community and more generally.

4. Regulation

It is submitted that ODR regulation ought to protect the rights of end users. At the same time, it is important to ensure that over-regulation does not stifle innovation. However, striking a proper balance between regulation and innovation can be challenging. This is because unduly rigorous rules could limit innovation, while inadequate supervision could expose users to avoidable bias. ODR centres should observe principles such as competence (ensuring the availability of skilled neutrals); confidentiality (and thus high levels of data protection); consent (ie, express, informed and continuous consent); fairness

* As one learned commentator has observed of the interaction between ODR and employment law: "An ODR system can provide an atmosphere of dispute resolution that involves less conflict and hence can more likely lead, not only to dispute resolution of disputes, but resolution accompanied, where appropriate, by a continuity of pre-existing relationships" (Ross, 306). Admittedly, there is a contrary view. Thus, it has been suggested that ODR works best when a dispute has no emotional elements (Bensley, 4).

(ie, ensuring due process and preventing bias); impartiality; neutrality; and transparency (so that parties understand the positive and negative attributes of ODR). If these principles are to be observed, it is necessary that adequate funding be made available for court and court-connected regulation.

5. Phased ODR

In India, it has been recommended that ODR be established in a phased manner – a model that may also suit other jurisdictions.[291] The Indian recommendations outline a three-phase progressive process: setting up the necessary infrastructure while leveraging existing capacity; 'mainstreaming' ODR within a supportive environment; and ultimately transitioning to ODR as the primary mode of dispute resolution. That said, phased rollout may impede the optimal usage of ODR from the 'get-go'. To harness the fullest benefits of ODR, governments must adopt a forward-looking approach, recognising that established norms of dispute resolution have already changed and are rapidly changing in a quickly evolving digital world. "In the dispute resolution ecosystem ... ODR is the future and that future is now."[292]

Appendix: ODR and international bodies

At present we are witnessing rapid growth of ODR around the world. The adoption of ODR requires sustained efforts to promote and improve the ODR processes … Recently, recognising the growth of ODR and its effectiveness in addressing cross-border disputes, supranational organisations such as United Nations and [the] European Union have taken initiatives to regulate and promote ODR processes.

NITI Aayog[293]

Improving ODR: 10 key lessons

- Leverage technology for justice.
- Prioritise user accessibility.
- Ensure secure and transparent communication.
- Adopt a clear and structured resolution process.
- Balance AI with human judgement.
- Integrate ODR with existing legal frameworks.
- Consider (and facilitate) cross-border interoperability.
- Standardise procedures for efficiency.
- Ensure ethical and competent neutral oversight.
- Promote public awareness and adoption of ODR.

1. Overview

This appendix examines the leading global frameworks and initiatives that are shaping the future of ODR. It explores the policy developments, best practices and regulatory frameworks shaped by key international organisations, such as APEC, ASEAN, the OECD and UNCITRAL – which has provided a global blueprint for ODR through its Technical Notes, setting out core principles such as impartiality, efficiency, transparency and technological integration. Each of the international frameworks discussed in this appendix reflects the unique challenges and opportunities of ODR in different legal and economic contexts. The APEC and ASEAN initiatives prioritise regional economic integration. The UNCITRAL Technical Notes seek to standardise best practices across multiple jurisdictions. The OECD recommendations emphasise consumer protection and cross-border cooperation. Despite differences in focus, all of these regional or global initiatives share a common goal: to create fast, fair and accessible digital dispute resolution systems that reflect the realities of a globalised, interconnected world.

2. Asia-Pacific Economic Cooperation

APEC is a regional economic forum established in 1989 to support sustainable economic growth and prosperity in the Asia-Pacific region. Its recent *Study on Best Practices in Using ODR* (2023)[294] is of interest as a study of ODR emanating from a prominent regional organisation.

The study begins by noting that the United Nations has recognised ODR as a viable solution to difficulties in accessing effective justice. It also notes that the development of ODR during the COVID-19 pandemic was critical to providing access to justice throughout this period. The study posits that simply adding Zoom to a current court system does not capitalise sufficiently on all that technology has to offer. Advanced technologies such as AI and machine learning, the study observes, remain largely untapped by justice systems. The pandemic-related technological shift, APEC suggests, has created an opportunity for greater use of ODR in the years ahead, both for domestic disputes and for commercial disputes involving micro, small and medium-sized enterprises – though also, it is submitted, more generally. The study identifies best practices for the use of ODR in commercial disputes, including the need for a user-focused approach. It also considers best practices in ODR platform design, basic principles relating to ODR providers and neutrals, and ODR use in courts and in consumer cases. The starting point in all of this, the study notes, is UNCITRAL's Technical Notes (considered separately in this appendix). In terms of best practices in designing ODR platforms, the study suggests the following:

- *E-resolution of disputes:* The study recommends that ODR include a platform that allows parties to resolve a dispute electronically. In other words, ODR must be (and is) more than e-ADR: it must involve a technological mechanism whereby communications may be generated, sent, received, processed and stored so as to facilitate dispute resolution.
- *Communications via platform:* The study recommends that all communications take place via an ODR platform. The idea behind this recommendation is to counter fraud and to promote confidentiality, fairness and data privacy/security.
- *Algorithmic tools:* The study recommends that ODR processes should include algorithmic tools that assist parties in finding a resolution without input from a neutral third party. The study is notably positive about the use of such tools.[295]

The study recommends that advanced technologies such as AI be incorporated into ODR platforms whenever possible, though it also suggests that systems be futureproofed to allow for ongoing exponential technological developments.

The study suggests that for ODR to assist in reducing difficulties in accessing justice, it must be user focused, accessible, affordable, efficient, flexible, usable and committed to capacity building. Each of these characteristics is considered below.

As to accessibility, the study notes that it does not just mean financial/geographical accessibility, but extends to digital accessibility/literacy, linguistic accessibility and a commitment to user capacity building. So, it has a very wide meaning. The study also points to the importance of mobile-friendly ODR platforms that do not require email. These, it observes, facilitate participation by those without computers and can also assist those with digital literacy challenges and those with physical disabilities.

As to affordability, the study recommends that ODR keep costs below the economic value under dispute. The study also notes that the value of procedural protections should be balanced against the need to provide a process the costs of which are commensurate with the sum in issue.

As to efficiency, the study suggests that if ODR processes are not efficient, reaching decisions promptly, they will soon lose credibility with users. Efficiency, the study notes, should be derived through the use of modern technologies, including algorithms and AI, integrated case management systems and recorded mediated settlement agreements.

As to flexibility, the study suggests that this is a key element of a user-focused ODR system. So, for instance, parties should be able to communicate synchronously or asynchronously and should be able to choose between, for example, email, electronic file transfer or text message as the means of communication.

As to usability – the measure of how easy it is to navigate an interface – clarity is a key facet. Users, the study suggests, should be able intuitively to navigate through the different options presented. Once a system is in operation, it should be subjected to usability testing. According to the US National Center for State Courts, having court proceedings that are accessible and usable is important to ensuring that they are just.[296]

As to capacity building, the study notes that ODR has been held back by a want of user familiarity, as well as related psychological barriers and data privacy concerns. The study suggests that APEC (for which one might reasonably substitute 'government') has a crucial role to play in promoting ODR.

In terms of best practices when it comes to ODR providers and neutrals, the study suggests the following. First, ODR platforms should be auditable, with such audits made publicly available. Second, ODR platform providers should ensure that neutrals have the necessary skillset to arbitrate/mediate a dispute and manage the platform technology. Third, ODR systems should be secure; have inbuilt encryption; maintain appropriate cybersecurity and data protection protocols; and promptly inform users about security breaches and steps taken to prevent reoccurrence. Fourth, in what seems almost a statement of the obvious, the study observes that ODR providers must treat parties equally, with each party given a full opportunity to present its case. Fifth, when it comes to fairness and impartiality, ODR operators should adopt a code of ethics for neutrals that covers, for example, conflicts of interest. Sixth, ODR providers should comply with and uphold the relevant laws and regulations governing an ODR process. Seventh, ODR provider should publish relevant data and statistics and other useful information in an accessible, user-friendly format.

In terms of best practices when it comes to ODR for B2C transactions, the study commences by noting a difference of opinion between the European Union and the United States which emerged during the negotiation of the UNCITRAL Technical Rules. Thus, the European Union was opposed to binding pre-dispute arbitration, wishing to preserve the right of the consumer to go to court. By contrast, the United States and some other economies considered that courts were unsuited to low-value cross-border disputes. This tension had the result that the UNCITRAL Technical Notes do not call for arbitration in the third stage of the ODR process (negotiation-facilitation-*court*.)[297] By contrast, the APEC ODR Collaborative Framework does provide for arbitration in the third stage (negotiation-facilitation-*arbitration*).[298] Turning to particular best practices, the study suggests enhancing e-platforms and e-stores with ODR; national small claims tribunals by ODR-enabling them; national dispute resolution by providing ODR platforms; and cross-border dispute resolution with ODR frameworks.

3. Association of Southeast Asian Nations

ASEAN was established in 1967. Today, it has 10 member states (Brunei, Cambodia, Indonesia, Lao, Malaysia, Myanmar, Philippines, Singapore, Thailand and Vietnam). Its founding declaration – the Bangkok Declaration of 1967 – commits member states, among other matters, to accelerate economic growth, social progress and cultural development in Southeast Asia; and to promote regional peace and stability through abiding respect for justice and the rule of law.

Consistent with ASEAN's founding declaration, the ASEAN Secretariat published the ASEAN Guidelines on Online Dispute Resolution in 2022. The guidelines seek to assist ASEAN member states with establishing or strengthening national ODR systems. The guidelines describe a systematic process for deciding on a suitable national ODR model in each ASEAN member state. One of the informing principles of the guidelines is to promote a certain degree of uniformity of ODR systems in the ASEAN region. They have a specific focus on ODR in the context of B2C commercial transactions. However, they have wider resonance as regards the design of ODR platforms.

The guidelines suggest that ODR offers a means of settling disputes in a speedy, inexpensive and impartial way; can increase transparency and flexibility; and can reinforce cooperation between state bodies whose responsibilities overlap through an alignment of their procedures.

In terms of existing ODR mechanisms in ASEAN countries, again in the consumer context, the ASEAN Secretariat found them to have the following principal characteristics: they were government-led; involved consumer protection authorities; offered flexible, voluntary mediation; applied to online and offline disputes; complemented offline mechanisms; and were interoperable across different sectors and jurisdictions.

In terms of the form of ODR contemplated by the guidelines, it is government or public body led; designed to assist consumers actively in accessing/using ODR; constructed to allow for mediation and arbitration; capable of dealing with both offline and online disputes; designed to complement existing offline/online mechanisms; capable of facilitating consumers with different preferences and needs; and futureproofed.

The guidelines focus on a number of key design criteria to which it considered that ASEAN member states could usefully attend. Each of these is considered below.

Scoping: The guidelines make a number of key recommendations in this regard. First, before commencing on the establishment of a national ODR system, its purpose should be identified by way of, for example, a national policy document. Second, establishing an ODR system need not involve setting up a new system from scratch. Third, states should carefully examine existing offline schemes to see what can be transposed into a more automated online system. Fourth, the widest consultation with stakeholders should precede/accompany the development of a national ODR system so as to build up the widest possible support. Fifth, extensive awareness building among potential users is advisable if, for example, the ODR system is not to suffer from public unawareness. Sixth, a single entity should be tasked with the rollout of a national ODR scheme. Seventh, the need for legislative changes should be factored in when devising a realistic rollout plan. Eighth, the preferred ODR option is a 'one-stop shop' that offers users the potential to engage with a single platform/system. Ninth, technical coordination between different elements of government is necessary to maximise efficiency. Tenth, futureproofing is recommended to allow for ongoing development and upgrading of the system.

Users and third-party participation: Identification of prospective disputants/users and their roles is of paramount importance.

Administration and accountability: Among other matters, the guidelines note that HR investment is required if the officials operating the ODR system are to be suitably competent. Additionally, the guidelines recommend that states organise regular capacity-building activities – for example, on online case management and/or mediation techniques – so that a high level of professionalism is attained and maintained. In terms of accountability (transparency), the guidelines indicate that trust in the effectiveness and fairness of ODR systems is enhanced through the public disclosure of case statistics and resolution rates.

Degree of automation: The guidelines caution against implementing fully automated and sophisticated systems from the outset, suggesting that this not only is expensive but also would require significant efforts to generate the necessary technology literacy among users, and indeed the necessary skills on the part of mediators (case managers). In terms of what might be done, the guidelines suggest the following. First, an assessment should be undertaken of appetite for (and skill in) digital technology, funding, data security and, for example, national policy objectives. Second, any existing online portals could usefully be upgraded from information portals to accommodate online complaints (and tracking of those complaints). Third, as well as online filing of complaints, there could and should be an algorithmic or human-driven process of filtering claims. Fourth, where there are multiple potential lines of complaint (potential avenues of adjudication), the guidelines suggest that a common form could be completed, with the complaint then directed to the most relevant decision-making body. Fifth, the ADR platform should enable parties to communicate virtually, either in real time or asynchronously. Sixth, when it comes to online proceedings, data privacy and security are critical. Seventh, while noting the potential of ODR to rely on AI and predictive justice,* the guidelines consider this to be something that could be looked into in the long term, suggesting that it would be most feasible for straightforward cases where the law and the reliefs available are clear.

---

* The European Ethical Charter on the Use of Artificial Intelligence in Judicial Systems and Their Environment (2018), which is considered at some length in Chapter 16, contains a glossary which contains the following helpful definition/commentary on the concept of 'predictive justice': "Predictive justice is the analysis of large amounts of judicial decisions by artificial intelligence technologies in order to make predictions for the outcome of certain types of ... disputes ... The term "predictive" used by legal tech companies comes from the branches of science (principally statistics) that make it possible to predict future results through inductive analysis. Judicial decisions are processed with a view to detecting correlations between input data (criteria set out in legislation, the facts of the case and the reasoning) and output data (formal judgment ...) Correlations deemed to be relevant make it possible to create models which, when used with new input data ... produce according to their developers a prediction of the decision ... Some authors have criticised both the form and substance of this approach. They argue that, in general, the mathematical modelling of certain social phenomena is not a task comparable to other more easily quantifiable activities (isolating the really causative factors of a court decision is infinitely more complex than playing the game of Go or recognising an image for example): here, there is a much higher risk of false correlations. In addition, in legal theory, two contradictory decisions can prove to be valid if the legal reasoning is sound. Consequently, making predictions would be a purely informative exercise without any prescriptive claim."

Funding: The guidelines accept that there is an upfront cost to ODR in terms of money and staffing commitment and a medium-term cost in terms of IT upkeep and staffing. So, they suggest that a longer-term perspective needs to be brought to bear when assessing the ongoing costs. In terms of recouping funding where full subsidisation is impracticable, the guidelines point to the potential for charging fees. However, the guidelines note that – in the consumer context in which the guidelines were focused – care would be required so as not to pitch fees at such a level that low-income persons seeking an alternative to court litigation would be disadvantaged or disincentivised from using an ODR system.

Accessibility: The guidelines make a variety of recommendations as regards accessibility. First, national ODR systems should allow for broad internet accessibility – for example, through the use of mobile phone 'apps' that require lower bandwidth. Second, a consumer-focused user interface design is an important consideration in terms of accessibility. Third, terms of use should be capable of being readily understood by consumers with different digital literacy levels and differing knowledge of the law. Fourth, multilingual needs should be met by IT or interpreters. Fifth, while a mobile phone may be useful for filing/tracking complaints and ongoing communication, for the settlement process, video calls should be possible, and signing should be done from a laptop or computer. Sixth, the costs of participation for disputants should be kept as low as possible. Seventh, procedural rules should enable users to pursue a claim without legal assistance if they feel confident to do so.

Due process and transparency: The guidelines make a variety of recommendations as regards due process and transparency. First, an ODR system should provide accessible/accurate information to users. Second, digital records should be kept and made accessible to disputants. Third, rules of procedure and other relevant information should be readily available to the public. Fourth, there should be regular reporting on ODR funding, success and use. Fifth, national ODR systems must respect basic principles of due process and fairness. Sixth, abuse of process by parties should be sanctionable. Seventh, sanctions should also be a possibility for non-compliance with ODR outcomes. Eighth, the qualifications, independence and integrity of neutrals should be vetted.

IT requirements: Because the guidelines are intended as a building block towards the longer-term objective of building an ASEAN ODR network, they mention the need for interoperability between national legal systems. They also emphasise the critical importance of data privacy and security.

Legal and procedural requirements: The guidelines make a variety of recommendations as regards legal and procedural requirements. First, for accountability/transparency reasons, the rules of procedure should be widely accessible – for example, on a public website. Second, the rules of procedure should be updated on an ongoing basis to allow for changed circumstances and to eliminate misunderstandings about the procedures. Third, dispute resolution should be staggered (negotiation-facilitation-arbitration/adjudication). Fourth, because ODR is e-based, states should ensure legal recognition of e-documents, e-communications and e-signatures in ODR proceedings. Fifth, it may be necessary to compel certain parties to join in proceedings. Sixth, as well as legal changes to establish/operate an ADR system, ASEAN states are encouraged to change their laws to facilitate cross-border cooperation, especially as regards data flows and sharing of confidential information.

4. Organisation for Economic Cooperation and Development

Founded in 1961, the OECD is a forum in which governments work together to address the economic, social and environmental challenges of, for example, globalisation and the information society, comparing policy experiences, seeking answers to common problems and identifying good practices. This section considers the OECD's Online Dispute Resolution Framework.[299]

The framework seeks to guide countries on how to implement ODR coherently across their justice systems and how to improve the seamless transfer of information between various dispute resolution mechanisms. In doing so, the document introduces a three-pillared framework aimed at providing guidance to countries on the development and integration of ODR within the broader gamut of digital transformation of justice systems. The framework is summarised in Figure 48 and is considered in more detail later below.

Despite its overall support for ODR, the OECD acknowledges that as a dispute resolution form, ODR does present with challenges, including the following. Its use is dependent on there being adequate access to infrastructure and public servants and final users with the necessary digital skills. Platforms require robust security systems to protect sensitive information and to prevent data breaches and unauthorised access. Challenges in ensuring the compatibility of ODR platforms with, and good integration into, existing systems (online and offline) can add complexity to the effective implementation of ODR. There is some concern from a transparency, fairness and equity perspective when it comes to the use of AI in ODR systems. ODR may not be suitable for all types of disputes – notably those involving complex legal issues or requiring detailed examination of evidence.

Figure 48: OECD's ODR framework (summary)

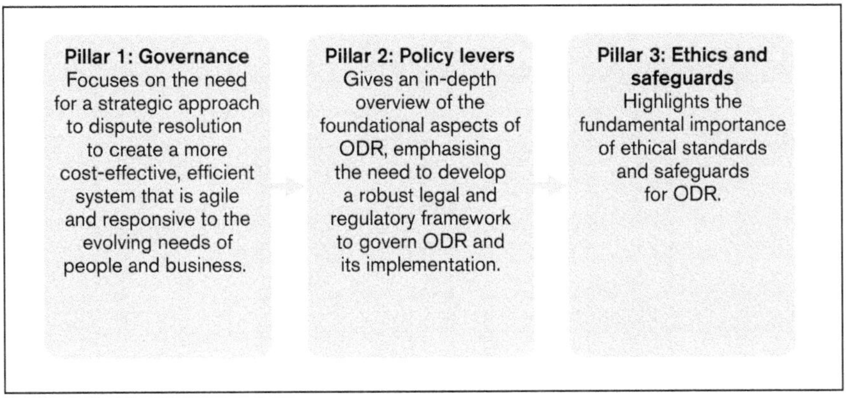

4.1 Pillar 1: Governance

Pillar 1 focuses on the need for a strategic approach to dispute resolution to create a more cost-effective, efficient system that is agile and responsive to the evolving needs of people and business:

- *Strategic approach to governance:* A dispute resolution strategy should, the OECD posits, have a clear vision of the future and well-defined goals; embed digital technologies and data in design and delivery from the outset; adopt a whole-of-government approach to the modernisation of dispute resolution; and involve all relevant stakeholders.
- *Personnel:* The OECD notes that developing the institutional, legal, technological and cultural requirements and changes within a coherent framework of ODR involves establishing institutions; (re)designing legal frameworks; recruiting, training and retaining skills and talent; strengthening and updating IT infrastructure; and integrating the cultural changes to increase stakeholder engagement and user buy-in for ODR.
- *Vulnerable groups:* The OECD makes a number of insightful observations concerning ODR and the 'vulnerable' – a grouping which it defines as including but not limited to children, indigenous groups, elderly, people with disabilities and women. Among the points made by the OECD concerning vulnerable groups are the following. ODR presents with opportunities and risks for people in vulnerable situations. By placing user needs at the centre of designing and delivering justice, services can be more easily adapted and tailored for the vulnerable. Increasing the accessibility and availability of online services can enhance access to justice for people with reduced mobility, living in remote or rural areas, or with certain health conditions. ODR has the potential to reduce the costs of justice services by enabling people to consult information and

services without having to travel long distances or take time out of their day to attend public facilities in-person. Digital technologies and data risk excluding users who cannot or do not wish to engage with justice services through online channels. Adopting a people-centred approach as early as possible in the design stage is the starting point for moving towards quality justice services that are more inclusive and equitable. Aiming for omni-channels can help with designing seamless user journeys across all channels (eg, screens, phone calls, virtual assistance or face to face). Streamlining channels, integrating online features and promoting interoperability can support increased coherence across service outcomes, irrespective of the channel used. Non-digital channels can be used as opportunities to engage with and inform users of the transition to the use of digital channels in the justice sector. The OECD suggests that interacting with consumers in this way can bring them closer to digital transformation in the medium to long term. Countries should view and treat data as a strategic asset, feeding it back into the service so as to enable continuous service improvement in line with the needs of vulnerable people.

- *Businesses as parties:* The OECD considers it important to adopt an agile approach to justice service design to ensure that services can provide swift and affordable solutions to businesses to resolve their conflicts. To do so, the OECD posits, it is essential to understand the specific legal and justice needs of businesses, especially smaller businesses.
- *Public bodies:* Dispute resolution mechanisms are often based on the assumption that the parties to a dispute share a private relationship. However, the OECD notes that ODR also has the potential to bring value to dispute settlements involving public bodies, saving on time and costs and increasing trust in public institutions. (Additionally, it might be noted, the sight of public bodies embracing ODR as a dispute resolution mechanism has the potential to legitimise the use of ODR in the eyes of the public.)
- *ODR and justice institutions:* The OECD suggests that to maximise the benefits of ODR, it is important to bridge the digital skills gap across justice institutions by equipping public sector staff with necessary digital skills and expertise.

4.2 Pillar 2: Policy levers

Pillar 2 emphasises the need to develop a robust legal and regulatory framework to govern ODR and its implementation:

- *Legal domains and claim types:* The OECD suggests that an effective approach to identifying legal domains and types of claims suitable for ODR involves considering whether an online process adequately addresses parties' needs and dispute concerns. The OECD notes that: "Conceptually, in civil and commercial law, all legal domains and all types of claims are potentially well suited to ODR."[300] Without qualifying this general observation, it notes also that ODR is particularly appropriate for certain types of case – namely, complaints that involve a small amount of money; consumer-trader disputes (given their often low value and standardised form); property disputes (eg, real estate conflicts – often between tenants and landlords or homeowner associations); and smaller civil infractions and minor misdemeanours, such as traffic and parking offences.

- *Managing technological advances:* The OECD makes a number of useful practical points about managing technological advances. Thus, it observes that ODR implementation should embrace technology and capacity building; centralised leadership is important to promote coherence; technology-neutral law making is a good practice to manage fast-paced changes; legal culture and traditions should be factored into ODR (and AI) integration; raising awareness about digital technologies in justice should enhance public support and understanding; it is important to minimise the risks of being tied to specific vendors or proprietary technologies; timely decommissioning of services can mitigate issues related to outdated technology; maintaining engagement with stakeholders is important; and some countries prefer to start with smaller initiatives and how to integrate ODR into less complex or contentious cases.
- *Data governance:* Data can be used to assess the functioning of ODR pre-court and court services. However, governments are urged by the OECD to develop legal and regulatory frameworks, data principles and guidelines to optimise such data utilisation while also maintaining and enhancing public trust.
- *Agile implementation:* The OECD recommends an agile approach to designing and delivering ODR, by which it means scoping a project; understanding user needs; designing dispute resolution functionalities; and testing, implementing, monitoring and evaluating outcomes.

4.3 Pillar 3: Ethics and safeguards

Pillar 3 highlights the fundamental importance of ethical standards and safeguards for ODR. To better ensure the ethical and trustworthy use of data in justice, the OECD suggests that countries may wish to consider using data to serve the public interest and deliver public value; managing data with integrity; ensuring that data is fit for purpose; integrating data ethics principles into governance and institutions; defining the boundaries of data collection, access sharing and use; communicating clearly and openly about the use of data in justice; allowing data subjects to exercise control over their data; and ensuring accountability and proactiveness in the management of risks.

5. United Nations Commission on International Trade Law

In 2016, the UN General Assembly adopted a series of technical notes on ODR that were prepared by UNCITRAL, headquartered in Vienna.[301] The motivations for the resolution are stated in its recitals. There had been a sharp increase in online cross-border transactions and hence a need for associated dispute resolution mechanisms. ODR is an attractive proposition as regards assisting parties in resolving disputes in a simple, fast, flexible and secure manner, without the need for physical presence at a meeting or hearing.

As to the substance of the notes, the recitals to the resolution make three general points. The notes are non-binding and descriptive and reflect the principles of impartiality, independence, efficiency, effectiveness, due process, fairness, accountability and transparency. The notes are expected to contribute significantly to the development of systems to enable the settlement of disputes arising from cross-border low-value sales or service contracts concluded using electronic communications. The UN General Assembly was convinced that the notes would significantly assist all states – in particular, developing countries and states whose economies are in transition – ODR administrators, ODR platforms, neutrals and the parties to ODR proceedings in developing and using ODR systems.

As to *transparency*, the notes suggest that an ODR administrator may wish to publish anonymised data or statistics on outcomes in ODR processes, to enable parties to assess its overall record, consistent with applicable principles of confidentiality. All relevant information, the notes state, should be available on the ODR administrator's website in a user-friendly and accessible manner.

As to *independence*, the notes suggest that it is desirable for an ODR administrator to adopt a code of ethics for its neutrals, in order to guide neutrals as to conflicts of interest and other rules of conduct. Additionally, they observe that it is useful for an ODR administrator to adopt policies dealing with identifying and handling conflicts of interest.

As to *expertise*, the notes indicate that an ODR administrator may wish to implement comprehensive policies governing the selection and training of neutrals. An internal oversight/quality assurance process may help an ODR administrator to ensure that a neutral conforms with the standards it has set for itself.

As to *consent*, the notes suggest that ODR processes should be based on the explicit and informed consent of the disputants.

The notes outline a three-stage process for ODR proceedings, as follows:

- Negotiation: The parties attempt to reach a mutually agreeable resolution without third-party involvement.

- Facilitated settlement: A neutral assists in mediating a resolution if negotiation fails.
- Final stage: If the dispute remains unresolved, adjudication or arbitration may be used to reach a binding decision.

This model is designed to promote efficiency while minimising costs and procedural complexity. UNCITRAL's framework identifies several key actors in an ODR process. These are depicted in Figure 49.

Figure 49: Key persons in the ODR process

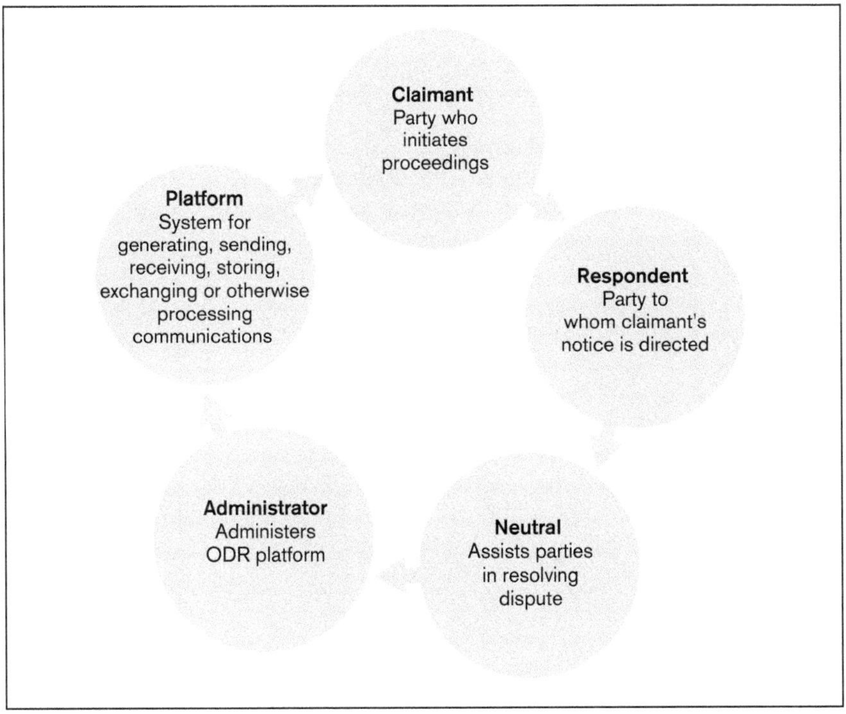

The notes consider the nature of the formal communications that may arise in ODR proceedings. In this regard, they make four observations. First, they identify the communications that may take place during the course of proceedings as comprising any communication made by means of information generated, sent, received or stored by electronic, magnetic, optical or similar means. Second, they suggest it to be desirable that all communications in ODR proceedings take place via the ODR platform. Third, they suggest that to enhance efficiency, an ODR administrator should promptly acknowledge (via the ODR platform) the receipt of any communication; notify the parties (via the ODR platform) of any communication; and keep the parties informed of the commencement/conclusion of different stages of the ODR proceedings. Fourth, they suggest that a communication should be deemed to be received by a party when the administrator notifies that party of its availability on the platform.

It is clear that once a dispute progresses to and beyond the facilitated settlement stage, the neutral has a significant role to play. The notes make a number of observations concerning this person. To enhance efficiency and reduce costs, it is preferable that an ODR administrator appoint a neutral only when required. Upon appointment, the ODR administrator must promptly notify the parties of the neutral's name and any other relevant information concerning that neutral. It is desirable that neutrals have relevant professional experience and dispute resolution skills, but they need not be lawyers. With regard to the appointment/functions of neutrals, the notes indicate that the following should apply: the neutral's acceptance of appointment should confirm that they have time to assist; they should declare impartiality/independence and disclose any later changes; the opposing parties should have a means of objecting to the chosen neutral; following any objection, the ODR administrator should rule on that objection; for reasons of cost efficiency, there must be only one neutral at any one time; and a party should be entitled to object to a neutral receiving negotiation stage material.

As regards the powers of a neutral, the notes suggest it to be desirable that the neutral have the power to conduct the ODR as they consider appropriate; be required to avoid unnecessary delay/expense; provide a fair, efficient process; remain independent and impartial, and treat parties equally; conduct proceedings based on the communications before them; allow the parties to provide additional information; and extend any deadlines for a reasonable time.

The notes also indicate that it is desirable that a party be able to indicate in a notice or response whether they wish to proceed in a different language, so that the ODR administrator can address this aspect.

Finally, the notes suggest that it is desirable for there to be guidelines and/or minimum requirements regarding the conduct of ODR platforms/administrators; and for ODR proceedings to be subject to the same confidentiality and due process standards that apply to offline proceedings – in particular independence, neutrality and impartiality.

Notes

1 Denning, 77.
2 Cardozo, 163.
3 Roberts, 4ff.
4 Civil Justice Council, 3.
5 Spaulding, 316.
6 381 US 532 (1965).
7 449 US 560 (1981).
8 Joint Technology Committee, ii. The Joint Technology Committee is a collaborative entity established by, among other things, the US National Center for State Courts.
9 NITI Aayog, 1. NITI Aayog is the premier thinktank of the government of India.
10 Katsh and Rule, 329.
11 OECD (2024), 10.
12 *Id.*
13 *Id.*
14 EBRD (1), 85.
15 Rainey and Bridgesmith, 4.
16 Syme, 343.
17 Rainey, 81.
18 OECD (2024), 9.
19 Winship, 38.
20 Condlin, 740
21 Ebner and Greenberg, 70.
22 Acosta *et al*, 135–137.
23 Greacen (2018).
24 Id, 3.
25 Joint Technology Committee (2017), 7.
26 NITI Aayog, 5.
27 Anon (4), 10.
28 Civil No 39301 (Erie City, Ct of Common Pleas), 6 December 1971.
29 McCrystal, 446.
30 Norton, 835.
31 Sharma *et al*, 225.
32 Hodson, 425.
33 Bulinski and Prescott, 245.
34 Galves, 43.
35 Rossner, 361.
36 Bannon and Adelstein, 1.
37 Id, 2.
38 *Id.*
39 Exon (2), 19.
40 Vieira de Carvalho Fernandes *et al*, 20.
41 318 US 332.
42 Id, 342.
43 Civil Justice Council, 26.
44 Briggs, Final Report, 2.
45 Civil Justice Council, 9-10.
46 Id, 18.
47 Id, 26.
48 House of Commons Library, 2.
49 *Id.*
50 See Vallance.
51 See Milmo.
52 Anon (7).

53 Briggs, Final Report, 37
54 See Hague Institute for Innovation of Law.
55 Joint Technology Committee, 24.
56 NITI Aayog, 3.
57 See www.gov.uk/service-manual/service-standard.
58 Joint Technology Committee, 11–14.
59 Wormington, 152–153.
60 Schmitz and Martinez, 2.
61 *Id.*
62 Rabinovich-Einy, 44.
63 Sela (1), 683.
64 Speech of US Vice President JD Vance to the AI Action Summit (Paris, 11 February 2025). The full text of the speech is available at the website of the American Presidency Project, www.presidency.ucsb.edu.
65 Witwer *et al*, 6.
66 *Id.*
67 Acosta *et al*, 135–136.
68 Witwer *et al*, Table A2.
69 American Bar Association Section of Dispute Resolution, 241.
70 Civil Justice Council, 4.
71 See www.security.gov.uk/policy-and-guidance/secure-by-design/principles/.
72 Schmitz and Wing, 261–262.
73 Susskind, 112.
74 National Center for Technology and Dispute Resolution, 2.
75 NITI Aayog, 13.
76 Schmitz and Wing, 259–260.
77 Goncalves and Vanenkova, 150.
78 Hornle, 289.
79 Rainey, 24.
80 Kumtepe and Riley, 156.
81 *Id.*
82 Civil Justice Council, 26.
83 Katsh and Wing, 43.
84 *Id.*
85 Shackelford and Raymond, 636.
86 Thornburg, 154.
87 Regulation (EU) No 2016/679 of the European Parliament and of the Council of 27 April 2016 on the protection of natural persons with regard to the processing of personal data and on the free movement of such data, and repealing Directive 95/46/EC (General Data Protection Regulation) (OJ L119, 4 May 2016, 1).
88 Draper and Raymond, 144.
89 Ebner and Greenberg, 88.
90 See California Access to Justice Commission (2).
91 NITI Aayog, 14.
92 Martinez, 141.
93 See Zoudoumis.
94 NITI Aayog, 10.
95 Salter and Thompson, 124.
96 *Id.*
97 *Id.*
98 See IEEE.
99 *Id.*
100 See Anon (8).
101 *Id.*
102 California Access to Justice Commission (2), 1.
103 *Id.*
104 Joint Technology Committee, 8.
105 NITI Aayog, 14.
106 See Anon (3).
107 *Id*, 20–23.
108 Larson (1), 101.
109 Butler *et al*, 72.
110 *Id*, 76.
111 *Id*, 79.
112 *Id*, 82.
113 *Id*, 84.
114 Joint Technology Committee, 19.
115 NITI Aayog, 15.
116 Regulation (EU) No 524/2013 of the European Parliament and of the Council of 21 May 2013 on online

dispute resolution for consumer disputes and amending Regulation (EC) No 2006/2004 and Directive 2009/22/EC (OJ L165 18 June 2013), 1.

117 European Commission, Proposal for a Regulation of the European Parliament and of the Council repealing Regulation (EU) No 524/2013 and amending Regulations (EU) 2017/2394 and (EU) 2018/1724 with regards to the discontinuation of the European ODR Platform, COM(2023) 647 final, Brussels, 17 October 2023.

118 Regulation (EU) 2022/850 of the European Parliament and of the Council of 30 May 2022 on a computerised system for the cross-border electronic exchange of data in the area of judicial cooperation in civil and criminal matters (e-CODEX system) and amending Regulation (EU) 2018/1726 (OJ L150, 1 June 2022, 1–19).

119 See the long title to the e-Codex Regulation.

120 Directive 2013/11/EU of the European Parliament and of the Council of 21 May 2013 on alternative dispute resolution for consumer disputes and amending Regulation (EC) No 2006/2004 and Directive 2009/22/EC (Directive on consumer ADR) (OJ L165, 18 June 2013, 63–79).

121 Stegner, 356.

122 Article 2(1).

123 Article 1.

124 *Id.*

125 Article 2.

126 Article 5.

127 Article 6.

128 Article 7.

129 Articles 8 and 9.

130 Article 11.

131 Article 12.

132 Article 13.

133 Article 19.

134 That is, Regulation (EU) 2019/1150 of the European Parliament and of the Council of 20 June 2019 on promoting fairness and transparency for business users of online intermediation services (OJ L186, 11 July 2019, 57).

135 Article 11.

136 Article 12(1).

137 Article 12(3).

138 Article 12(4).

139 Specifically, in Central Europe and the Baltic states, the countries of Estonia and Poland; in Central Asia, the countries of Kazakhstan, Kyrgyz Republic, Mongolia and Uzbekistan; in Eastern Europe and the Caucasus, the countries of Armenia, Azerbaijan, Georgia, Moldova and Ukraine; in Southeastern Europe, the countries of Albania, Bulgaria and Serbia; in the southern and Eastern Mediterranean, the countries of Morocco and Tunisia; and Türkiye.

140 Joint Technology Committee, 17. Curiously, although China is to the fore in terms of ODR provision, it actually came somewhat late to ODR and then "steamed ahead" of other jurisdictions which had previously entered the field of ODR (Tahura and Selvadurai, 14).

141 NITI Aayog, 60.

142 Ballesteros, 94.

143 Anon (5).

144 https://english.court.gov.cn/pdf/Topic3DigitalEconomyE-commercealongtheSilkRoadandOnlineDisputeResolution.pdf.

145 Ballesteros, 92.

146 Cooper, 282.

147 Lin, 537.

148 *Id.*

149 *Id.*

150 *Id.*

151 Ballesteros, 93.

152 *Id*, 92.

153 Cooper, 283.

154 Tahura and Selvadurai, 16.

155 Liebman *et al*, 2410.

156 *Id*, 2413.

157 *Id*, 2420.

158 *Id*, 2426.

159 Cao, 316.

160 Tahura and Selvadurai, 17.

161 Abdullah, 1.

162 Available on Project Gutenberg (www.projectgutenberg.org).

163 Bol, 69–70.

164 *Id.*

165 Bell *et al*, 15.

166 *Id*, 2. Generative AI is a form of AI which generates new content.
167 Baker *et al*, 22–30.
168 UNCTAD, 13.
169 Bell *et al*, 15–28.
170 Gingras and Morrison, 228.
171 OECD (2024), 22–23.
172 Abdullah, 9.
173 *Id*, 12.
174 Joint Technology Committee, 8.
175 NITI Aayog, 6.
176 Schmitz and Rule, 108.
177 Article I.
178 Janssen and Vennmanns, 57.
179 *Id*.
180 Van Den Herik and Dimov, 104.
181 Ast and Deffains, 9.
182 Bergquist, 1273.
183 Anon, (1).
184 *Id*.
185 See generally Kumtepe, 143–145.
186 *Id*.
187 Ortolani, 628.
188 Van Den Herik and Dimov, 100.
189 See Dimov.
190 The facts of the case are based on the example in Lesaege *et al*.
191 Summarises the process described in Cuende and Izquierdo.
192 Joint Technology Committee, 15.
193 NITI Aayog, 62.
194 Thomas, 159.
195 Salunke, 1572.
196 Directive (EU) 2022/2555 of the European Parliament and of the Council of 14 December 2022 on measures for a high common level of cybersecurity across the Union, amending Regulation (EU) No 910/2014 and Directive (EU) 2018/1972, and repealing Directive (EU) 2016/1148 (OJ L333, 27 December 2022, 80–152).
197 Directive (EU) 2022/2557 of the European Parliament and of the Council of 14 December 2022 on the resilience of critical entities and repealing Council Directive 2008/114/EC (OJ L333, 27 December 2022, 164).
198 Regulation (EU) 2019/881 of the European Parliament and of the Council of 17 April 2019 on ENISA (the European Union Agency for Cybersecurity) and on information and communications technology cybersecurity certification and repealing Regulation (EU) No 526/2013 ('Cybersecurity Act') (OJ L151, 7 June 2019, 15–69).
199 See Regulation (EU) 2022/2554 of the European Parliament and of the Council of 14 December 2022 on digital operational resilience for the financial sector and amending Regulations (EC) No 1060/2009, (EU) No 648/2012, (EU) No 600/2014, (EU) No 909/2014 and (EU) 2016/1011 (OJ L333, 27 December 2022, 1, and Directive (EU) 2022/2256 of the European Parliament and of the Council of 14 December 2022 amending Directives 2009/65/EC, 2009/138/EC, 2011/61/EU, 2013/36/EU, 2014/59/EU, 2014/65/EU, (EU) 2015/2366 and (EU) 2016/2341 as regards digital operational resilience for the financial sector (OJ L333, 27 December 2022, 153).
200 Regulation (EU) 2024/2847 333, 27 December 2022, of the European Parliament and of the Council of 23 October 2024 on horizontal cybersecurity requirements for products with digital elements and amending Regulations (EU) No 168/2013 and (EU) 2019/1020 and Directive (EU) 2020/1828 (Cyber Resilience Act) (OJ L, 2024/2847, 20 November 2024.
201 Proposal for a Regulation of the European Parliament and of the Council laying down measures to strengthen solidarity and capacities in the Union to detect, prepare for and respond to cybersecurity threats and incidents (COM(2023) 209 final, 18 April 2023).
202 Mignanelli, 299–300.
203 See Roos.
204 See Zhang, 113–117.
205 Joint Technology Committee, 19.
206 NITI Aayog, 7.
207 Council of Europe (1).
208 Joint Technology Committee, 14.
209 NITI Aayog, 90.
210 The European Ethical Charter on the Use of Artificial Intelligence in Judicial Systems and Their Environment (2018).
211 Speech of US Vice President JD Vance to the AI Action Summit (Paris, 11 February 2025). (The full text of the speech is available at the website of the American Presidency Project, www.presidency.ucsb.edu.)
212 Joint Technology Committee, 6.

213 NITI Aayog, 91.
214 Norton, 779.
215 See Tillman.
216 *Id*, 60.
217 Washington, DC: 2021.
218 Tiamiyu, 125.
219 *Id*.
220 NLADA, 32.
221 See California Access to Justice Commission (2).
222 NLADA, 34.
223 Civil Justice Council, 2.
224 NLADA, 34.
225 Civil Justice Council, 5.
226 Briggs, Final Report, 38.
227 NLADA, 48.
228 *Id*, 49.
229 *Id*, 55.
230 *Id*, 55–56
231 *Id*, 56.
232 *Id*, 58.
233 *Id*, 59–61.
234 *Id*, 61.
235 Anderson and Cole, 256.
236 Grabowski, 1.
237 Woodard, 1171.
238 Lifshitz, 529.
239 Sacoff, 20.
240 141 F3d 1316.
241 Sacoff, 22.
242 Hassan, 9–10.
243 Joint Technology Committee, 12–14.
244 Administrative Conference of the United States, 1.
245 *Id*, 572.
246 Administrative Conference of the United States, 1.
247 *Id*.
248 296 F3d 316 (4th Cir 2002).
249 *Id*, 322.
250 See Exon (2).
251 See Zoudoumis.
252 *Id*.
253 *Id*.
254 Marouf and Herrera, 525. There are also apps that enable illegal immigrants to engage better with ICE and to notify friends and family if they have been arrested or deported (*id*, 525–526).
255 *Id*, 534–535.
256 *Id*, 532.
257 *Id*, 565.
258 Brennan, 198.
259 Schmitz and Wing, 252–254.
260 See Sorensen.
261 See www.gov.uk/get-a-divorce.
262 Calliess, 660.
263 Sang, 140.
264 See Colee.
265 *Id*, 2–3.
266 National Consumer Law Center, 7.
267 *Id*.
268 See Gibb.
269 Ferguson, 1462.
270 *Id*, 1464.
271 *Id*.
272 Bender, 6.
273 NACDL, 4.
274 Bender, 35.
275 *Id*.
276 *Id*, 36.
277 See Exon (2).
278 See generally id, 53.
279 On the potential for cost reduction, see, eg, id, 58–59.

280 *Id*, 54.
281 *Id*, 36.
282 *State v Loomis*, 2016 WI 68.
283 *Id*, 13–17.
284 *Id*, 19.
285 *Id*, 27.
286 *Id*, 1–4.
287 European Committee on Crime Problems, "Discussion Paper on Criminal Liability Related to AI systems" CDPC (2024)09 (2024).
288 Sartor *et al*, 537.
289 European Committee on Crime Problems, "Discussion Paper on Criminal Liability Related to AI systems" CDPC(2024)09. (2024), 10–11.
290 Wing *et al*, 61–62.
291 NITI Aayog, 105.
292 *Id*, 107.
293 *Id*, 43.
294 APEC (2023).
295 *Id*, 9.
296 *Id*, 17.
297 *Id*, 28.
298 *Id*.
299 OECD (2024).
300 *Id*, 23.
301 See UNCITRAL.

Bibliography

Abdullah, Aedit, "The 30th Singapore Law Review Annual Lecture: The Obsolescent Judge" (2018-19) 36 *Singapore Law Review* 1.

Acosta, Michelle *et al*, "ODR Best Practices for Court-Connected Programmes from Our Experiences with Court-Based ODR Design Processes" (2019) 6(2) *International Journal of Online Dispute Resolution* 134.

Administrative Conference of the United States, "Administrative Conference Recommendation 2011-4: Agency Use of Video Hearings: Best Practices and Possibilities for Expansion" (2011).

American Bar Association Section of Dispute Resolution, Guidance for Online Dispute Resolution (2023) 38(3) *Ohio State Journal on Dispute Resolution* 241.

Anon,

- (1) "Beijing Internet Court introduces automated case filing with blockchain tech", Beijing Internet Court Press Release, 4 November 2019. https://english.bjinternetcourt.gov.cn/2019-11/04/c_234.htm#:~:text=With%20only%20a%20click%2C%20the,smart%20contract%20technology%20in%20China.
- (2) Courts Deliver Justice Virtually Amid Coronavirus Outbreak, *United States Courts,* 8 April 2020. www.uscourts.gov/news/2020/04/08/courts-deliver-justice-virtually-amid-coronavirus-outbreak.
- (3) *Evaluation of Two Statewide Virtual Dispute Resolution Services in Michigan,* Final Report (2022). www.courts.michigan.gov/49c110/siteassets/reports/odr/sji-evaluation-report-final-report.pdf.
- (4) "Microphones in Court", *The Times*, 30 December 1931, 10.
- (5) "SPC head stresses construction of one-stop dispute solving, litigation service system", 3 September 2023. https://english.court.gov.cn/2020-09/03/c_769817.htm.
- (6) "SPC launches new online platform for dispute resolution". https://english.court.gov.cn/2025-01/26/c_1067336.htm.
- (7) "The Guardian view on the digital divide: a growing problem that must be taken seriously", *The Guardian,* 6 August 2023.
- (8) "Turning America's Digital Divide into Digital Dividends" (2021). https://digitalplanet.tufts.edu/us-digital-divide/.

Anderson, Edward C and Timothy S Cole, "The UDRP – A Model for Dispute Resolution in E-Commerce" (2002) 6(1) *Journal of Small and Emerging Business Law* 235.APEC, *APEC Collaborative Framework for Online Dispute Resolution of Cross-Border Business-to-Business Disputes*

– *Endorsed* (2019) (2019/SOM3/EC/022).

– *Stocktake of APEC Online Dispute Resolution Technologies* (APEC, 2022).

– *Study on Best Practices in Using ODR* (2023).

ASEAN, *Guidelines on Online Dispute Resolution* (2022).

Ast, Federico and Bruno Deffains, "When Online Dispute Resolution Meets Blockchain: The Birth of Decentralized Justice" (2021) 4(2) *Stanford Journal of Blockchain Law & Policy* 1.

Baker, James *et al*, *An Introduction to Artificial Intelligence for Federal Judges* (Federal Judicial Center, 2023).

Ballesteros, Teresa, "International Perspectives on Online Dispute Resolution in the E-Commerce Landscape" (2021) 8(2) *International Journal of Online Dispute Resolution* 85.

Bender, Matthew, "Unmuted: Solutions to Safeguard Constitutional Rights in Virtual Courtrooms and How Technology Can Expand Access to Quality Counsel and Transparency in the Criminal Justice System" (2021) 66(1) *Villanova Law Review* 1.

Bannon, Alicia and Janna Adelstein, "The Impact of Video Proceedings on Fairness and Access to Justice in Court" (Brennan Center for Justice, 2020).

Bell, Felicity *et al*, *AI Decision-Making and the Courts* (AIJA, 2019).

Bensley, Norman, "Online Dispute Resolution" (2004) 6(4) *TortSource* 1.

Bergquist, Chantell, "Virtual Hearings and Blockchain Technology Solutions in Criminal Law" (2021) 47(3) *Mitchell Hamline Law Review* 1248.

Bhalla, Deepakshi and Kriti Sharma, "ODR – An Impending Solution to Disputes" (2022) 4 *Indian Journal of Law and Legal Research* 1.

Biskup, Bartosz, "Two Senses of Law as an Artefact" (2034) 50(3) *Monash University Law Review* 1.

Boehme, Simon J, "Sceptics of the Screen: Irish Perceptions of Online Dispute Resolution" (2015) 2(2) *International Journal of Online Dispute Resolution* 156.

Bol, Stephanie H, "Online Dispute Resolution, Resolving Conflicts in Cyberspace" (2003) 11(1) *Artificial Intelligence and Law* 69.

Branting, Karl *et al*, "A Computational Model of Facilitation in Online Dispute Resolution" (2023) 31(3) *Artificial Intelligence and Law* 465.

Brennan, Rebecca, "Mismatch.com: Online Dispute Resolution and Divorce" (2011) 13(1) *Cardozo Journal of Conflict Resolution* 197.

Briggs, Michael, *Civil Courts Structure Review: Final Report* (Judiciary of England and Wales, 2016).

– *Civil Courts Structure: Interim Report* (Judiciary of England and Wales, 2015).

Bulinski, Maximilian A and JJ Prescott, "Online Case Resolution Systems: Enhancing Access, Fairness, Accuracy, and Efficiency" (2016) 21(2) *Michigan Journal of Race & Law* 205.

Butler, Stacy *et al*, *The Utah Online Dispute Resolution Platform: A Usability Evaluation Report* (University of Arizona, 2020).

California Access to Justice Commission,

- (1) *Remote Hearings and Access to Justice During Covid-19 and Beyond* (2020).
- (2) *The Role of Technology in Enhancing Rural Access to Justice* (2020).
- (3) *Final Report on the Pilot Program: Remote Services by Urban Pro Bono Lawyers for Rural Small Business Clients* (2023).

Calliess, Gralf-Peters, "Online Dispute Resolution: Consumer Redress in a Global Market Place" (2006) 7(8) *German Law Journal* 647.

Cao, Zhixun, "Evolution of Online Courts in China: Situation and Challenges", (2021) 11(2) *International Journal of Procedural Law* 300.

Cardozo, Benjamin Cardozo, *The Nature of the Judicial Process* (Yale University Press, 1921).

CEPEJ, *European Ethical Charter on the Use of AI In Judicial Systems and Their Environment* (2018).

Civil Justice Council, *Online Dispute Resolution for Low Value Civil Claims* (Civil Justice Council, 2015).

Cole, Sarah R and Amanda Spangler, "Virtual Mediation: The Only Door Needed in the Multi-Door Courthouse?" (2023) 52(3) *Stetson Law Review* 477.

Colee, Christopher H, "Alabama – Online Dispute Resolution", *The Alabama Lawyer*, 21 July 2022. www.alabar.org/news/from-the-alabama-lawyer-alabama-online-dispute-resolution/.

Condlin, Robert J, "Online Dispute Resolution: Stinky, Repugnant, or Drab?" (2017) 18(3) *Cardozo Journal of Conflict Resolution* 717.

Council of Europe,

- (1) *Electronic Evidence in Civil and Administrative Proceedings* (2019) (2019).
- (2) *European Ethical Charter on the Use of AI in Judicial Systems and Their Environment* (2018).
- (3) *Guidelines on Online Dispute Resolution Mechanisms in Civil and Administrative Court Proceedings* (2021). https://search.coe.int/cm/Pages/result_details.aspx?ObjectId=0900001680a2cf96.

Cuende, Luis and Jorge Izquierdo, "Aragon Network: A Decentralised Infrastructure for Value Exchange" (Version 1.1, 20 April 2017).

Denning, Alfred, *Freedom Under the Law* (Stevens & Sons, 1949).

Dimov, Daniel, "Crowdsourced Online Dispute Resolution" (Leiden University Centre for Law and Digital Technologies, SIKS Dissertation Series 2017-17, 2017).

Draper, Chris and Angie Raymond, "Ethical Technology Risk: How to Identify What Is Reasonable Data Protection for ODR" (2019) 6(2) *International Journal of Online Dispute Resolution* 144.

Dykes, Taylor, "Rewriting Digital Content for Brevity", 10 September 2023, www.nngroup.com/articles/rewriting-content-brevity/.

Ebner, Noam and Elayne E Greenberg, "Strengthening Online Dispute Resolution Justice" (2020) 63 *Washington University Journal of Law & Policy* 65.

Ebner, Noam and John Zeleznikow, "Fairness, Trust and Security in Online Dispute Resolution" (2015) 36(2) *Hamline Journal of Public Law & Policy* 143.

– "No Sheriff in Town: Governance for Online Dispute Resolution" (2016) 32(4) *Negotiation Journal* 297.

EBRD, *Are You Ready for Online Courts? Guide on Readiness for the Introduction of Online Courts* (EBRD, 2023).

– *What Is an Online Court?* (2023).

European Committee on Crime Problems, "Discussion Paper on Criminal Liability Related to AI Systems" CDPC(2024)09, (2024).

Exon, Susan Nauss, "The Internet Meets Obi-Wan Kenobi in the Court of Next Resort" (2002) 8(1) *Boston University Journal of Science & Technology Law* 1.

– "Next Generation of Online Dispute Resolution: The Significance of Holography to Enhance and Transform Dispute Resolution" (2010) 12(1) *Cardozo Journal of Conflict Resolution* 19.

Federal Trade Commission, *Consumer Protection in the Global Electronic Marketplace* (2000).

Ferguson, Andrew, "Courts without Court" (2022) 75(5) *Vanderbilt Law Review* 1461.

Galves, Fred, "Virtual Justice as Reality: Making the Resolution of E-Commerce Disputes More Convenient, Legitimate, Efficient, and Secure" (2009) 1 *University of Illinois Journal of Law, Technology & Policy* 1.

Gibb, Frances, "The Rule of Law is under Serious Threat", *The Times*, 23 May 2019, 54.

Gingras, Darren and Joshua Morrison, "Artificial Intelligence and Family ODR" (2021) 59(2) *Family Court Review* 227.

Goncalves, Ana and Irena Vanenkova, "From Practice to Profession: The ODR Community's Next Vital Step" (2016) 3(2) *International Journal of Online Dispute Resolution* 146.

Grabowski, Mark, "Should the U.S. Reclaim Control of the Internet: Evaluating ICANN's Administrative Oversight Since the 2016 Handover" (2018) *Nebraska Law Review Bulletin* 1.

Greacen, John, "Supporting Self-Represented Litigants and Access to Justice: How Does ODR Fit in?" (2019) 6(2) *International Journal of Online Dispute Resolution* 170.

– *18 Ways Courts Should Use Technology to Better Serve Their Customers* (IAALS, 2018).

Hague Institute for Innovation of Law, *ODR and the Courts: The Promise of 100% Access to Justice* (HiiL, 2016).

Hill, Chloe, "Litigants in Person in Judicial Review Cases: Lessons from the Wider Legal Context and Ways to Improve the Process for Litigants in Person" (2019) 24(4) *Judicial Review* 258.

Hodson, David, "The Role, Benefits, and Concerns of Digital Technology in the Family Justice System" (2019) 57(3) *Family Court Review* 425.

Hornle, Julia, "The Uniform Domain Name Dispute Resolution Procedure: Is Too Much of a Good Thing a Bad Thing?" (2008) 11(3) *SMU Science and Technology Law Review* 253.

House of Commons Library, *Access to Broadband Services* (No. 2023/176) (2023).

ICCA/NYC Bar/CPR, *Protocol on Cybersecurity in international Arbitration* (2019).

IEEE, "Connecting the Unconnected". https://ctu.ieee.org/blog/2023/02/03/solutions-to-the-digital-divide-moving-toward-a-more-equitable-future/.

Janssen, AU and Tom J Vennmanns, "Smart Dispute Resolution in the Digital Age: The Potential of Smart Contracts and Online Dispute Resolution for Dispute Prevention and Resolution in Consumer Law Cases" (2021) 9 *International Journal on Consumer Law and Practice* 52.

Joint Technology Committee, *JTC Resource Bulletin: ODR for Courts*, Version 2.0 (2017).

Kadioglu Kumtepe, Cemre C, "A Brief Introduction to Blockchain Dispute Resolution" (2021) 14(2) *John Marshall Law Journal* 138.

Kadioglu Kumtepe, Cemre C and Stephen Riley, "Digital Dignity: The Shibboleth of Digitalization in Europe?" (2024) 6(3) *Law, Technology and Humans* 156.

Katsh, Ethan and Colin Rule, "What We Know and Need to Know about Online Dispute Resolution" (2016) 67(2) *South Carolina Law Review* 329.

Katsh, Ethan and Leah Wing, "Ten Years of Online Dispute Resolution (ODR): Looking at the Past and Constructing the Future" (2006) 38(1) *University of Toledo Law Review* 19.

Keegan, Siobhán, "The Duties and Joys of Digital Judging, Artificial Justice? The Integrity Problem Facing Judicial AI" (2024) 8(1) *Irish Judicial Studies Journal* 19.

Khatam, Abdul Hassan, "Evaluation of ICANN's Uniform Domain-Name Dispute-Resolution Policy" (2021) 24(6) *Journal of Legal, Ethical and Regulatory Issues* 1.

Krupa, Jacob, "UK Refusal to Sign AI Summit Declaration to Do with Weak Language on Security, Government Source Says", Europe Live with Jacob Krupa blog, *The Guardian,* 11 February 2025.

Larson, David Allen,

– (1) "Designing and Implementing a State Court ODR System: From Disappointment to Celebration" (2019) 2 *Journal of Dispute Resolution* 77.

– (2) "Resolving Disputes Online? Ensure Your Services Are Disability Accessible". https://nysba.org/resolving-disputes-online-ensure-your-services-are-disability-accessible/?srsltid=AfmBOorEH0VppgRSKUk4nIS_P9JzzJyCBEpr0nHWqulI8nVjQFj_Higm.

Lesaege, Clément *et al, Kleros, Long Paper v.2.0.2* (2021). https://kleros.io/yellowpaper.pdf.

Liebman, Benjamin *et al*, "Rolling Back Transparency in China's Courts" (2023) 122(8) *Columbia Law Review* 2407.

Lifshitz, Allon, "Cybersquatting" (2001) 38(2) *Harvard Journal on Legislation* 529.

Lin, Yang, "China's Three Internet Courts" (2021) 2(3) *Amicus Curiae* 531.

Macmillan, Hugh, *Law and Other Things* (Cambridge University Press, 1937).

Malik, Rohan, "The Advancement and Role of Artificial Intelligence in Online Dispute Resolution" (2024) 7 *International Journal of Law Management & Humanities* 3309.

Martinez, Janet K, "Designing Online Dispute Resolution" (2020) 1 *Journal of Dispute Resolution* 135.

McCrystal, James, "The Videotape Trial Comes of Age" (1974) 57(10) *Judicature* 446.

McMurry, Julie J, "The UDRP v. Traditional Litigation: May the Best Process Win" (2001) 20(2) *Saint Louis University Public Law Review* 379.

Mignanelli, Nicholas, "The Legal Tech Bro Blues: Generative AI, Legal Indeterminacy, and the Future of Legal Research and Writing" (2024) 8(2) *Georgetown Law Technology Review* 298.

Milmo, Dan, "Millions in UK are Being Left Behind as World Moves Online, Say Peers", *The Guardian*, 29 June 2023.

Moran, Lyle, "Lawyers and Judges Optional? Online Dispute Resolution Promises to Increase Access to Justice, but Challenges Remain" (2021) 107(5) *ABA Journal* 58.

Murray, Sarah, "'A Letter to the Loser?' Public Law and the Empowering Role of the Judgment" (2014) 23(4) *Griffith Law Review* 545.

NACDL, *Criminal Court Reopening and Public Health in the Covid-19 Era* (2020).

National Center for State Courts, "JTC Resource Bulletin: ODR for Courts" Version 2.0, (2017), 7. https://ncsc.contentdm.oclc.org/digital/collection/tech/id/909/.

National Center for Technology and Dispute Resolution, "Framing the Parameters of Online Dispute Resolution" (2022).

Nguyen Thao, Vy Ngo, "AI Implementation in ODR: A Game-Changer or a Troublemaker of Data Protection" (2023) 1 *Vietnamese Journal of Legal Sciences* 1.

NITI Aayog Expert Committee on ODR, *Designing the Future of Dispute Resolution: The ODR Policy Plan for India* (NITI Aayog, 2021).

Norton, Katherine, "Avoiding the Great Divide: Assuring Court Technology Lightens the Load of Low-Income Litigants Post-COVID-19" (2021) 88(4) *Tennessee Law Review* 771.

OECD, *Schooling for Tomorrow: Learning to Bridge the Digital Divide* (2000).

– *Building Trust to Reinforce Democracy: Main Findings from the 2021 OECD Survey on Drivers of Trust in Public Institutions, Building Trust in Public Institutions* (2022).

– *OECD Framework and Good Practice Principles for People-Centred Justice* (2021).

– *OECD Online Dispute Resolution Framework* (2024).

Oh, Nayon, "On Online Dispute Resolution: Current Limitations on Enforcing Transnational B2C Online Arbitration Awards" (2023) 32(2) *Transnational Law and Contemporary Problems* 299.

Palfi, Dora, "Internal Dispute Resolution Systems: Do High Promises Come with Higher Expectations?" (2023) 64(3) *Hungarian Journal of Legal Studies* 391.

Rabinovich-Einy, Orna, "Beyond Efficiency: The Transformation of Courts through Technology" (2008) 12(1) *UCLA Journal of Law and Technology* 1.

Rainey, Daniel, "Conflict Engagement and ICT: Evolution and Revolution" (2016) 3(2) *International Journal of Online Dispute Resolution* 77.

– "Creating Standards for ODR" (2018) 4(2) *International Journal of Online Dispute Resolution* 21.

Rainey, Daniel and Larry Bridgesmith, "Bits and Bytes and Apps – Oh My! Scary Things in the ODR Forest" (2021) 8(1) *International Journal of Online Dispute Resolution* 3.

Roberts, John, *Year-End Report on the Federal Judiciary* (2023). www.supremecourt.gov/publicinfo/year-end/2023year-endreport.pdf.

Roos, Hanna, "Arbitration Tech Toolbox: Let's Chat Some More About ChatGPT and Dispute Resolution", *Kluwer Arbitration Blog*, 8 April 2023.

Ross, Graham, "Online Dispute Resolution and Business" (2004) 8(2) *Vindobona Journal of International Commercial Law and Arbitration* 301.

Rossner, Meredith, "Remote Rituals in Virtual Courts" (2021) 48(3) *Journal of Law and Society* 334.

Rule, Colin, "Using Online Dispute Resolution to Expand Access to Justice" *Oklahoma Bar Journal*, August 2019 (www.okbar.org/barjournal/aug2019/obj9006rule/)

Sacoff, Robert W, "A Consumer's View of UDRP Actions" (2005)23(4) *IPL Newsletter* 20.

Salter, Shannon and Darin Thompson, "Public-Centered Civil Justice Redesign: A Case Study of the British Columbia Civil Resolution Tribunal" (2016–2017) 3 *McGill Journal of Dispute Resolution* 113.

Salunke, Smruti Abhijit, 'Online Dispute Resolution System for Digital Payments in India" (2022) 5 *International Journal of Law Management & Humanities* 1552.

Sang, Jianing, "International Online Consumer Contracts: Jurisdiction, Enforcement and Online Dispute Resolution" (2024) 34(1) *Swiss Review of International and European Law* 139.

Sartor, Giovanni *et al*, "Thirty Years of Artificial Intelligence and Law: The Second Decade" (2022) 30(4) *Artificial Intelligence and Law* 521.

Schmitz, Amy J, "Expanding Access to Remedies through E-Court Initiatives" (2019) 67(1) *Buffalo Law Review* 89.

Schmitz, Amy J and Jan Martinez, "ODR and Innovation in the United States" (SSRN Draft Paper, 2020).

Schmitz, Amy J and Colin Rule, "Online Dispute Resolution for Smart Contracts" (2019) 2 *Journal of Dispute Resolution* 103.

Schmitz, Amy J and Leah Wing, "Beneficial and Ethical ODR for Family Issues" (2021) 59(2) *Family Court Review* 250.

Sela, Ayelet,

– (1) "The Effect of Online Technologies on Dispute Resolution System Design: Antecedents, Current Trends, and Future Directions" (2017) 3 *Lewis & Clark Law Review* 635.

– (2) "Diversity by Design: Improving Access to Justice in Online Courts with Adaptive Court Interfaces" (2021) 15(1) *Law & Ethics of Human Rights* 125.

Shackelford, Scott J and Anjanette H Raymond, "Building the Virtual Courthouse: Ethical Considerations for Design, Implementation, and Regulation in the World of ODR" (2014) 3 *Wisconsin Law Review* 61.

Sharma, Sugam *et al*, "Emerging Legal Informatics towards Legal Innovation: Current Status and Future Challenges and Opportunities" (2021) 21(3–4) *Legal Information Management* 218.

Sorensen, Martin Selsoe, "Fast Online Divorce? Nothing Denmark", *New York Times*, 1 April 2018, 9.

Spaulding, Norman W, "The Enclosure of Justice: Courthouse Architecture, Due Process, and the Dead Metaphor of Trial" (2012) 24(1) *Yale Journal of Law & the Humanities* 311.

Stegner, Marianne, "Online Dispute Resolution: The Future of Consumer Dispute Resolution?" (2017) *Yearbook on International Arbitration and ADR* 347.

Steinberg, Jessica K, "Demand Side Reform in the Poor People's Court" (2015) 47(3) *Connecticut Law Review* 741.

Susskind, Richard, *Online Courts and the Future of Justice* (Oxford University Press, 2019).

Syme, David, "Keeping Pace: On-line Technology and ADR Services" (2006) 23(3) *Conflict Resolution Quarterly* 343.

Thomas, Ryan, "Password Sharing and Online Dispute Resolution Systems" (2021) 5(2) *Business, Entrepreneurship & Tax Law Review* 147.

Thornburg, Elizabeth G, "Going Private: Technology, Due Process, and Internet Dispute Resolution" (2000) 34(1) *UC Davis Law Review* 151.

Tiamiyu, Oladeji M, "The Impending Battle for the Soul of ODR: Evolving Technologies and Ethical Factors Influencing the Field" (2022) 23(1) *Cardozo Journal of Conflict Resolution* 75.

Tillman, Zoe, "Going to Court Without a Lawyer Was Always Hard. The Pandemic Has Made It Much Harder", *Buzzfeed*, 15 May 2020. www.buzzfeednews.com/article/zoetillman/coronavirus-courts-closed-civil-court-legal-help.

Traffic Penalty Tribunal, *Dispute Resolution through the Fast Online Appeals Management (FOAM) System* (Traffic Penalty Tribunal, 2021).

– *Revolutionising a Service: Creating a World-Leading Online Tribunal Service through a Fresh Approach to Digital Transformation* (Traffic Penalty Tribunal, 2020).

Ummey Sharaban Tahura and Niloufer Selvadurai, "The Use of Artificial Intelligence in Judicial Decision-Making: The Example of China" (2022) 3 *International Journal of Law, Ethics, and Technology* 1.

UNCITRAL, *Technical Notes on Online Dispute Resolution* (2017).

UNCTAD, *Technology and the Future of Online Dispute Resolution (ODR) Platforms for Consumer Protection Agencies* (2023) (UNCTAD/TCS/DITC/INF/2023/5), 13.

Vallance, Chris, "One Million Cancel Broadband as Living Costs Rise", BBC News, 18 May 2023.

Van Den Herik, Jaap and Daniel Dimov, "Towards Crowdsourced Online Dispute Resolution" (2012) 7(2) *Journal of International Commercial Law and Technology* 99.

Vermeys, Nicolas and Jean-Francois Roberge, "ODR as a Public Service: The Access to Justice-Driven Canadian Experience" (2019) 6(2) *International Journal of Online Dispute Resolution* 227.

Vieira de Carvalho Fernandes, Ricardo *et al*, "The Expansion of Online Dispute Resolution in Brazil" (2018) 9(2) *International Journal for Court Administration* 20.

Wing, Leah *et al*, "Designing Ethical Online Dispute Resolution Systems: The Rise of the Fourth Party" (2021) 37(1) *Negotiation Journal* 49.

Winship, Sarah, "Can We Consciously Stop Unconscious Bias?" (2017) *Solicitors' Journal* 38.

WIPO,

– (1) *Alternative Dispute Mechanisms for Business-to-Business Digital Copyright-and-Content-Related Disputes* (2021).

– (2) *The Management of Internet Names and Addresses: Intellectual Property Issues* (1999).

Witwer, Amanda R *et al*, "Online Dispute Resolution: Perspectives to Support Successful Implementation and Outcomes in Court Proceedings" (RAND, 2021).

Woodard, Elizabeth C, "The UDRP, ADR, and Arbitration: Using Proven Solutions to Address Perceived Problems with the UDRP" (2009) 19(4) *Fordham Intellectual Property, Media & Entertainment Law Journal* 1169.

Wormington, Emma, "Why Missouri State Courts Should Implement an Online Dispute Resolution Platform to Resolve Traffic Tickets, Warrants and Pleas, and Misdemeanors" (2023) 1 *Journal of Dispute Resolution* 148.

Zhang, Jiawei, "Regulating Chatbot Output via Inter-Informational Competition" (2024) 22(1) *Northwestern Journal of Technology and Intellectual Property* 109.

Zoudoumis, Petros, "ODR4Refugees through a Smartphone App" (2017) 4(1) *International Journal of Online Dispute Resolution* 3.

Index

About the author

The Honourable Mr Justice Max Barrett is a judge of the High Court of Ireland. He holds a degree in law from Trinity College Dublin, a first-class master's in competition law from King's College London, a PhD in law from the University of Salford (having won a full scholarship) and a first-class master's in children's literature from Dublin City University. He also holds a variety of postgraduate diplomas on various aspects of law. He has written and spoken widely on all manner of legal topics.

When not lawyering or writing, Max is a keen amateur watercolourist.

By the same author: *The Art and Craft of Judgment Writing: A Primer for Common Law Judges, Second Edition*

If you enjoyed this book, you may also enjoy Max Barrett's *The Art and Craft of Judgment Writing: A Primer for Common Law Judges, Second Edition* (Globe Law and Business, 2025, https://www.globelawandbusiness.com/TACJW2).

1. Overview

Court systems are increasingly being shaped by digital processes. Even so, the task of writing judgments should not be viewed as an anachronism from the offline era but as an opportunity for the writing judge (whether acting online or offline) to reaffirm the values of rationality, fairness and transparency that have traditionally informed the task of judgment writing. In a sense, judgments written by judges – whether those judgments issue online or offline – stand as permanent witnesses to the benefit of human agency in decision making. As Dame Keegan, the Lady Chief Justice of Northern Ireland, has recently observed:

> *[W]hile law is, to some extent, an algorithmic process, it is a very human one too. To my mind, judges know when to be rigid with the law, but they also know how to display compassion, restraint, and reserve. In a debate that is encompassed by preference-based utilitarianism, we would do well to remember that, at the end of the day, judges are asked to deal with ordinary people at their most vulnerable. In my experience, a little bit of humanity goes a long way.*[1]

Whereas this book has charted the mechanisms and ethical foundations of ODR, *The Art and Craft of Judgment Writing* focuses on the judgment itself – that is, the textual context where law, fact and authority converge. Both books, however, are informed by the same key assumption: that justice, to be legitimate, must be accessible. This is a repeated theme in multiple judgments from across the common law world. To give one recent example, in *State Bank of India v Ajay Kumar Sood*,[2] the Supreme Court of India was critical as to the incomprehensibility of certain language used by a trial judge, observing:

---

1 Keegan, 29.
2 Unreported, Supreme Court of India, 12 March 2021.

> *Judgments are intended to convey the reasoning and process of thought which leads to the final conclusion of the adjudicating forum. The purpose of writing a judgment is to communicate the basis of the decision not only to [1] the members of the Bar, who appear in the case and [2] to others to whom it serves as a precedent but above all, [3] to provide meaning to citizens who approach courts ... Such orders of the High Court as in the present case do dis-service to the cause of ensuring accessible and understandable justice to citizens.*[3]

As can be seen, the Supreme Court of India invoked what it described as the "cause" of making sure that citizens of India enjoy "accessible and understandable justice".

Judges communicate to the public uniquely through their judgments. In ODR systems, where parties may never enter a courtroom or hear a judge speak, the written judgment is arguably the court's most significant and consequential interaction with online court users. Fundamentally, a judgment is where the law becomes tangible. In the age of apps, that tangibility is often (ironically) sought via the intangible online environment. (Millennials, it has been observed, often take the view that if something is not available via an app, they are just not interested.)[4] But while a judgment that issues via an app or pursuant to an online process may and does require a different stylistic approach, it is substantively no different in terms of impact and effect from a traditional-form judgment that issues following an offline process. As a consequence, the art and craft of good judgment writing is or should be a subject of interest to judges who work via ODR processes or in a more traditional offline court environment.

2. The judgment as digital interface

The renowned English judge Lord Mansfield (a Scotsman by birth) famously observed in *Morgan v Jones* (1773),[5] a case concerning the proper meaning of a will, that: "Most of the disputes in the world arise from words."[6] The English philosopher John Locke touches in greater detail on the frailty of words in his essay *Concerning Human Understanding* (1690).[7] Coming closer in time, the Scottish law lord Lord Macmillan observes how words suffer from the defects which affect all human currency: their value in exchange is unstable.[8]

One of the insights offered by *The Art and Craft of Judgment Writing* is that a judgment, a standalone communicative artefact,[9] is capable of bearing multiple layers of meaning to multiple audiences. But whereas courtroom dynamics

---

3 *Id*, §5.
4 See Rule.
5 98 ER 587, 596 (KB).
6 *Id*, 596.
7 See especially Book 3, Chapters 9–11.
8 Macmillan, 154.
9 On the notion of law (not just judgments) as an artefect (whether social or natural), see, eg, Biskup.

might once have compensated for opacity or poor structure in judgment writing, *digital* justice places the full burden of intelligibility on the text itself. Research suggests that everyday internet users read only about 20% of a webpage and are intimidated by long words, making the need to edit down content especially important.[10] So, a whole new mode of communication is called for, in which structure, clarity and tone in writing cease to be (if they ever were) 'mere' aesthetic preferences and assume instead the standing of ethical and practical imperatives.

Summaries at the outset of a judgment, thematic signposting, tables of contents and consistent terminology – all matters considered in *The Art and Craft of Judgment Writing* – assume new importance in a digital space where brevity, clarity and simplicity are important presentational virtues. If disputants, the legal community and the wider audience are to be served optimally, such features must also be deployed along with the design imperatives that inform good digital interfaces – for example, hierarchical information layout, summary boxes and the plainest of language.

3. On reasons and reasoning

A recurring topic in both books is that of reasoning: who are judgments for and how might they best be expressed? In ODR, this concern often finds expression in debates about algorithmic transparency, explainability and due process. In the offline judgment-writing context, perhaps five key interlocking justifications are offered for giving a reasoned judgment: to explain a decision; to discipline the judge's thought process; to facilitate scrutiny by the appellate courts; to guide future decision makers; and to maintain public trust in the judiciary.

What unites these online and offline justifications for reasoned judgments is a commitment to dialogue in the rhetorical and institutional sense. A judgment may assume the form of a monologue, but it is dialogical in function. A well-written judgment responds to whatever arguments have been made, addresses the questions arising in any one and invites critique of the law as regards both its specific application and its wider orientation. These features of the traditional well-written offline judgment offer reasons as to why a well-written judgment is also important in the online (ODR) context.

As noted in this book, and also in *The Art and Craft of Judgment Writing*, AI can assist in research and drafting. Caution, however, is required. The *Guidance for Judicial Office Holders on Artificial Intelligence* (2025), published for judges in England and Wales, suggests that AI is presently good at summarising large bodies of text, assisting in the writing of presentations and undertaking administrative tasks; however, it is not recommended for legal research ("AI tools are

---

10 See in this regard, eg, Dykes.

a poor way of conducting research to find new information you cannot verify independently")[11] or legal analysis ("[T]he current public AI chatbots do not produce convincing analysis or reasoning").[12]

Any ODR system must find a means of arriving at and offering reasons that satisfy the ethical and communicative functions traditionally fulfilled in the offline world by the judge-written judgment. This is not 'merely' a technical challenge; it is also one that goes to the very heart of the overarching obligation to protect the integrity of the administration of justice.

4. Writing for the reader

Both this book and *The Art and Craft of Judgment Writing* place special emphasis on audience. In ODR, user experience is perhaps paramount in terms of arriving at a solution that is most likely to meet with general acceptance. But when it comes to judgment writing, the audience is (or can be) more diffuse, comprising disputants, the legal profession, the appellate courts and the wider public. Yet in both domains – online and offline – the same basic writing principle applies: a judgment must always be oriented towards ensuring reader comprehension. Its primary aim is not to enable the writing judge to display their legal, linguistic and literary expertise; rather, it is to produce a judgment that is comprehensible by the many, with its credibility enhanced by its clarity.

The Art and Craft of Judgment Writing emphasises that the losing party ought perhaps to be viewed as the primary audience for a judgment. This is not a new concept. Some 4,000 years ago, Ptah-Hotep, an insightful ancient Egyptian politician and philosopher, observed that: "[A] good hearing soothes the heart."[13] A judgment written for the loser will suggest that such a hearing is precisely what has been afforded, hopefully with like effect. For the writing judge to proceed so does not mean that they are proceeding partially. Rather, it means that they are showing a deep respect for the emotional and cognitive demands placed on someone who must accept an unfavourable decision.

In the ODR context, litigants may feel even more distant from the adjudicative process than the traditional disputant. In a recent report on the provision of remote services by certain urban lawyers to rural businesses, the California Access to Justice Commission identified, among others, the following learnings: "An online ... process can be daunting for some and [a source of] concern for others";[14] "Use of remote, digital communication for the topics involved in getting legal help exacerbates cultural and trust barriers";[15] and, critically:

11 §5.
12 *Id.*
13 Murray, 545.
14 California Access to Justice Commission (3), 5.
15 *Id.*

> *People and firms in small communities are accustomed to engaging in direct dealings. Additional effort is required to convince prospective clients that they will benefit enough to justify investing their time in dealing with distant lawyers (whom they probably will never meet in person), an impersonal … process, and learning how to use digital means.*[16]

In terms of online and offline judgment production and form, it is submitted that an empathetic and transparent judgment assumes particular importance as a compensatory mechanism whereby a deciding judge can signal that the process undertaken online was a serious one; the issues raised were understood; and sound reasoning underpins the conclusions reached – even if the loser might have wished for different conclusions. In this way, writing becomes not only a form of expression, but an instrument of justice.

5. Structure, simplicity and visual aids

The Art and Craft of Judgment Writing offers detailed guidance on structural techniques that enhance readability, such as use of headings, summary introductions and, in some cases, visual aids such as timelines or diagrams. These techniques mirror best practices in digital communication and user interface design. As more judgments are delivered via screen rather than print, these methods, it is submitted, will move – arguably they have already moved – from being optional enhancements to being practical necessities.

Visual aids are not about simplification in the pejorative sense; they are all about clarity. Where a chronology is complex, a timeline clarifies. Where multiple parties or legal issues intersect, a diagram assists. These are not replacements for legal reasoning, but facilitators of optimally clear communication. And just as an ODR interface must be readily navigable, so too (it is submitted) a written judgment must be thoroughly comprehensible and easily readable.

6. Literary lessons

In its fourth section, *The Art and Craft of Judgment Writing* draws lessons from literary authors – Orwell, Woolf, Hazlitt, James and others – whose informed insights into style, voice and narrative offer a rich resource for judicial writers. These chapters underscore a fundamental point: that the discipline of legal writing benefits from the learnings which fall to be derived from all good writing. Clarity, brevity, rhythm, empathy and audience awareness are not optional virtues in a judgment; they are essential to a judgment's success and its persuasiveness. In the digital justice context, where much of the process is purely textual, these lessons are even more critical. The judgment may be the only place where the legal system reveals the reasoning process to the parties. If

16 *Id.*

it is cold, convoluted or self-referential, it undermines trust. If it is clear, structured and respectful, it enhances the legitimacy of the decision-making process.

7. A shared ethos of justice and communication

Both this book and *The Art and Craft of Judgment Writing* are animated by the same ethos: a belief that justice must not only be done, but also be seen and understood to be done. The judgment is where that belief is tested. It is where technology meets tradition; where law meets language; and where procedure meets principle. *The Art and Craft of Judgment Writing* does not offer firm rules for judgment writing. It offers something more valuable: a set of frameworks, reflections and tools for improving the clarity, integrity and accessibility of legal writing. For those working in or thinking about ODR, it provides a grounding in the communicative obligations that have survived technological change. Justice is no longer confined to courtrooms. But, whether despatched online or offline, judgments will continue to need to be written. As a book, *The Art and Craft of Judgment Writing* offers a thoughtful and engaged guide to how the task of judgment writing is best accomplished.

About Globe Law and Business

Globe Law and Business was established in 2005. From the very beginning, we set out to create legal books that are sufficiently high level to be of real use to the experienced professional, yet still accessible and easy to navigate. Most of our authors are drawn from Magic Circle and other top commercial firms, both in the United Kingdom and internationally.

Our titles are carefully produced, with the utmost attention paid to editorial, design and production processes. We hope this results in high-quality publications that are easy to read and a pleasure to own.

In 2021, we were very pleased to announce the start of a new chapter for Globe Law and Business following the acquisition of law books under the imprint Ark Publishing. Our law firm management list is now significantly expanded with many well-known and loved Ark Publishing titles.

We have also launched an online content platform, Globe Law Online, which allows for easy access across firms. Details of all titles included can be found at www.globelawonline.com. Email glo@globelawandbusiness.com for further details and to arrange a free trial for you or your firm.

We'd very much like to hear from you with your thoughts and ideas for improving what we offer. Please do feel free to email me on sian@globelawandbusiness.com. Happy reading and thank you for your time.

Sian O'Neill
Managing director
Globe Law and Business
www.globelawandbusiness.com

www.ingramcontent.com/pod-product-compliance
Ingram Content Group UK Ltd.
Pitfield, Milton Keynes, MK11 3LW, UK
UKHW062037180526
471212UK00003B/8